SECOND EDITION

EXPLORE THE ANCIENT WORLD

Ballard &
Tighe

Brea, California

Leila A. Langston, B.A., is a graduate of Occidental College, California. She has extensive teaching experience and also has served as a learning specialist and ESL program coordinator in the public schools. Ms. Langston is the author of *Explore the United States* and co-author of *Explore America* and the *Explore Geography Picture Dictionary.*

CONSULTING EDITORS

Explore the Ancient World benefited greatly from the assistance of talented and distinguished consulting editors:

Dr. Lanny Fields, Department of History, California State University, San Bernardino
Dr. George Giacumakis, Department of History, California State University, Fullerton
Rabbi Devora Jacobson, The Claremont Colleges
Dr. Hugh La Bounty, California State University, San Marcos
Mary Leakey, Nairobi, Kenya
Dr. Kim Martin, Department of Behavioral Sciences, University of LaVerne
Dr. Cheryl Riggs, Department of History, California State University, San Bernardino
Dr. Kent Schofield, Department of History, California State University, San Bernardino
Dr. Robert Simonds, National Association for Christian Education
David Vigilante, Associate Director of the National Center for History in the Schools,
    University of California, Los Angeles
Dr. Dale Wright, Department of Religious Studies, Occidental College

REVIEWERS

The author and publisher express grateful appreciation to the teachers who carefully reviewed the textbook in manuscript form and provided helpful comments and suggestions:

Kelly Andrews, Santa Barbara, California
Blaine Buchenau, Arlington Heights High School, Fort Worth, Texas
Jan Burns, William James Middle School, Fort Worth, Texas
Patricia Garcia, Riverside Middle School, Fort Worth, Texas
Phyllis Greenberg, Virginia Polytechnic Institute and State University
Mary Haldorsen, San Bernardino, California
Rosa Ruiz Hernandez, Dallas Independent School District, Dallas, Texas
Duane Magoon, Lower Kuskokwim School District, Bethel, Alaska
Nancy Miller, L.V. Stockard Middle School, Dallas, Texas
Lisa Thwing, Santa Barbara, California
Paul Watlington, Falls Church High School, Falls Church, Virginia

An IDEA® Content Program from Ballard & Tighe

Managing Editor: Patrice Gotsch
Editors: Dr. Roberta Stathis and Rebecca Ratnam
Editorial Staff: Kristin Belsher and Linda Mammano
Art Directors: Nancy Wright and Danielle Arreola
Contributing Writers: Carin Dewhirst and Lou Robinson
Desktop Publishing Coordinator: Kathy Styffe
Graphic Designer: Ronaldo Benaraw
Printing Coordinator: Cathy Sanchez

2005 Printing

ISBN 1-55501-652-9   Catalog #2-853

Brea, California • (800) 321-4332 • www.ballard-tighe.com

Table of Contents

CHAPTER 1
Clues to the Ancient Past

2 Million Years Ago	1 Million Years Ago	B.C. 0 A.D.

Australopithecus boisei (2.2-1.2 million years ago)
Homo habilis (1.75-1.2 million years ago)

ERA: Prehistoric Times
PLACE: East Africa
PEOPLE: Mary and Louis Leakey
THEME: Ingenuity—being resourceful, inventive, and skillful

CHAPTER FOCUS: Mary and Louis Leakey studied fossils from the past to find out about life before written history.

◀ *Mary and Louis Leakey are studying*
fossils found during the day.

Anthropologists study human cultures to find out how people live. They want to know how people get their food, what kinds of tools they use, what their religious beliefs are, and how they live together in groups. This information helps us understand other people as well as ourselves.

Some anthropologists study the ways people live now. Others study people who lived in the past. One way to learn about the past is to study old newspapers, letters, and diaries. However, people have only known how to write since about 3000 B.C.

Anthropologists who study people who lived before that time must look for other clues to find out how people lived. These anthropologists are called archaeologists. They dig up fossils and other clues from the past to learn about life before written history. In this chapter, you will read about some of the fossils and clues that archaeologists have found. As you read, think about how people in the past interacted with their environment to meet their needs.

The World

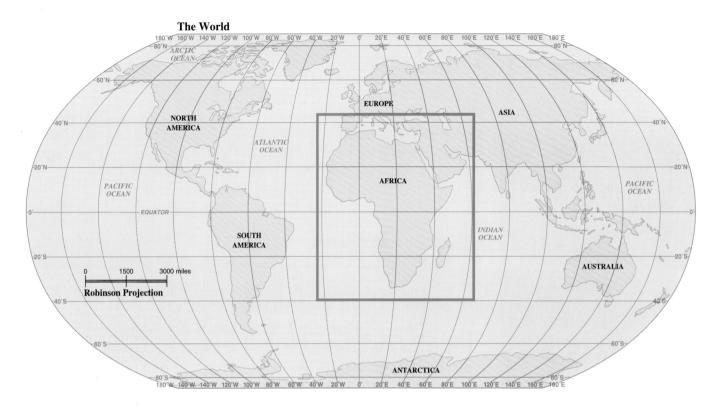

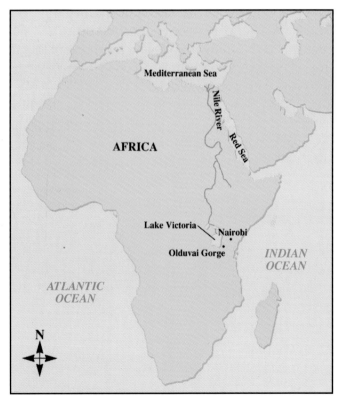

▲ Olduvai (OL-duh-vy) Gorge is located in East Africa near Lake Victoria.

gorge: a deep, narrow pass with steep sides

Mary and Louis Leakey found fossil bones in Olduvai Gorge.

THE STONE AGE

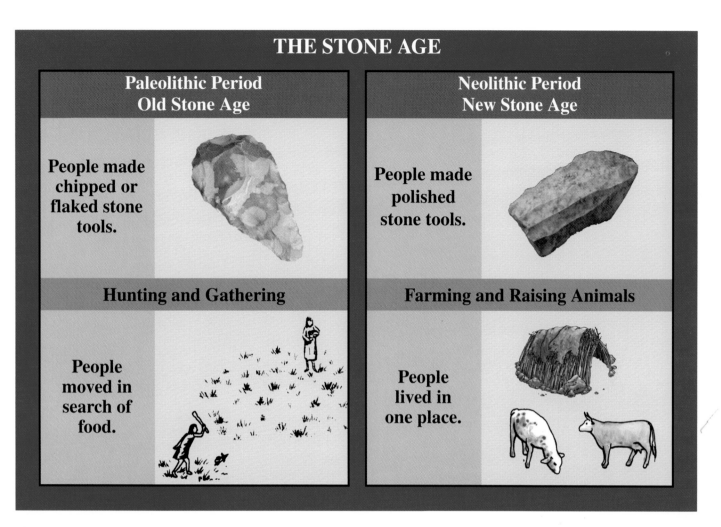

Paleolithic Period **Old Stone Age**	**Neolithic Period** **New Stone Age**
People made chipped or flaked stone tools.	People made polished stone tools.
Hunting and Gathering	**Farming and Raising Animals**
People moved in search of food.	People lived in one place.

▲ *Scientists have divided the Stone Age into two periods: the Paleolithic Period, or Old Stone Age; and the Neolithic Period, or New Stone Age.*

The Stone Age

Anthropologists sometimes describe societies by the kinds of tools they make. When people make their tools and weapons from stone, bone, **antler**, **ivory**, or wood, anthropologists call this stage the "Stone Age." Anthropologists think the Stone Age began about two million years ago when people began to make and use tools made of stone.

The Stone Age ended at different times around the world. Some societies continued to use stone tools for many years. In fact, in parts of the world, there are still groups of people who use only stone tools.

antler: a bone on the head of animals in the deer family

ivory: the hard, white material of which the tusks of elephants and walruses are made

? THINK ABOUT IT:

Why do some people still use stone tools?

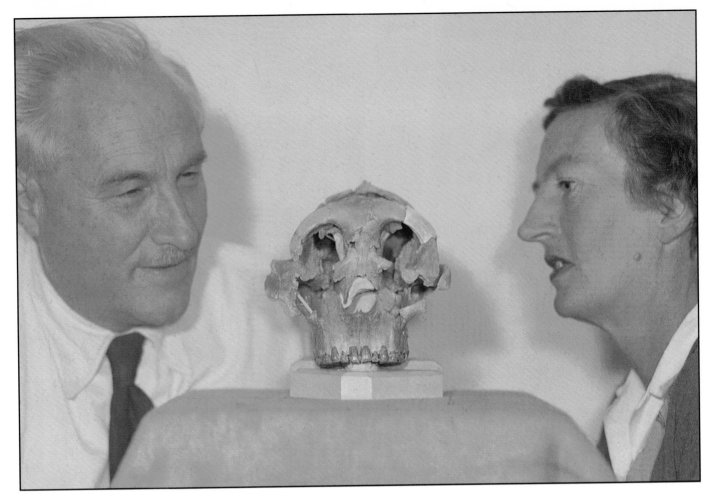

▲ *Louis and Mary Leakey are studying a fossil skull.*

Choosing a Site

Mary and Louis Leakey were archaeologists. They had been looking for **fossils** in Africa for many years. In the summer of 1959, they decided to make a short trip to Olduvai Gorge to search for fossils and **artifacts**.

They came with a small team of helpers and set up camp near where they were going to work. This trip was especially exciting because a cameraman was going to film the **excavation** for television.

Louis and Mary were hoping to find fossils or artifacts of **prehistoric** people. Two **sites** looked promising, but the sites covered miles of the gorge. They wondered where to begin.

artifact: an object made by humans

excavation: a hole made by digging

fossil: hardened remains of a plant or animal

prehistoric: the time before written history

site: a place; location

? THINK ABOUT IT:

How is an archaeologist like a detective?

A Lucky Find

One morning, in July of 1959, Mary and her two dogs walked to a site where she knew there were **fragments** of bones and stone artifacts. It had rained and some of the soil had washed away. As she walked along, Mary saw a piece of bone. She wrote later, "It seemed to be part of a skull . . . I carefully brushed away a little of the deposit, and then I could see parts of two large teeth in place in the upper jaw . . . I rushed back to camp to tell Louis."

Louis and Mary now knew where to begin their excavation. They covered the skull carefully with stones to protect it and waited for the cameraman to arrive.

fragment: broken piece

? THINK ABOUT IT:

How can weather help and hurt in a hunt for artifacts?

▶ *This is a photograph of some of the bone fragments Mary Leakey found.*

The Excavation

Mary and Louis spent 19 days removing the pieces of the skull from the ground. They used dental tools and paintbrushes to remove the pieces of bone. Then Mary, Louis, and their team **sifted** tons of dirt through a wire screen to get every fragment of bone they could find. They discovered that the skull was on a **living-floor** that contained many stone artifacts and animal bones.

The Leakeys and their helpers carefully dug a **trench** and began to sift the dirt looking for more bones and other artifacts. The cameraman found a leg bone that the Leakeys thought belonged with the skull.

Mary drew pictures of the skull and the other artifacts. She also drew a map to show the location of the skull on the living-floor. The photographer took many pictures. It was important to make drawings and photographs of the fossils, artifacts, and the site itself so that there would be a permanent record of the way everything was found. By this time, the season to look for fossils was over and Mary and Louis returned home to Nairobi.

living-floor: a place where people lived or camped

sift: to pass through a screen; to separate

trench: a long narrow ditch

? THINK ABOUT IT:

How could they find out if the leg bone belonged with the skull?

▲ *This photograph shows Mary starting to uncover the skull. Her dogs, Sally and Victoria, are with her.*

◀ *Louis Leakey is measuring the depth of the excavation.*

The Excavation Continues

The next year the Leakeys returned to Olduvai Gorge. At a site not far from where Mary found the skull, they found stone artifacts, parts of another skull, 21 small bones from a hand, and 12 bones from a foot. These were the remains of two **skeletons**. At another site they also found a circle of **lava** stones.

The Leakeys began to study these fossil bones and stone artifacts. Mary spent many hours fitting the pieces of bone together. It was like putting together a puzzle, but most of the pieces were missing.

Scientists gave the first skull found by the Leakeys the name **Australopithecus boisei** (aw-stray-loh-PITH-uh-kus BOI-see-iy). Many people think Australopithecus boisei was not a human **ancestor** because its jaws and teeth were quite different from those of modern humans.

ancestor: a family member who lived long ago

Australopithecus boisei: called "southern ape" because the first fossils were found in the southern part of Africa; Charles Boise helped pay for the Leakeys' exploration and they named the fossil after him

lava: melted rock from a volcano

skeleton: the bones of an animal or person

? THINK ABOUT IT:

What information on this page is fact? What is opinion? What is judgment?

Homo Habilis

Louis and Mary also studied the bones that went with the second skull. From the shape of the foot bones, they believed this creature walked **fully upright**. From the shape of the hand bones, they knew it could do many things with its hands.

The second skull was named Homo habilis (HOH-moh HAB-il-us). "Homo" means it is in the same **genus**, or group, as human beings. The **species**, "habilis," means it was able to **grip** with its hand. People usually call Homo habilis "handy human" because of its ability to make tools.

Because they found these bones in the same **level** of rock, the Leakeys decided Homo habilis lived at the same time as Australopithecus boisei. They believed that Homo habilis was an ancestor of modern humans.

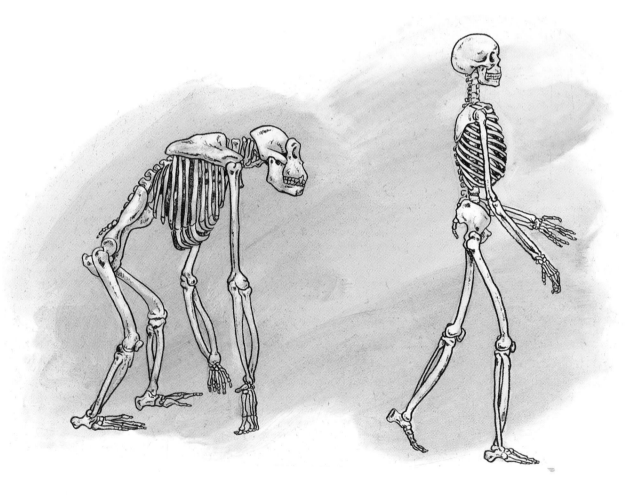

▲ *Gorillas have a spine that causes them to be bent over as they move around.*

▲ *The Leakeys believed that both Australopithecus boisei and Homo habilis walked fully upright like modern human beings.*

Studying the Artifacts

The stone artifacts found on the living-floor turned out to be simple stone choppers and small stone **flakes**. The choppers were large and pear-shaped. They were made by chipping off flakes of stone. One end was pointed and the other rounded. The sides were thin to make a good cutting edge. Homo habilis probably used these tools for chopping and scraping and to cut meat for food and branches for shelter.

The Leakeys decided the lava stones may have been the base for a simple **hut**. The hut might have been made of branches with a roof of grass or animal skins. Did Homo habilis make it? No one knows for sure. There are a few **nomadic** peoples in Africa who still use huts like this today. The hut the Leakeys found is believed to be the oldest known human structure in the world.

> **flake:** a thin piece cut from something
>
> **hut:** a small house made of wood or branches
>
> **nomadic:** having no permanent home; moving about in search of food

▲ *Some nomadic people in Africa still live in huts like this one.*

▼ *Mary and Louis Leakey are carefully removing the fossils and artifacts.*

? **THINK ABOUT IT:**

Did Homo habilis live during the Paleolithic or Neolithic Period? What artifacts let you know this?

▲ *Mary Leakey is studying fossils and rocks that are almost two million years old. These rocks provide clues about the first known tool-making.*

butcher: to cut up animals for meat

? **THINK ABOUT IT:**

Was Homo habilis more like an ape or a human? What is the evidence?

How Did Homo Habilis Live?

The skull, leg, and foot bones each told Louis and Mary something about what Homo habilis looked like and what they could do. The stone tools also gave some clues about what their life was like.

Anthropologists believe that Homo habilis probably gathered fruits, nuts, seeds, and other plants to eat. Homo habilis also may have eaten some meat.

Anthropologists think it is possible that groups of Homo habilis lived together and shared their food with each other. Anthropologists think Homo habilis may have had certain places where they **butchered** animals and where they made their tools.

Chapter Summary—Ingenuity

Because they lived so long ago, and because there are so few clues, no one knows much about Australopithecus boisei and Homo habilis. However, the simple stone tools found with Homo habilis suggest that they were resourceful. It appears that they took materials around them and used these materials in new ways to make their lives easier and better.

Mary and Louis Leakey continued to study fossils in Africa for many years. Their work helped us learn more about prehistoric life. Archaeologists continue to search for clues to help us learn more about Australopithecus boisei and Homo habilis and how they lived.

? THINK ABOUT IT:

If you were an archaeologist, what part of the world would you want to study? Why?

▲ *Archaeologists help us learn more about prehistoric life. These archaeologists are searching for fossils and artifacts.*

CHAPTER 2
The Neanderthals

ERA: Prehistoric Times
PLACE: The Neander Valley, Germany
PEOPLE: The Neanderthals
THEME: Ingenuity—being resourceful, inventive, and skillful

CHAPTER FOCUS: The Neanderthals adapted to life in a cold climate.

2 Million Years Ago	1 Million Years Ago	B.C.	0	A.D.

Neanderthals (100,000-30,000 years ago)

LINK

In the last chapter, you read about Louis and Mary Leakey and their discovery of fossil bones in East Africa.

In this chapter, you will read about the discovery of more fossil bones, this time in Germany and in other parts of the world. These bones belonged to a group called the Neanderthals. Anthropologists believe the Neanderthals lived thousands of years ago during the Ice Age. As you read, think about how the Neanderthals interacted with their environment to meet their needs.

◀ *This drawing shows an artist's idea of Neanderthals hunting rabbits.*

The World

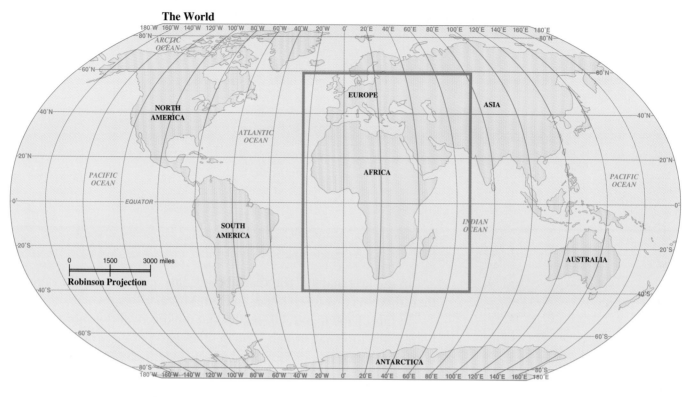

▶ *Many Neanderthal remains have been found in Europe. There are also important sites in Africa and Southwest Asia. Some of the Neanderthal sites are identified on this map by dots.*

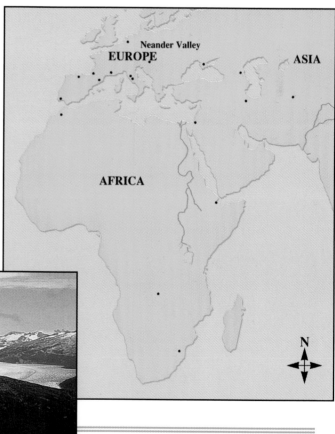

glacier: a large mass of ice and snow that forms faster than the snow can melt

The Neanderthals lived when there were glaciers covering parts of Europe.

◀ *This model shows one scientist's idea of how a Neanderthal man looked.*

▶ *This is a drawing of the Neanderthal skull found in a cave in the Neander Valley in Germany. Scientists believe that skull is 50,000 years old.*

Bones in a Quarry

In 1856, workers found pieces of a skull in a **limestone quarry** in the Neander Valley in Germany. The workers gave the fragments of bone to the owner of the quarry. The owner thought the bones were from a bear, but he showed them to a local school teacher. The school teacher did not know what they were, but he thought the bones were very old.

The **experts** disagreed about what the bones were. Some thought they were the bones of a modern man who had been sick. Some thought they belonged to a very early apelike man. Today we call this group of apelike men the Neanderthals. Scientists now know that the Neanderthals were not close or direct ancestors to modern human beings.

expert: a person who knows a lot about a subject

limestone: a kind of rock

quarry: a place from which stone is cut

▲ *This picture shows part of a 60,000-year-old Neanderthal skeleton.*

? THINK ABOUT IT:

What kinds of things can we know about Neanderthals? What things are impossible to know?

Why do anthropologists think the Neanderthals were hunter-gatherers?

Studying the Clues

Who were these ancient people? What were they like? Since 1856, many more fossil bones and other artifacts from the Neanderthals have been found. Anthropologists and other scientists have studied these bones, stone tools, and other artifacts. From these clues, they have put together a picture of what life might have been like for the Neanderthals.

By studying the fossils, scientists think the Neanderthals lived from about 100,000 to 30,000 years ago. Anthropologists believe that the Neanderthals were hunter-gatherers.

Neanderthal Society

Anthropologists study groups of modern hunter-gatherers to get more ideas of what life was like for the Neanderthals.

In most hunter-gatherer societies, the **elders** pass on to the younger people knowledge and **traditions**. However, anthropologists believe that Neanderthals usually did not live long enough to become grandparents. Scientists have compared Neanderthal bones with bones of mammals alive today. Based on this comparison, they believe that most Neanderthals probably lived less than 40 years.

Anthropologists believe that Neanderthals probably cared about each other and took care of one another, even people who had **handicaps**. One of the fossil skeletons was of a man who had a **paralyzed** arm. Even though the man had not been able to hunt, he had been taken care of until he died.

elder: an older person (with some authority)

handicap: something that makes life difficult for a person

paralyzed: not able to move

tradition: a story, belief, or custom handed down from parents or grandparents to children

▼ *Neanderthals probably lived in groups of 35 to 40. Each group lived in an area so large that it took them several days to go from one part to another. They may have seen people in another group only once or twice in their lives.*

? THINK ABOUT IT:

What traditions have you learned from an elder in your family?

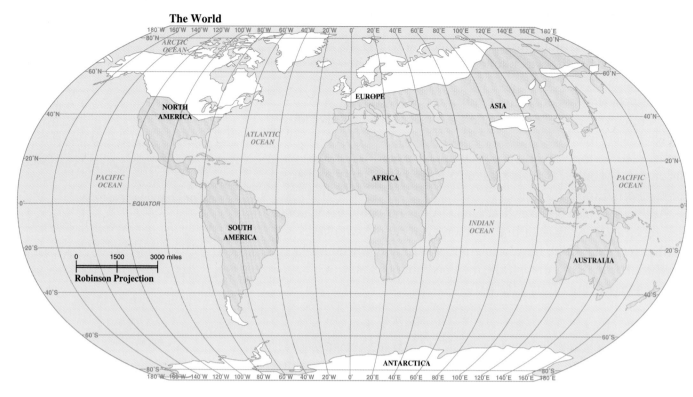

The World

▲ *Glaciers covered much of North America, Europe, and Asia during the Ice Age.*

geologist: a person who studies the earth's crust (the outer layer)

? THINK ABOUT IT:

How are these warming times between the Ice Ages like the "global warming" environmentalists talk about today? How are they different?

The Ice Age

Neanderthals lived in Europe before and during the last Ice Age. **Geologists** believe that at least four times in the past, large parts of the earth were covered with ice. The most recent Ice Age began about 75,000 years ago and ended about 10,000 years ago.

When the last Ice Age began, the earth became colder. Snow began to fall in the mountains. There was so much snow it did not melt in the summer. Year after year it piled up and became ice. Glaciers began to form in the mountains and near the North and South Poles. The glaciers grew thick. They flowed slowly down the mountains, covering the northern part of Europe with a thick sheet of ice. In some places the ice was more than a mile thick.

The winters were long and very, very cold. Summers were short and cool. The hottest summer days were probably only about 50° F. However, between the long cold periods there were warmer times, and the glaciers would melt. But then the ice would come again and freeze everything.

Adapting to the Cold

Several things helped the Neanderthals survive in the cold climate of the Ice Age. Their thick bodies may have helped them keep warm. Anthropologists also think Neanderthals wore loose-fitting animal hides.

In the areas where the Neanderthals lived, there are many caves in the cliffs. Anthropologists believe Neanderthals probably found shelter from the cold inside the caves. One cave in France has a post hole at the opening. Another cave in Russia has marks in the dirt that make a circle. These might be clues that Neanderthals put up a wall of skins or built huts to protect themselves from the cold.

Neanderthals had something else to keep themselves warm. In the mouths of the caves, archaeologists have found **hearths**, charcoal, and ashes. This tells us that Neanderthals knew how to use fire.

hearth: the stones the fire sits on

? THINK ABOUT IT:

Why have anthropologists never found clothing with Neanderthal bones? What are some other things they would not find?

▲ *Archaeologists found the remains of a stone hearth in France. They believe Neanderthals cooked meat on the stones.*
1. *First, they built a fire over the rocks.*
2. *Next, they pushed the fire to one side.*
3. *Then, they put chunks of meat on hot stones.*
Neanderthals were not the first people to use fire. Anthropologists believe other early human ancestors living in China used fire around 500,000 years ago.

Cave Bear

Mammoth

Musk Ox

Woolly Rhinoceros

▲ *Neanderthal fossils have been found with the remains of cave bears, mammoths, musk oxen, and woolly rhinoceroses. Woolly rhinoceroses, mammoths, and cave bears are now **extinct**.*

extinct: none living

preserve: to keep from spoiling or going bad

Hunting and Gathering

From the many animal bones found in their caves and other living areas, anthropologists think that Neanderthals ate the meat of different kinds of animals. Groups of Neanderthal hunters probably worked together, waiting at places where the animals passed by. Sometimes they forced animals off cliffs and then killed them with clubs and spears. They may have used spears with stone points.

After the men brought the animals back to the home camp, the women probably scraped the meat from the hides and cut it up. They may have stored meat in the ice to **preserve** it for the winter.

From studying modern hunter-gatherer societies, anthropologists think Neanderthals also gathered plants and seeds to eat. Anthropologists do not know much about the kinds of plants Neanderthals ate because they have not found any preserved plant foods. However, archaeologists have found stones that may have been used to grind seeds.

Tools

Neanderthals used many different kinds of stone tools. Archaeologists have found more than 50 different types of tools with Neanderthal bones. These tools are more carefully made than the tools found with Homo habilis. Neanderthals made spear points for hunting. They had scrapers to clean animal hides. They used piercing tools to make holes in hides. Then they laced the hides together to make simple clothing.

Archaeologists studied the types of tools found together and discovered that Neanderthals may have had different "tool kits" for different activities. For example, Neanderthals seem to have used one tool kit to make clothes and another for killing and butchering animals.

? THINK ABOUT IT:

What kinds of tool kits do you have?

▲ *Neanderthal women probably made clothing from animal skins.*
1. *First, the women cleaned the skin with a stone scraper.*
2. *Next, they punched holes along the edge with a pointed stone.*
3. *Then, they laced the skin together with strips of animal hides.*

What Did Neanderthals Look Like?

When Neanderthal fossils were first discovered, anthropologists thought they were primitive creatures. They drew pictures of hairy men and women, stooped over and apelike. However, recent research shows that Neanderthals actually looked very much like modern people.

Neanderthals were shorter and broader than modern humans. Most Neanderthals had bigger heads than ours, with broad faces and heavy **brow ridges**. Their arm and leg bones also were shorter and thicker than ours. They probably could lift twice as much as modern humans. From studying their hand and finger bones, scientists know that Neanderthals had a powerful grip.

Anthropologists now believe that some of the Neanderthals suffered from **arthritis**, **rickets**, and **malnutrition**. The results of these diseases caused early archaeologists to think all Neanderthals walked stooped over.

In addition, studies of skulls seem to indicate that Neanderthals probably used language. Their brains may even have been larger than those of today's humans.

arthritis: a disease of the joints

brow ridge: the part of the forehead just above the eyes

malnutrition: a condition caused by lack of healthy food

rickets: a disease of the bones

? THINK ABOUT IT:

Of all the information we have about the Neanderthals, what is fact? What is opinion? What is judgment?

▶ *Neanderthals probably looked very similar to modern human beings.*

◀ *This Neanderthal hunter is following the tracks of a cave bear.*

Chapter Summary—Ingenuity

The Neanderthals lived in a **harsh**, cold world. Sometimes there was not enough food to eat. They did not have many things to make their lives comfortable. However, they were strong and they were good at hunting and gathering food. Neanderthals worked together to find food, and they took care of each other when they were sick. They showed ingenuity.

The Neanderthals survived until around 35,000 years ago when suddenly they became extinct. No one knows why. In the next chapter, you will read about the Cro-Magnons, the ancestors of modern people.

harsh: extreme; severe; cruel

? THINK ABOUT IT:

What are some things that might have caused Neanderthals to become extinct?

CHAPTER 3
The Cro-Magnons

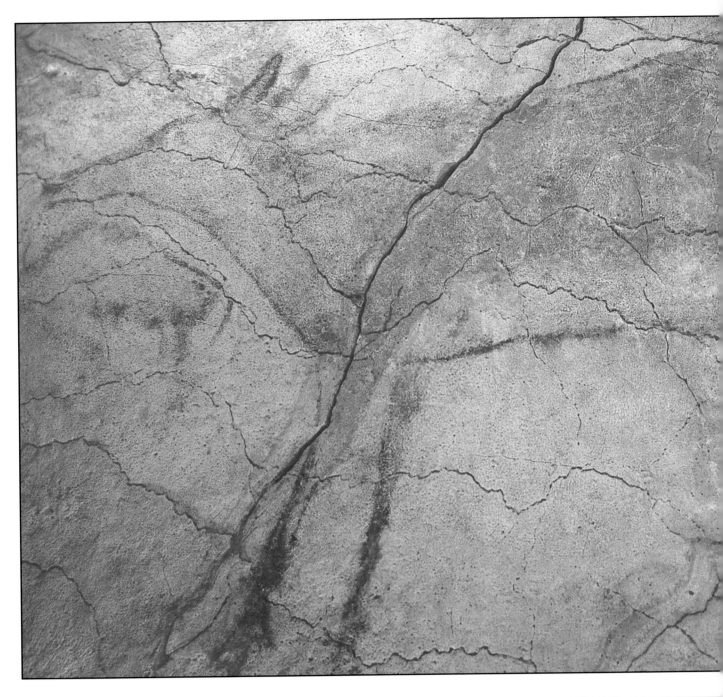

2 Million Years Ago	1 Million Years Ago	B.C. 0 A.D.

Cro-Magnons (40,000-10,000 years ago)

ERA: Prehistoric Times
PLACE: Altamira, Spain
PEOPLE: The Cro-Magnons
THEME: Ingenuity—being resourceful, inventive, and skillful

CHAPTER FOCUS: Prehistoric artists painted pictures of bison and other animals in caves.

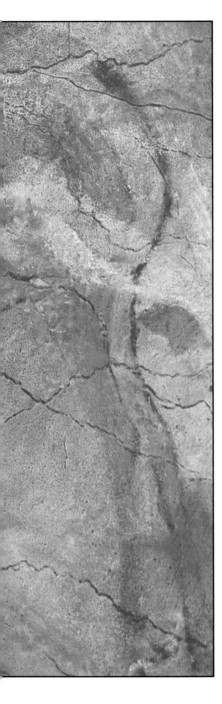

◀ *A young Spanish girl was the first person in thousands of years to see this cave painting of a deer.*

LINK

In the last chapter, you read about the Neanderthals, a group of people who lived in Europe, Africa, and parts of Asia for thousands of years until they mysteriously disappeared.

During the last 10,000 years or so that the Neanderthals were living, another group of people, called the Cro-Magnons, lived alongside them. Although they lived in the same places and during the same general time period, the Cro-Magnons were different from the Neanderthals in many ways.

In this chapter, you will read about the Cro-Magnons—their tools, their beliefs, and most of all, their works of art. As you read, think about how the Cro-Magnons interacted with their environment to meet their needs.

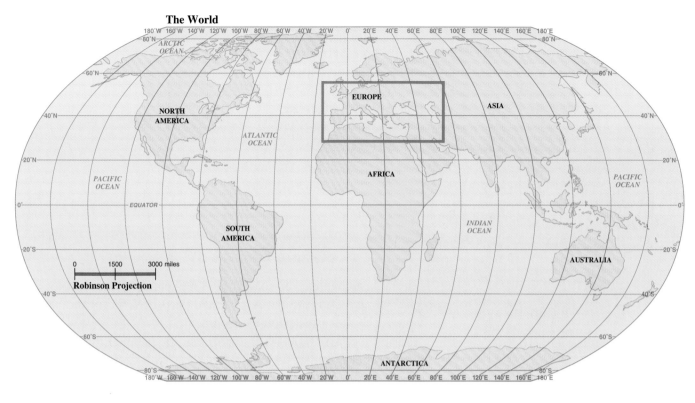

The World

Robinson Projection

0   1500   3000 miles

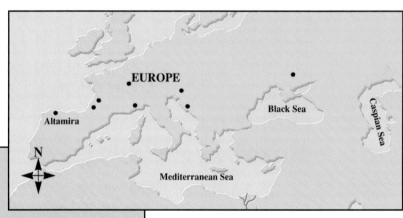

EUROPE

Altamira

Black Sea

Caspian Sea

Mediterranean Sea

N

▶ *Cro-Magnons lived on every continent and in every environment, from tropical Africa to the Arctic Ocean. The dots show major Cro-Magnon sites in Europe.*

HOW A CAVE IS MADE

◀ *1. Water dissolves limestone. It makes an underground cave.*

◀ *2. The water level drops, leaving the cave dry.*

◀ *3. Rocks fall and cover the mouth of the cave.*

◀ GEOGRAPHY IN FOCUS

cave: an opening in a hillside

The Cro-Magnons painted pictures inside caves.

Toros in a Cave in Altamira

Many caves with prehistoric art have been found by **accident**. Marcelino de Sautuola's cave at Altamira, Spain was one of these. Thousands of years ago, the mouth of this cave was closed when rocks fell and covered the entrance. No one had been inside since then. Then one day in 1868, a hunter's dog fell into a hole. The hunter looked for his dog and found the opening to the cave, but he did not think the cave was important. Years later someone told Marcelino de Sautuola, an **amateur** fossil hunter, about the cave.

Marcelino decided to look for prehistoric stone tools in the cave. He spent many days digging in the dirt on the floor of the cave. The **ceiling** of the cave was so low that Marcelino had to crawl on his hands and knees. Sometimes he took his daughter, Maria, with him.

One day Maria wandered off farther into the cave. She looked up at the ceiling and suddenly cried, "¡Papá, mira, toros pintados!" ("Papa, look, painted bulls!") Her father hurried over and saw the painted figures of animals. There on the ceiling were 25 painted animals, mostly bison. Some of the animals were life-size or even larger. They were colored in rich browns, reds, yellows, and black.

accident: something that happens by chance

amateur: a person who does something for the fun of it, not for money

ceiling: the top of a room

▼ *This picture of a horse is probably one of the oldest paintings at Altamira.*

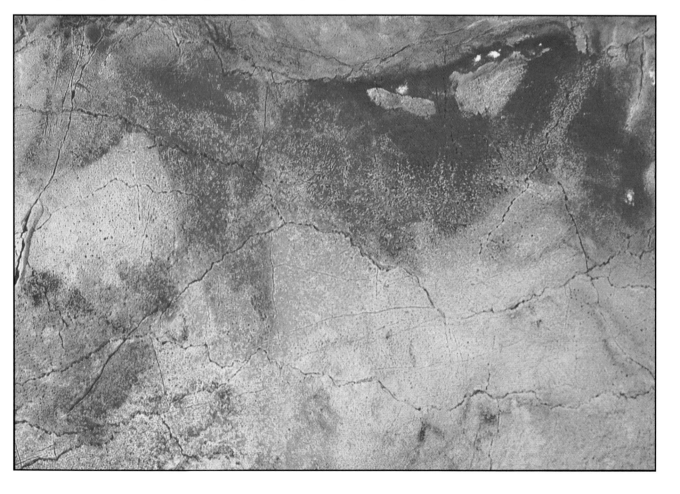

Pictures from the Past

The animals were painted in bright colors and looked as if they had been painted that day. However, Marcelino knew that these animals had not lived in the area for years. He had seen small **carved** animals made by people living in France and Spain thousands of years ago. The paintings he saw in the cave looked just like the carvings. He **realized** that these paintings were probably made by people who lived long ago.

For many years, archaeologists did not believe that the paintings had been done by artists thousands of years ago. People did not think the colors could have stayed so bright or that people of long ago were **capable** of creating such good art. Archaeologists now have evidence that these pictures were drawn by people who lived as many as 30,000 years ago.

capable: able

carve: to make a statue by cutting wood, bone, or stone

realize: to understand

? THINK ABOUT IT:

Why didn't archaeologists think ancient people were capable of creating good art?

▲ *This picture shows one of the bison painted on the ceiling of the cave at Altamira, Spain.*

Cro-Magnons ate a lot of fish. They may have trapped them in pools of water and then speared them. Men, women, and children probably worked together to catch the fish.

The Cro-Magnons

The people who painted these cave pictures are called Cro-Magnons because the first bones were found in the Cro-Magnon caves in Southwestern France. These people lived about 40,000 to 10,000 years ago and were the ancestors of modern people.

Just like Neanderthals, the Cro-Magnons were hunter-gatherers who lived during the Ice Age. The Cro-Magnons and the Neanderthals lived alongside each other for at least 10,000 years. No one knows if they **interacted** or not. Both groups probably spent most of their time finding enough to eat. However, the Cro-Magnons had better tools and weapons than the Neanderthals, and they were probably more successful hunters.

This grindstone and pestle were used to grind wild grain about 17,000 years ago.

? THINK ABOUT IT:

Do you think the Neanderthals and Cro-Magnons interacted with each other? Why or why not?

---

interact: to do things together

▲ *These hunters are using spear throwers to attack a herd of reindeer. Cro-Magnon hunters used the meat, hides, bones, and antlers of reindeer.*

harpoon: a spear with a rope tied to it

stampede: to cause a sudden running away of a group of frightened animals

? THINK ABOUT IT:

What can modern people learn from the Cro-Magnons?

Hunting

The Cro-Magnons were successful hunters because they had very good weapons. They made many different kinds of flaked stone tools and weapons for hunting. Anthropologists believe that Cro-Magnons threw spears to kill animals. They also had fishhooks and **harpoons** to catch fish, and they probably made traps to catch birds and animals.

They made tools of stone, wood, antler, bone, and ivory. Anthropologists have found more than 100 types of tools in Cro-Magnons' tool kits.

Cro-Magnons also learned to herd animals to places where they could kill them for food. In France, anthropologists found the fossil bones of 10,000 wild horses at the bottom of a high cliff. Year after year, Cro-Magnon hunters had **stampeded** the horses off the cliff.

Tools

Much skill and patience was needed to make the Cro-Magnons' stone tools. It took more than 250 blows with a rock to make a **flint** flake knife. The toolmaker had to know just where to strike the blow to shape the flint. The Cro-Magnons' flint knives were sharp. They were as good for cutting as steel knives, except that they broke more easily.

These tools allowed Cro-Magnons to have much more control of their environment and made their lives better. Spear throwers made it possible to kill animals from farther away. The Cro-Magnons' scrapers, cutters, and sewing needles helped them make more comfortable clothing and living shelters. They also were able to make **luxuries** such as jewelry.

The Cro-Magnons often were able to stay in one place and find enough food because they had good weapons and tools and there were so many animals. This made it possible for them to build more **permanent** living places and also to have more **possessions**.

flint: a very hard stone

luxury: something you would like to have, but don't need

permanent: made to last a long time

possession: something a person owns

▶ *Cro-Magnons put rows of barbs down the sides of harpoons to make them better for catching fish.*

embroider: to make a design on material using a needle and thread

functional: doing a certain job

stencil: to make a pattern by covering up places that will not be painted

? THINK ABOUT IT:

Why do you think hunting was so important to the Cro-Magnons?

Cro-Magnon Art

The Cro-Magnons' tools were not just **functional**. Often they also were beautiful. Many of the Cro-Magnons' tools were carved with decorations. The Cro-Magnons also made pottery, wove baskets, painted pictures, and carved sculptures. Some of their paintings and sculptures are considered to be among the best in the world.

Cro-Magnon artists painted lively, well-drawn figures of animals. They also carved animals and female figures out of stone, ivory, bone, and antlers. Most of their pictures had animals in them, probably because hunting was so important in their lives.

In some caves, there are hand prints. These hand prints were usually **stenciled** around the paintings of animals. Anthropologists think that may have been the artist's way of signing the painting or possibly a way of showing power over the animal.

Cro-Magnon Burials

Anthropologists think the Cro-Magnons, like the Neanderthals, believed in life after death. They have found stone tools in some graves. They also have found necklaces of bone beads, and rings and bracelets of ivory. Some of the dead were buried with fur clothes **embroidered** with shells and beads. This shows that some Cro-Magnons were considered more important than others.

▲ *This shows a stencil of a hand print.*

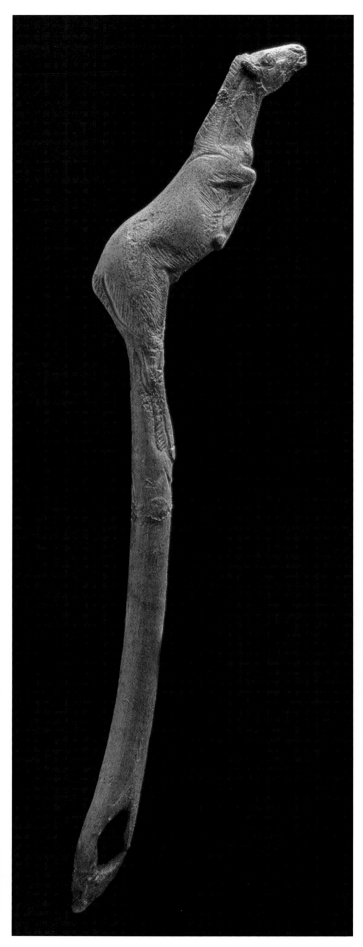

◄ *Spear throwers were about a foot long, with a hook at one end. This one is carved from a reindeer antler in the shape of a horse.*

▼ *A Cro-Magnon artist carved this small head from ivory.*

End of the Ice Age

About 10,000 years ago, the climate in Europe warmed up. Many of the herds of animals moved farther north. Some of the animals could not adjust to the changes in weather and became extinct.

Most of the hunters followed the herds north. Some stayed behind and **adapted** to new conditions. People began to keep herds of cattle, sheep, and other animals to use for food, clothing, and shelter. In some parts of the world, people began to farm for the first time. In the next chapter, you will read about the first farmers.

▲ *The woolly mammoth lived in Asia and North America during the Ice Age. It weighed eight tons and was 12-feet tall. It disappeared about 10,000 years ago, probably because it could not adapt to warmer temperatures after the Ice Age ended.*

Chapter Summary—Ingenuity

Just like the Neanderthals, the Cro-Magnons lived during the Ice Age. The climate was very cold. They had to hunt for all their food and make all their own tools, weapons, clothes, and shelters from things they could find around them. The Cro-Magnons were resourceful. They became excellent hunters. They may have been the most successful hunters of all time. They were also very good artists. Their drawings still are considered among the best in the world.

The Cro-Magnons' excellent tools made it possible for them to find plenty of food and live in very cold parts of the world. Because of their success in finding food and adapting to their environment, their population grew.

? THINK ABOUT IT:

How did the tools of each group of people in this unit influence their survival?

▼ *These Cro-Magnons are getting ready for the long, cold winter. They will stay in the shelter made from three tepee-like parts.*

CHAPTER 4
The People of Çatal Hüyük

ERA: Prehistoric Times
PLACE: Çatal Hüyük
PEOPLE: The people of Çatal Hüyük
THEME: Ingenuity—being resourceful, inventive, and skillful

CHAPTER FOCUS: Villages and towns grew as people began to raise animals, grow crops, and trade goods with one another.

LINK

For thousands, perhaps even millions of years, people were hunters and gatherers. They moved from place to place in search of food. In the last chapter, you read about one of these groups of people, the Cro-Magnons. Then after the last Ice Age, about 9000 B.C., people began to settle down. In this chapter, you will read about the people of Çatal Hüyük (chah-TUL hoo-YUK) who were one of the first groups to settle down, grow food, and raise animals. As you read, think about how the people of Çatal Hüyük interacted with their environment to meet their needs.

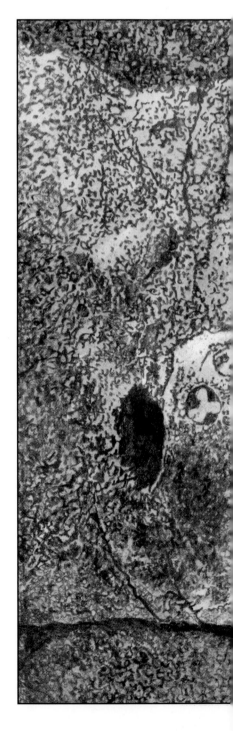

▲ *These leopard figures were on a wall in Çatal Hüyük.*

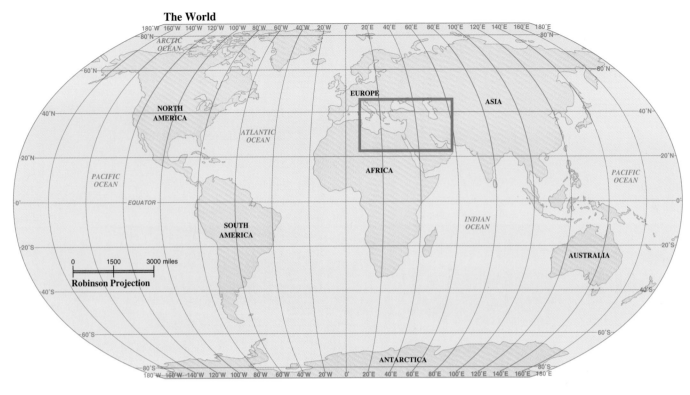

The World

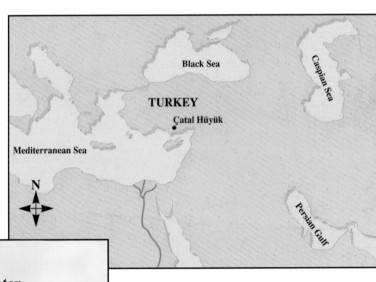

▶ *Çatal Hüyük is located in present-day Turkey.*

Black Sea

Caspian Sea

TURKEY

Çatal Hüyük

Mediterranean Sea

Persian Gulf

N

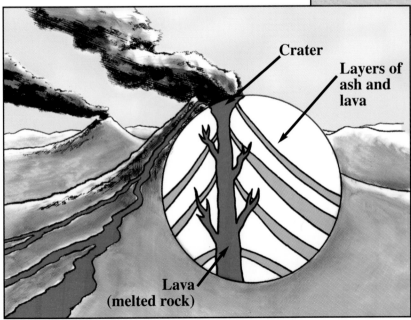

Crater

Layers of ash and lava

Lava (melted rock)

◀ GEOGRAPHY IN FOCUS

volcano: a hole in the earth's crust through which hot ashes or lava (melted rock) come out

After the lava cooled, the people of Çatal Hüyük gathered a hard black rock, called obsidian, from the volcanoes.

▲ *Modern farmers harvest grain in Turkey with a machine called a combine.*

The Beginning of Farming

In many parts of southwestern Asia, wheat and barley grow naturally. About 10,000 years ago, people put pieces of flint into wooden handles and **reaped** these grains. They ground the wild wheat and barley and probably used them for a kind of cereal. Then one year, they began to save some of the seeds for planting. This was the beginning of farming.

After they began farming, people no longer moved around from place to place as much because they had a steady source of food. They built more permanent houses and small villages. One of these villages was **Çatal Hüyük**.

Çatal Hüyük: in the Turkish language, *Çatal* means "fork" and *Hüyük* means "mound"

reap: to gather a crop by cutting

? THINK ABOUT IT:

What are some ways people's lives changed when they began to farm?

The Mounds of Çatal Hüyük

In 1961, a team of archaeologists came to two large **mounds** on a **plain** in Turkey. They had come to excavate the **ruins** of the Neolithic, or New Stone Age, town of Çatal Hüyük. The mounds were covered by grass and weeds, except on one side where the winds had uncovered some mud-brick buildings.

The archaeologists began their excavation at the older of the two mounds. As they began to dig, they discovered that there were 12 levels of the town. The first level probably was built around 6500 B.C. or even earlier. When a building **collapsed** or burned down, people just built new buildings on top of the ruins. Each time they rebuilt, the town was a little higher above the plain. In time, Çatal Hüyük was on a mound, or a small hill.

The Beginning of Çatal Hüyük

Probably a group of about 50 people began the **settlement** of Çatal Hüyük. They chose a spot near a river. The area had hot summers and very cold winters, but the people could get water from the river. There also were many animals in the area.

The population grew. By around 5800 B.C., as many as 5,000 or 6,000 people lived there. By this time, Çatal Hüyük was the largest town in southwestern Asia.

---

collapse: to fall in

mound: a pile of dirt; a small hill

plain: a stretch of flat, level country

ruins: the remains of a building or city

settlement: a village

? THINK ABOUT IT:

What are some things that make a place good for settlement?

◀ *In Çatal Hüyük, there was no space between the houses. People spent much of their time on the roofs, eating, sleeping, and talking.*

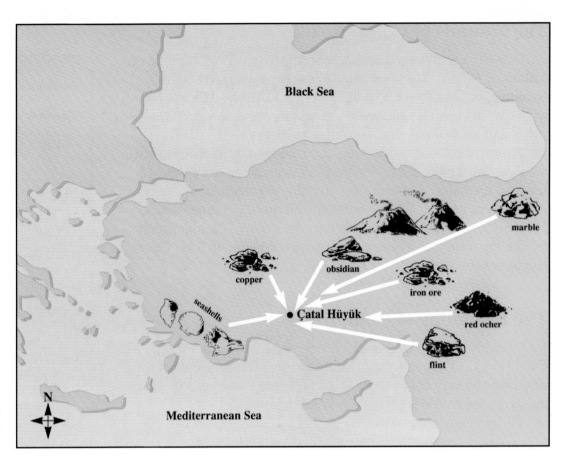

The people of Çatal Hüyük imported materials from surrounding areas.

boar: a wild hog (with a hairy coat and a long snout)

dagger: a short weapon with a sharp point

export: to send goods to another place to sell or trade

import: to bring goods into one place from another

prosperous: successful; well-off

Trade Center

Çatal Hüyük was a **prosperous** town. Farmers grew many different crops, including wheat, barley, and peas. People raised sheep and cattle and hunted wild cattle, red deer, **boars**, wild donkeys, and leopards.

As the town grew, groups of people left and built small villages around Çatal Hüyük. The people who lived in Çatal Hüyük traded with people in these villages and with people in other towns. Trade may have been the most important way for the people of Çatal Hüyük to make a living. They probably **imported** marble and other kinds of stone and **exported** finished goods such as marble bowls, beads, and small statues.

One item they probably traded was a hard, black rock called obsidian. Ancient people used obsidian for mirrors, spearheads, and also as a kind of money. The people of Çatal Hüyük gathered obsidian from two active volcanoes at the east end of the plain. They traded it for other things they needed, such as flint for **daggers** and other tools.

◄ *The picture shows the ruins of a religious shrine at Çatal Hüyük. Archaeologists knew this was a shrine because of the sculpture of the bull head on the wall. The bull was used in religious ceremonies at Çatal Hüyük.*

Houses in Çatal Hüyük

The people of Çatal Hüyük built their houses from materials they could find nearby. They brought oak and juniper wood from the hills for the frames of their houses. They made mud bricks for the walls. Then they covered the brick walls, inside and out, with white **plaster** made from clay. They made roofs from **bundles** of reeds covered with mud on top.

All the houses were very much alike. Most of them were one-story high, and each house had two rooms. One room was for living. The other room was for storing things. The rooms were rectangular in shape. Archaeologists think there might have been small windows high in the walls. The floors and the ceilings were covered with mats.

Each room had **platforms** and benches made of wood. People sat, worked, and slept on the platforms. They went in and out through a hole in the roof. Smoke from their fires and ovens also went out this hole.

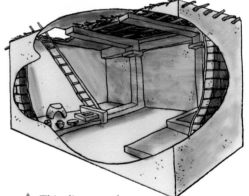

▲ *This diagram shows the inside of a room. You can see the platforms, hearth, and the ladder that people used to go in and out.*

? THINK ABOUT IT:

What information is fact? What is judgment?

> **bundle:** a number of things tied together
>
> **plaster:** a mixture of clay, sand, and water
>
> **platform:** a part of the floor that is higher than the rest

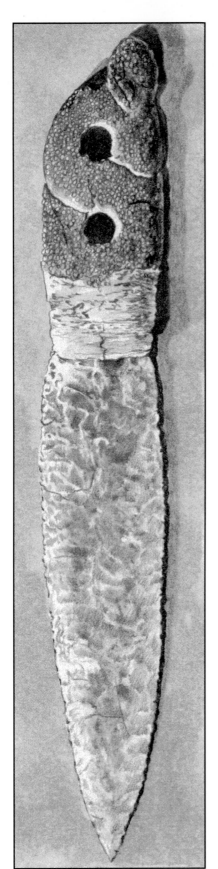

Specialization

In time, farmers grew more food than they needed for their own families. They had extra food to trade with other families. That meant some families did not have to farm. They could do other things to trade for food. Many of the people at Çatal Hüyük became **specialists**. There were probably farmers who raised crops and people who raised cattle and sheep.

Other specialists might have been bakers or people who made weapons such as slingshots, bows and arrows, and spears. Still others wove cloth or made baskets or wooden containers. Each person became very good at a certain skill.

Although the people of Çatal Hüyük were experts at many things, they did not seem to have any form of writing, **bookkeeping**, or music.

bookkeeping: a record of trading or buying and selling

specialist: a person who does a certain kind of work

? THINK ABOUT IT:

In what ways would your life be different if we did not have writing or bookkeeping?

◀ *The people of Çatal Hüyük become specialists. Some specialists made weapons such as this dagger to trade with other people.*

Crafts from Materials at Hand

Artisans used materials they found close to home to make many things. They gathered wood, animal bones, and antlers to make boxes and other kinds of containers. These boxes are better than any others that have been found in southwestern Asia from this time period. Artisans wove baskets from straw and other plants that grew near the town.

The people of Çatal Hüyük also made and used pottery. They exported the pottery to people in other villages. However, they also continued to use containers made from wood and other materials.

> **artisan:** a person skilled at making things

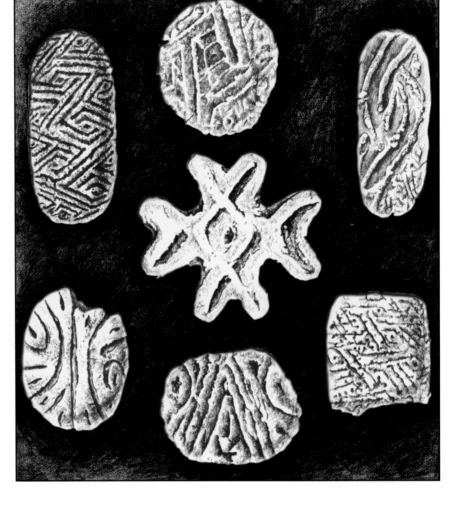

▶ *The people of Çatal Hüyük made many clay seals. No one knows how they were used, but people may have used them to decorate cloth or to decorate their bodies.*

? THINK ABOUT IT:

What kinds of things could you make from materials that can be found near your home?

▶ *These drawings show what the wooden containers of Çatal Hüyük looked like.*

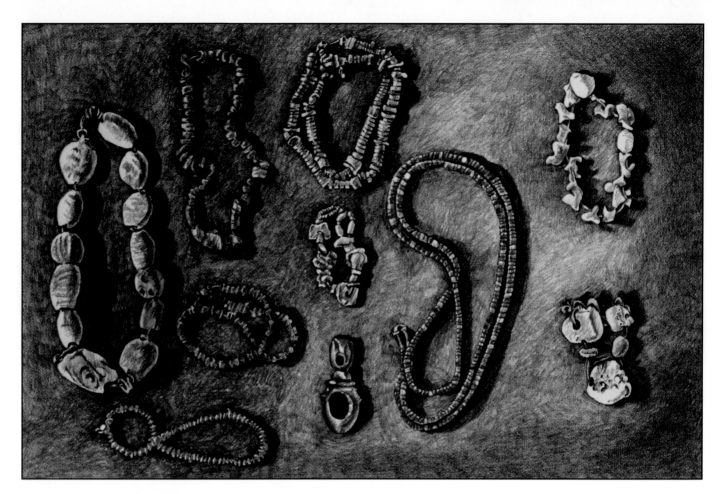

▲ *The people of Çatal Hüyük made jewelry from stone beads.*

Crafts from Imported Materials

The people of Çatal Hüyük also used materials from farther away to make things. For example, they used seashells from the Mediterranean Sea to make beads. They used stones such as alabaster, marble, and limestone, to make jars, beads, grinding stones, and small religious statues.

Artisans **polished** the obsidian they gathered and put it in holders of limestone plaster to make mirrors. They made beads and rings from imported copper and lead.

Chapter Summary—Ingenuity

The people of Çatal Hüyük are a good example of human ingenuity. They learned how to adapt to their environment and to use the available resources to the **maximum**. The town of Çatal Hüyük prospered for around 1,000 years. Then around 5600 B.C., the town was **abandoned**. No one knows why.

In the years that followed, other villages and towns grew up. Some of these towns grew into cities. In the next unit, you will read about the people of Sumer who built great civilizations in the "Fertile Crescent."

abandon: to leave

maximum: the greatest amount possible

? THINK ABOUT IT:

What are some reasons the people of Çatal Hüyük might have abandoned their town?

The Resourceful People of Çatal Hüyük

TOOK RAW MATERIALS		AND MADE	
Cattle		Meat and Leather	
Obsidian		Mirrors	
Reeds		Mats	
Stones and Seashells		Statues and Jewelry	
Sheep		Wool	
Mud		Bricks	
Leopards		Clothes	
Clay		Pottery and Plaster	

UNIT 2: RIVER VALLEY CIVILIZATIONS IN THE MIDDLE EAST AND AFRICA

CHAPTER 5

The Sumerians

ERA: Early Civilizations
PLACE: Sumer
PEOPLE: King Ur-Nammu of Ur and the Sumerians
THEME: Power—the ability to control others

CHAPTER FOCUS: The Sumerians developed the world's first known civilization.

3500 B.C.	3000 B.C.	2500 B.C.	2000 B.C.	1500 B.C.	1000 B.C.	500 B.C.	0	A.D. 500

King Ur-Nammu rebuilds the walls of Ur (2100 B.C.)

▼ *The city of Ur was one of the great cities of Sumer. This is how Ur might have looked when Ur-Nammu was king.*

LINK

In the last unit, you read about fossil discoveries and early human societies. Each group had its own accomplishments: Homo habilis used stone tools; the Neanderthals buried their dead; the Cro-Magnons created beautiful cave art; and the people of Çatal Hüyük built a large town, grew crops, and became specialists in different jobs. However, none of these groups developed a civilization.

In this chapter, you will read about the Sumerians, who lived in an area of southwestern Asia commonly called the Middle East. The Sumerians were good at thinking up new ways to do things. This chapter tells about many beginnings, including the beginning of the world's first known civilization. As you read, think about how the Sumerian rulers showed their power by building monuments.

The World

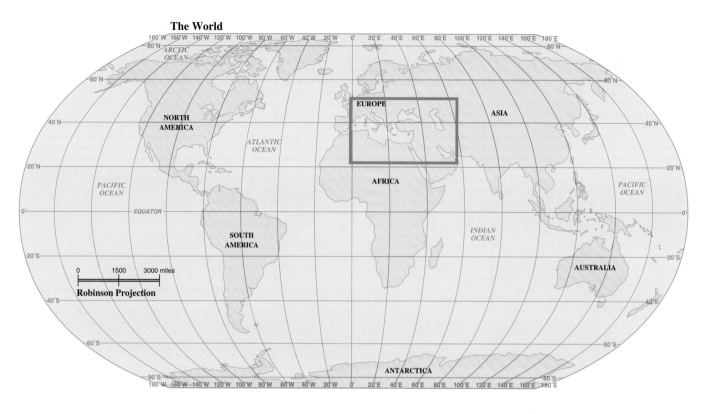

▶ *Sumer (SOO-mur) was part of a larger area called Mesopotamia. Mesopotamia is a Greek word meaning "the land between two rivers." Sumer was located between the Tigris and Euphrates rivers.*

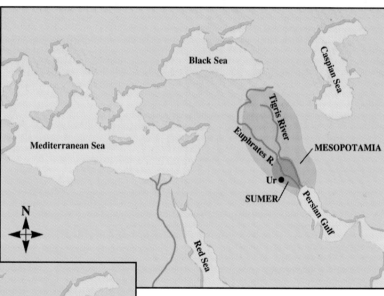

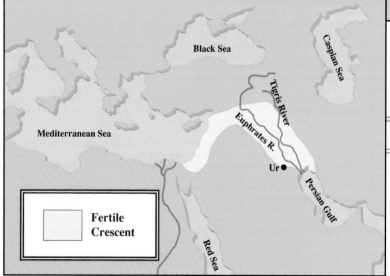

Fertile Crescent

◀ **GEOGRAPHY IN FOCUS**

Fertile Crescent: *a region of rich, fertile soil that stretched from the Mediterranean Sea, between the Tigris and Euphrates rivers, to the Persian Gulf*

The Sumerians are one of the groups that developed their civilization in the Fertile Crescent.

The Beginning of the City-State

Sometime after 4000 B.C., groups of people called Sumerians settled along the **banks** of the Tigris and Euphrates rivers. At first they probably lived in small villages made up of mud huts. However, by 3000 B.C., they had built great cities.

There were 15 to 20 cities in Sumer. Each city had its own **independent** government and its own army. Each city also controlled the villages around it. These were not just cities, they were city-states. The city-states of Sumer were constantly at war with one another. Most of their battles were over rights to use the water of the rivers.

bank: the side of a river

independent: not under the control of another

? THINK ABOUT IT:

Why do you think the Sumerians built cities?

How is a city-state like a state? How is it different?

Differences Between a City and a City-State	
CITY	**CITY-STATE**
A city is a large, important town. It has the following characteristics: • Permanence (people stay in the same place for a long time) • Size (population is over 5,000) • Specialization of jobs (people perform different jobs) • Organized religion (religious leaders direct worship) • Cooperative services (people work together on large projects)	A city-state is made up of an independent city and the areas the city directly controls. A city-state has all the characteristics of a city, but it also has three additional characteristics: • Independent government • Army for defense • Control over surrounding villages

▲ *Sumerian artisans created beautiful objects such as this dagger and* **lyre**.
The lyre is decorated with gold and a blue stone called lapis lazuli.

canal: a waterway built for irrigation

irrigate: to supply with water

lyre: a musical instrument

practical: useful

temple: a building for the worship of a god or gods

The City-State of Ur

One of the most famous of the Sumerian city-states was Ur. Ur was surrounded by brick walls. Inside the walls were large **temples**, palaces, and comfortable houses. Carpenters, glass-workers, jewelers, and other artisans made objects that were both beautiful and **practical**. Outside the walls were huge fields **irrigated** by long **canals**. By 2100 B.C., almost 40,000 people lived inside the city walls.

The walls of Ur were important because they protected the people from attacks by armies from the other city-states and also by tribes from the mountains.

The Beginning of Kings

At first, the **citizens** of Ur met as a group to make decisions. There was no king or president. Sometimes, however, they chose one man to be in charge for a short time. This person might lead a religious celebration or lead the army to fight an enemy. They called this leader *lugal*, which means "a great man."

After the ceremony or the battle, the lugal went back to his regular job in the community. In time, these leaders wanted to keep their jobs permanently. Eventually, the lugal became a king.

The **priests** began to tell the story that the gods had given the people kings. They said that kings ruled by "**divine right**."

> **citizen:** a member of a state or nation who has certain duties, rights, and privileges, such as the right to vote
>
> **divine right:** the god-given right to be king
>
> **priest:** a religious leader
>
> **standard:** an object such as a flag or banner, used as a symbol of a group of people

▼ *This "**Standard** of Ur" is a mosaic picture. It tells the story of a successful battle that happened around 2500 B.C. In the top row, a king stands in the center.*

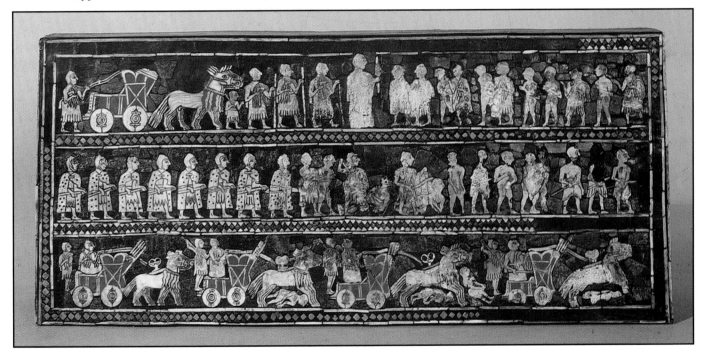

? THINK ABOUT IT:

What are some reasons the priests might have wanted people to believe kings ruled by "divine right"?

▲ *The ziggurat was the largest building in the city. It could be seen from 20 miles away.*

The Beginning of Monumental Building

For many years the people of Ur did not take care of their city. The walls and the irrigation canals needed to be **repaired**. Then, around 2100 B.C., Ur-Nammu became king.

Ur-Nammu organized the people to rebuild the walls of the city, repair the irrigation canals, and build a large brick palace for him. The Sumerians also built temples to honor the gods of Ur. These were the first **monumental** buildings.

The walls of the temples were built of mud bricks. Whenever the walls of one temple fell down, a new temple was built on the ruins. In time, this made a building of giant steps called a **ziggurat**. A small temple was built on top of the ziggurat.

monumental: very large, solid, and long-lasting

repair: to put back in good condition; to fix

ziggurat: a type of temple with a one-room shrine at the top

? THINK ABOUT IT:

How would you describe King Ur-Nammu?

The Beginning of Organized Religion

Religion was very important to the Sumerians. People in Ur worshiped thousands of gods and goddesses. The four most important gods were the god of heaven, the god of air, the god of water, and the god of earth. In addition to these gods, each city had a god or goddess. The god of Ur was Nanna. Each person had a personal god. There also were gods or goddesses for everyday objects such as plows and pick-axes.

The people of Sumer thought their gods ate, got married, and fought among themselves, just like people. They believed that if the gods were unhappy, they caused floods, withheld rains, and brought attacks by enemies. According to a Sumerian **myth**, the gods had made people out of clay to serve them.

To keep the gods happy, priests gave them **offerings** from the people. They praised the gods with songs and music. Priests also gave food to needy people, especially women and children. In time, many people worked for the priests at the temple. There were cooks, maids, and weavers. There were farmers growing crops and artisans making pottery, furniture, and small statues of the gods. The priests became very **influential**.

influential: powerful; having power over people because of one's position

myth: a story told over and over that explains something about nature, the customs, or religious beliefs of a people

offering: a gift made in worship

? THINK ABOUT IT:

Were the Sumerians the first people to have religious beliefs? Explain your answer.

What makes the Sumerians' religion organized?

▼ *This statue is of a worshiper holding a candle. People used statues like this in religious ceremonies at the temples.*

*The Sumerians worked together to build irrigation systems. In this picture, you can see a man lifting water with a **shadoof**. The Sumerians **invented** the shadoof.*

ditch: a long, narrow cut in the earth for carrying water

flow: to move in a stream

invent: to think up new ideas or ways to do things

levee: a special wall built along a river to keep water from flooding the land

shadoof: a device that consists of a long pole with a bucket on one end and a weight on the other to draw water to irrigate the fields

? THINK ABOUT IT:

How was the river's overflow both good and bad for the Sumerians?

What did the Sumerians do that made it possible to build irrigation canals?

The Beginning of Irrigation

Every spring the Euphrates River overflowed its banks and left a rich layer of soft soil on the fields. Even though the soil between the Tigris and Euphrates rivers was fertile, the summers were long, dry, and hot.

The people of Ur needed to use water from the rivers to irrigate their crops. At first they carried the water to their small fields. Later they cut **ditches** in the **levees** so the water could **flow** to their crops. By 2100 B.C., when Ur-Nammu was king, the people of Ur had built long canals to bring water to fields far from town. This was the beginning of irrigation.

The Beginning of Community Cooperation

One family could not build the canals and manage a large farm alone, so the Sumerians learned to cooperate and work together.

Some people became managers in charge of building the canals and keeping the canals working for the farmers. Other people became carpenters, artisans, merchants, or **scribes**. However, in an **emergency**, these workers came back to help in the fields.

Just like at Çatal Hüyük, the farmers at Ur often had more grain than they needed for their families. Farmers traded their **surplus** grain for goods and services from the workers.

emergency: a sudden situation that needs immediate action

scribe: a person who does the writing for others

surplus: more than what is needed; extra

? THINK ABOUT IT:

What services would be missing if people in a city did not work together?

Community Cooperation

1

This farmer has more grain than he needs, but he does not have any containers to store them. The man on the right is an artisan who makes containers.

2

The farmer trades his grain for containers. The artisan now has grain to feed his family. Both men are happy.

▲ *The bronze blade of the plow helped farmers cultivate hard soil.*

alloy: a metal that is a mixture of two or more metals

cultivate: to prepare soil for planting

plot: an area of ground

technology: progress in the use of tools

? THINK ABOUT IT:

What are some ways the plow probably changed the lives of the Sumerians?

The Beginning of Technology

The Sumerians were always looking for better ways to do things. Many of the Sumerians' inventions helped them become more successful farmers. This was the beginning of **technology**.

They invented the plow to dig through the hard soil. The first plow the Sumerians used was just a crooked tree branch. By the time Ur-Nammu was king, the Sumerians were using an **alloy** of copper and tin to make bronze. Bronze is a hard metal, and it makes a strong plow. This plow made it possible for the Sumerians to **cultivate** large **plots** of land.

The Beginning of the Wheel

The Sumerians invented many other things, including the wheel. The first wheels were made of solid wood. The Sumerians probably first used the wheel in making pottery. Later, farmers discovered it could help them, too. An ox or a donkey **hitched** to a cart with wheels could carry three times as much as an animal could carry on its back.

The Sumerians made carts with two or four wheels. Sometimes they even hitched wild donkeys to these carts and raced them.

hitch: to fasten or hook onto something

? THINK ABOUT IT:

What are some ways your life would be different without wheels?

▲ *This is a model of a two-wheeled Sumerian chariot that is being pulled by wild donkeys. The Sumerians sometimes raced chariots like this to see whose team was the fastest.*

▼ *A bulla and tokens like those below could help a merchant keep track of trade.*

syllable: a group of letters that make one sound

symbol: a written mark that stands for an object or idea

token: a piece of clay that stands for something else (one token for each cow or sheep)

The Beginning of Writing

The priests and merchants of Sumer needed a way to keep records. Priests wanted to remember who had made their yearly contributions to the temple. Merchants needed to list the goods they had sent for trade.

Around 8000 B.C., merchants put small clay **tokens** in hollow clay balls called "bullas" to keep track of the goods they had traded. They made a mark on the outside to show how many tokens were inside.

Later, scribes used sharpened reeds to make marks on small tablets of clay. These marks showed small pictures, called pictographs, and the number of the objects traded. The problem with this system was that it left bumps on the clay. Also, there were thousands of pictographs to learn because each pictograph stood for a different idea, place, or object.

By 2500 B.C., scribes stopped using the pointed reed and used one shaped like a triangle that left a neat, wedge-shaped mark. This kind of writing is called "cuneiform" (kyoo-NEE-uh-fohrm). The pictographs stood for **syllables** or sounds and ideas instead of just one object. This meant that they only needed to learn about 600 **symbols**. These pictographs marked the beginning of writing. Most Sumerians, however, did not know how to read and write.

The Beginning of Written Laws

At first, writing was used only to record the business of priests and merchants. Later, kings used writing to record laws, military leaders used it to **communicate** orders on the battlefield, and scribes began to write down stories.

King Ur-Nammu wrote the first law **code** that has been found. The tablet has been **damaged** so most of the laws cannot be read. However, one of the laws we can read says: "If a man has severed with a weapon the bones of another man, he shall pay one mina of silver." This was the beginning of written laws.

code: a group of rules

communicate: to give information

damage: to harm or injure something; to break

? THINK ABOUT IT:

What would our life be like without written laws?

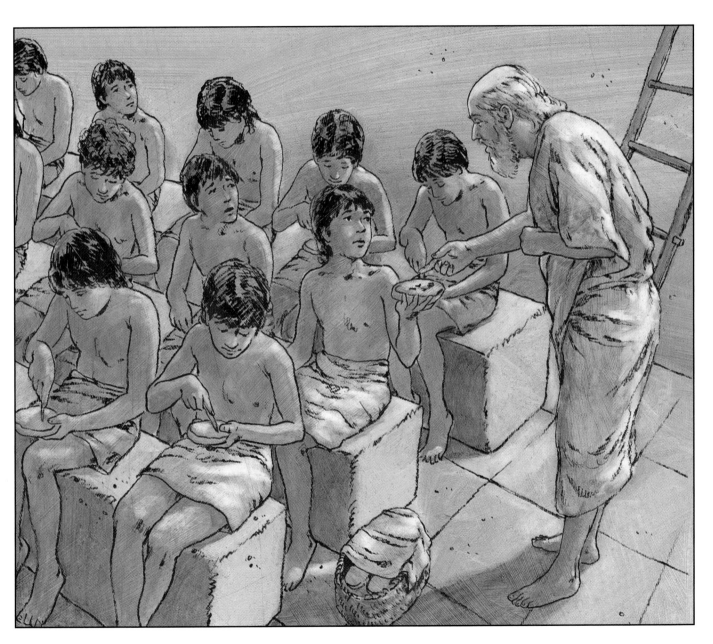

▲ *Boys went to school for many years to learn to write.*

CIVILIZATION

POPULATION

SPECIALIZATION OF JOBS

RELIGION & GOVERNMENT

WRITING

▶ *A civilization can be defined as a highly-developed culture that includes at least three of the following: cities with populations of 5,000 or more; specialization of jobs; organized religion and government; and a system of writing.*

The Beginning of Civilization

The first known civilization in the history of the world was in Sumer. The Sumerians built large cities. Farmers traded their surplus crops for goods made by artisans and for services by such people as carpenters. The people worshiped their gods and goddesses at large temples. Kings ruled the people according to written laws.

Perhaps most importantly, the Sumerians developed a system of writing. Because of all these things, we can say that the Sumerians developed the world's first known civilization.

Chapter Summary—The Sumerians: Inventive, but Hungry for Power

Both the geography of the river valley and the inventiveness of the Sumerians made it possible for the Sumerian civilization to develop. The **fertile soil** only needed water to make it grow an **abundance** of crops.

The Sumerians were determined to think of new and better ways to do things. They invented many useful things to make their lives easier. Their ideas and inventions soon spread to other people and places. However, the Sumerian city-states could not get along with each other. Each city-state wanted to be in control. For 1,000 years they fought with each other. In time, enemies from the east and from the west destroyed their cities.

In the next chapter, you will read about another group of people who developed a great civilization along the banks of the Nile River in Egypt.

abundance: a great supply; more than is needed

fertile soil: soil good for growing food

? THINK ABOUT IT:

What are some ways your life would be different if we did not have the things invented by the Sumerians?

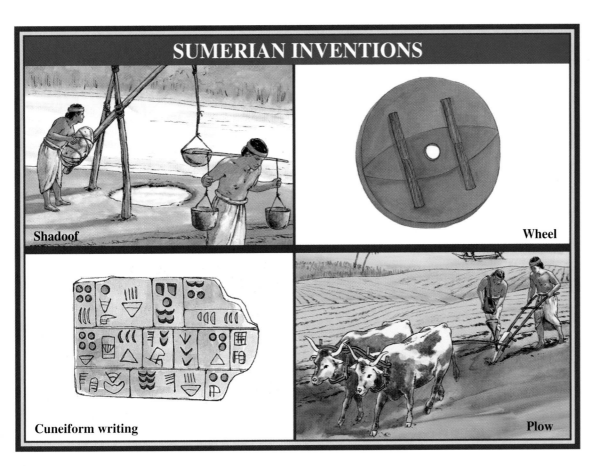

This chart shows some of the Sumerian inventions.

CHAPTER 6
Egypt: The New Kingdom

ERA: Early Civilizations
PLACE: Egypt
PEOPLE: Hatshepsut, pharaoh of Egypt, and the Egyptians
THEME: Power—the ability to control others; and Stability—the quality of being permanent, not changing easily

CHAPTER FOCUS: Hatshepsut was the first woman to call herself pharaoh. She helped ancient Egypt remain peaceful and prosperous for 20 years.

LINK

In the last chapter, you read about the Sumerians and the beginning of civilization along the Tigris and Euphrates rivers. Now you will read about another great civilization and another great river.

The history of Egypt is a story of kings and pharaohs. In this chapter, you will read about Hatshepsut (hat-SHEHP-soot), the first woman to call herself pharaoh. As you read, think about how the Egyptian rulers showed their power by building monuments.

Reign of Hatshepsut (1490-1468 B.C.)

▲ *Hatshepsut built this huge temple on the Nile River next to a temple built by an earlier ruler.*

The World

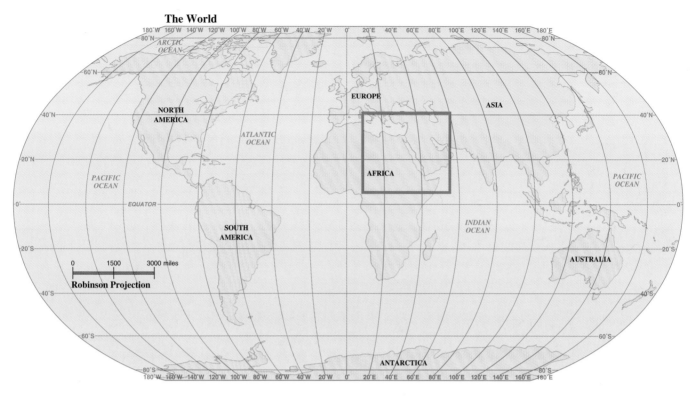

▼ GEOGRAPHY IN FOCUS

delta: *a deposit of sand and soil at the mouth of some rivers; the delta is usually shaped like a triangle*

The Nile River spreads out into a delta when it reaches the Mediterranean Sea.

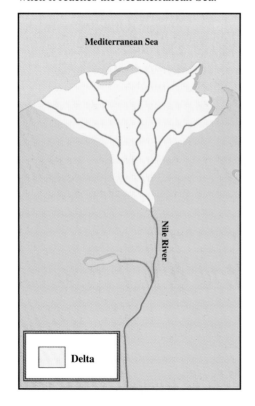

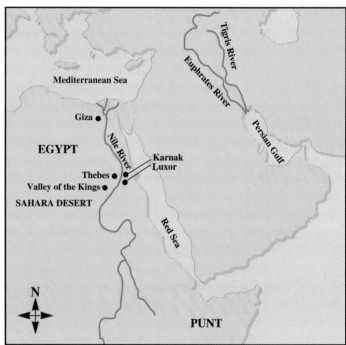

▲ *Egypt is in the northeastern corner of Africa. It is surrounded by the largest desert in the world, the Sahara. Ancient Egypt developed along both banks of the Nile River, the longest river in the world. The Nile River is 4,145 miles long. It begins south of Egypt. While most rivers flow south, the Nile flows north to the Mediterranean Sea.*

Black Land and Red Land

Almost every year beginning in August, the water level in the Nile River rose slowly. The water rose higher and higher until it overflowed the banks and flooded the land. In October the flooding gradually stopped, and the river slowly returned to its normal level. The flood waters left a rich, dark mud on the land. Long ago, people called the areas of dark soil in the Nile Valley the Black Land. They called the dry desert around the fertile valley the Red Land.

Five thousand years ago, ancient Egypt developed along the Nile River. It **remained** strong for 3,000 years.

Sometimes Egypt is called "the gift of the Nile" because the Nile River provides water for plants, animals, and people. Without the Nile River, Egypt could not have grown and prospered.

remain: to stay

? THINK ABOUT IT:

What question would you like to ask someone who lived near the Nile River in ancient Egypt?

▲ *The land along the banks of the Nile River is green and fertile. The land beyond the river is a dry desert.*

Three Kingdoms

The history of ancient Egypt is divided into three major time periods: the Old Kingdom, the Middle Kingdom, and the New Kingdom. The Old Kingdom lasted about 500 years, from 2750 to 2260 B.C. During this period, Egypt first became powerful. Kings began building **pyramids**.

The Middle Kingdom lasted about 300 years, from 2061 to 1784 B.C. During this period, Egypt became rich. Rulers improved the irrigation system. Farmers grew more crops. Trade increased with other countries.

The New Kingdom lasted about 500 years, from 1570 to 1070 B.C. Some say that this was the most **glorious** period in Egypt's history.

These three periods mark the times when powerful **dynasties** ruled Egypt. Egypt was more stable during these periods. The years in between were unstable.

▼ *This shows the pyramids at the Giza necropolis. "Necropolis" means "city of the dead." Throughout Egypt's 3,000-year history, **pharaohs** were buried in pyramids.*

dynasty: a line of rulers from the same family

glorious: being at the height of prosperity or achievement

pharaoh: the leader or king of ancient Egypt

pyramid: an ancient building where a dead body is placed; most are found in Egypt

? THINK ABOUT IT:

The largest pyramid at Giza is called the Great Pyramid and stands 450-feet high. How many students would you need to reach the top of the pyramid if they stood on each other's shoulders?

▲ *This drawing shows Thutmose I "raging like a panther."*

The New Kingdom Pharaohs

During the New Kingdom, Egyptians began calling their ruler "pharaoh." Before that time, they called their ruler "king."

Egyptian **society** had many levels and the pharaoh was at the very top. The pharaoh controlled and owned everything. Ancient Egyptians believed that the pharaoh was a god in human form. When the pharaoh died, his oldest son usually became the next ruler. In this way, power was kept in the family.

About 30 dynasties ruled ancient Egypt during its 3,000-year history. Thutmose I (thoot-MOH-suh) was one of the pharaohs who ruled during the New Kingdom period. One of his advisors wrote, "His Majesty, **raging** like a panther, transfixed his enemy … and carried him off … " This might have been an **exaggeration**, but Thutmose I did win back Egyptian lands from outsiders. His army also **conquered** new lands.

conquer: to take over someone else's land

exaggeration: a statement that makes a thing seem bigger or better or smaller or worse than it really is

rage: to show violent anger

society: a community having shared traditions, activities, or interests

? THINK ABOUT IT:

How were ancient Egyptian and Sumerian societies alike? How were they different?

▲ *These statues show two of the many ways artisans depicted Hatshepsut. In one, she looks like a woman. In the other, she wears the traditional **false** beard and dress of a pharaoh and looks like a man.*

boldly: to do something strongly and without fear

false: not real; not true

throne: the chair of a king, but also a symbol of the power of the king

? THINK ABOUT IT:

Did Hatshepsut have the right to rule ancient Egypt? Why or why not?

Hatshepsut Becomes Pharaoh

When Thutmose I died, his son, Thutmose II, became pharaoh. Thutmose II married Hatshepsut, and they ruled Egypt for about 18 years.

According to custom, when Thutmose II died, his son Thutmose III should have taken the **throne**. However, Thutmose III was very young, so Hatshepsut ruled for him. Later, she pushed him aside and **boldly** called herself pharaoh. Hatshepsut felt she had the right to rule because she was the daughter of one pharaoh and the wife of another.

Women had taken over for kings before, but Hatshepsut was the first woman to call herself pharaoh.

Hatshepsut's Tomb

Hatshepsut began building her **tomb** soon after she became pharaoh. She did this for several reasons. A huge tomb would be a symbol of her power. In addition, ancient Egyptians believed in an **afterlife**. They believed that if they prepared **properly**, their spirits would live forever. Rich Egyptians built tombs to protect their preserved bodies, or **mummies**, and their **treasures** after they died. It took a long time to build a tomb, so work began while the person was still alive.

Hatshepsut wanted to have her mummy placed in her tomb in the Valley of the Kings after her death. The Valley of the Kings in Thebes is where many of the tombs of the pharoahs are found. However, when archaeologists excavated her tomb, they could not find her mummy. To this day, no one knows what happened to it.

afterlife: life after death

mummy: a dead body that is handled in a special way to keep it from decaying

properly: correctly; to do something as it should be done

tomb: a building where a dead body is placed; grave

treasure: valuables such as gold, silver, and jewels

▲ *Wealthy Egyptians put models like this one of a building for storing grain in tombs. They thought they would need these things in the afterlife.*

Building a Temple and a Tomb

Hatshepsut built her temple and tomb near the Valley of the Kings. Some people think that Hatshepsut's temple is the most beautiful one in Egypt.

All levels of Egyptian society were probably involved in the building of Hatshepsut's temple. Government officials organized the project. Priests approved the design. Scribes kept records of the whole process. Artisans made **relief sculptures** and statues. Hundreds of workers built the temple. Hatshepsut paid for this work from her **royal** treasure.

Some of the workers were farmers. Farmers could not work in the fields when the Nile flooded. During the yearly floods, many worked on royal building projects such as Hatshepsut's temple, other tombs, or irrigation projects.

▲ *This model of Hatshepsut's temple shows what it probably looked like during the New Kingdom.*

? THINK ABOUT IT:

Compare the picture of Hatshepsut's temple on pages 68-69 with the picture on this page. Why does it look so different? What caused the changes?

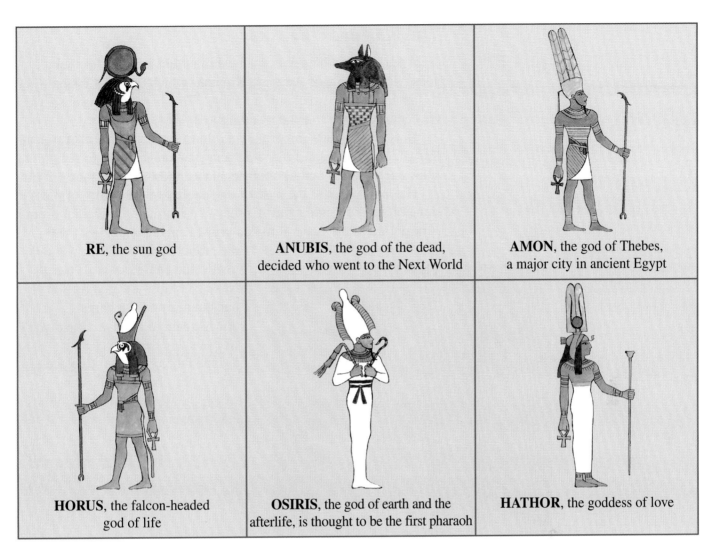

RE, the sun god

ANUBIS, the god of the dead, decided who went to the Next World

AMON, the god of Thebes, a major city in ancient Egypt

HORUS, the falcon-headed god of life

OSIRIS, the god of earth and the afterlife, is thought to be the first pharaoh

HATHOR, the goddess of love

▲ *These are just a few of the many gods and goddesses the Egyptians worshiped.*

Many Gods and Goddesses

There were many **shrines** in Hatshepsut's temple. Each shrine was **dedicated** to a different god. The ancient Egyptians worshiped many gods and goddesses. These **deities** were sometimes represented as humans, sometimes as animals, and sometimes as both. Egyptians believed that gods controlled everything. Just like the Sumerians, the Egyptians had deities for everyday activities, and each city had its own special god.

Although there were many Egyptian gods, Re, the sun god, became the official god during the Old Kingdom. During the Middle Kingdom, Amon became very important. Amon and Re were sometimes worshiped together as the deity Amon-Re. The largest shrine in Hatshepsut's temple was dedicated to Amon.

dedicate: to address a piece of art, music, or a book to a person (or deity) to honor or thank that person

deity: a god or goddess

shrine: an altar, chapel, or other place of worship

? THINK ABOUT IT:

Why do you think the ancient Egyptians and the Sumerians had deities for everyday activities? How does this compare with other religions you know about?

The Karnak Obelisks

Ancient Egyptians built many shrines and temples for their gods. The Temple of Amon at **Karnak**, which began as a small shrine, ended up as the largest temple. This happened because over the centuries, pharaohs kept adding to it.

Hatshepsut made important additions to the Temple of Amon at Karnak. She added a stone **sanctuary** and dedicated it to Amon. In addition, she had two tall **obelisks** placed there in his honor.

Hieroglyphics at the base of one obelisk tell the story of these stone pillars. The red **granite** pillars were brought to Karnak from almost 150 miles away. It took a year to carve the obelisks out of the granite quarry. Then, workers loaded the obelisks onto a **barge**. Next, 27 ships powered by 846 **oarsmen** towed the barge downstream to Karnak. Finally, workers dug deep holes and dropped the obelisks into place. One of the obelisks still stands where the workers placed it almost 3,500 years ago.

▶ *This photograph shows an obelisk at the Temple of Amon in Karnak.*

barge: a large, flat-bottomed boat for carrying goods on rivers

granite: a hard stone used for building

hieroglyphic: a picture or symbol used in ancient Egyptian writing

Karnak: a city in Egypt

oarsman: a person who rows a boat

obelisk: a tall pillar set up in honor of a special event, person, or deity

sanctuary: a part of a church or temple

? THINK ABOUT IT:

Name some of the monuments we have built to honor people or events in this country or other countries.

Making a Mummy

Ancient Egyptians believed that without a body the spirit would die. They thought that making a mummy was a way to preserve both the person's body and spirit.

It took more than two months to prepare a mummy. First, **embalmers** used special tools to remove all the **organs** inside the body, except the heart. The embalmers then dried the organs and placed them in special jars. Meanwhile, they kept the body covered for 40 days with a natural salt to dry it.

After the body was dried, embalmers toughened and **waterproofed** the skin with hot **resin**. Finally, they wrapped the body in linen strips. They might have used up to 400 yards of **fabric**! For extra protection, they put **amulets** or magic charms into the linen wrappings next to the body.

amulet: a magic charm to keep away evil

embalmer: a person who preserves a dead body from decay by using special salts or chemicals

fabric: cloth

organ: a part of the body which does certain work; the stomach, liver, heart, and lungs are organs

resin: a sticky material that comes from trees and plants

waterproof: to make something so that it cannot soak up any water

? THINK ABOUT IT:

What can we learn about people from studying their graves?

▼ *This Egyptian mummy is on display at the Field Museum in Chicago. The body was preserved so well that it still exists today.*

Voyage to the "Incense Land" of Punt

We know about some of Hatshepsut's great **deeds** from the stone monuments, or relief sculptures, that artisans carved into the walls of her temple. One wall shows a famous voyage to **Punt**. Five ships sailed south on the Red Sea to Punt. They were gone for two years.

Hatshepsut sent beautiful jewelry, axes, daggers, and other gifts to the rulers of Punt. In return, they gave her many gifts, including live **myrrh** trees. Hatshepsut had these trees planted outside the Temple of Amon. Myrrh from the trees was made into sweet smelling incense and used in temple **rites**.

The Power of the Pharaoh

Unlike many pharaohs before her, Hatshepsut did not conquer other lands. She used her power in peaceful ways. During her 20-year reign, Hatshepsut directed the people to build new monuments. These were symbols of her power. She also directed workers to repair the older buildings and temples. As a result, she helped preserve Egypt's history.

Hatshepsut sent explorers on **expeditions** to other lands. Explorers brought back incense, leopard skins, gold, ivory, and even monkeys. Hatshepsut's reign was a peaceful and prosperous time for Egypt.

---

deed: something done; an act

expedition: a trip made to explore

myrrh: a kind of gum or resin from a tree used in perfumes, medicines, or incense

Punt: probably present-day Somalia

rite: a religious ceremony

? THINK ABOUT IT:

Do you think Hatshepsut and other rulers exaggerated their deeds? Do leaders do this today?

Why do some leaders want to use their power in peaceful ways and some want to fight and conquer? Is it ever a good idea to fight and conquer?

◀ *This is a close-up picture showing the oarsmen.*

▼ *This is an ancient model of an Egyptian ship that was found in the tomb of an important person.*

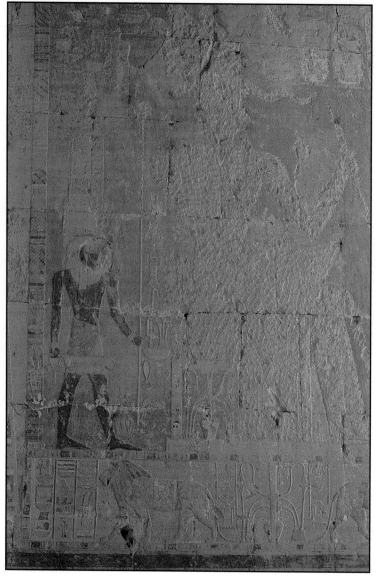

▶ *Thutmose III had Hatshepsut's picture erased from this relief sculpture.*

▼ *This shows an enlarged section from the photograph.*

Hatshepsut's Reign Ends

After Hatshepsut died, Thutmose III took over. Under his rule, the Egyptian army conquered lands to the Euphrates River. The people living in the conquered lands had to send slaves, gold, and raw materials to Egypt as a kind of tax. Egypt became richer and even more powerful.

Unfortunately, Thutmose III also destroyed almost all of Hatshepsut's statues, relief sculptures, and other monuments. In ancient Egypt, if the new ruler disliked the ruler before, he or she erased the name of the previous ruler from most monuments or simply destroyed these objects.

Hatshepsut's temple was not destroyed because it was dedicated to Amon and considered **sacred**.

sacred: belonging to a god or goddess; holy

? THINK ABOUT IT:

How was Hatshepsut different from other pharaohs you have read about? What was her greatest accomplishment?

▲ *The Great Sphinx has a lion's body and a man's head. It guards a pyramid at Giza. Built during the Old Kingdom, the Great Sphinx is 240-feet long. You can see that it is very tall by looking at the man standing next to its paw.*

Chapter Summary—Power and Stability

Ancient Egypt was powerful and stable during the New Kingdom. During this period, some pharaohs **expelled** outsiders and conquered lands to the north and south. Under Hatshepsut's 20-year rule, ancient Egypt continued to prosper. By the end of the New Kingdom, ancient Egypt's territory was the largest in its 3,000-year history.

Over time, the power and stability of ancient Egypt weakened. Egypt lost control of lands to the north and south. About 1070 B.C., the New Kingdom period ended. Several hundred years later, armies from the Kingdom of Kush conquered Egypt. You will read about Kush in the next chapter.

expel: to force out

? THINK ABOUT IT:

What helped make Egypt powerful and stable?

CHAPTER 7
The Kingdom of Kush

ERA: Early Civilizations
PLACE: Meroë, the capital of the Kingdom of Kush
PEOPLE: The Kushites, the people of Kush
THEME: Power—the ability to control others; and Stability—the quality of being permanent, not changing easily

CHAPTER FOCUS: Kush became an important trade center for goods from other parts of Africa.

This wall painting shows princes from Kush with rings and bags of gold.

LINK

In the last chapter, you read about ancient Egypt and the reign of Hatshepsut. Now you will learn about a kingdom south of Egypt called Kush. Like ancient Egypt, the Kingdom of Kush was a gift of the Nile. The river's yearly flooding made the Kingdom of Kush possible. However, Kush was very different from Egypt.

Kush was the most important trade route between Africa and the world to the north. The people from different cultures who traded in Kush influenced its development. In this chapter, you will read about what the Kushites learned from others and how they made these ideas their own. As you read, think about how the Kushite rulers showed their power by building monuments.

3500 B.C.	3000 B.C.	2500 B.C.	2000 B.C.	1500 B.C.	1000 B.C.	500 B.C.	0	A.D. 500

Kingdom of Kush at its height (300 B.C.-A.D. 400)

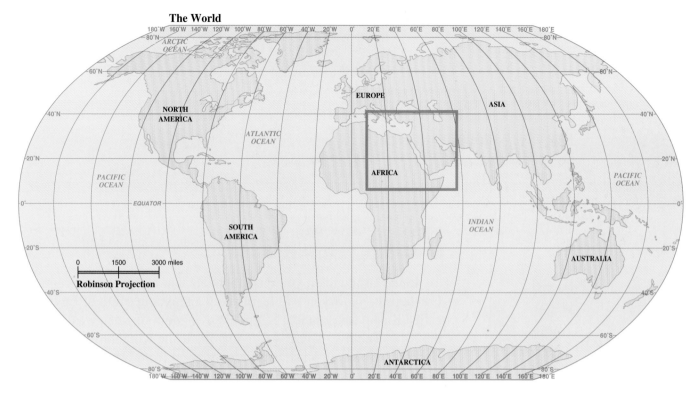

The World

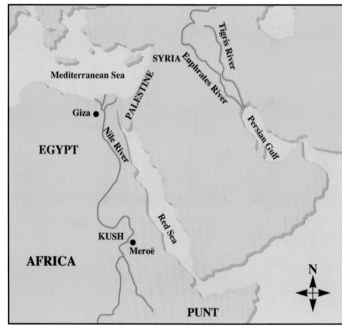

▲ *In ancient times, the trade route to Africa was through the Nile River Valley and Kush.*

◄ **GEOGRAPHY IN FOCUS**

cataract: a large waterfall

Six tall waterfalls stop travel at points along the Nile River. These waterfalls are called cataracts. Cataracts are natural boundaries. The First Cataract was the boundary between Egypt and Kush.

Kush: Center of Trade

The pharaohs of Egypt and other early civilizations wanted **exotic** goods such as gold, **ebony**, and incense from Africa. Kush was close to the source of these items, so it became a trade center for African goods.

During the New Kingdom, pharaohs such as Thutmose III took control of Kush. Later, when Egyptian leaders became less powerful, armies from Kush conquered Egypt. The leaders of Kush then ruled Egypt.

After a short time, however, a group of people from the region of the Tigris River **drove** the Kushites from Egypt. The leaders of Kush moved their **capital** south to a city called **Meroë** (MAYR-uh-wee). There, Kushites built an **empire** in northeast Africa.

capital: the main city of a country or state

drive: to force out

ebony: a hard, dark wood

empire: a group of states or people ruled by one person or government

exotic: from another place; not native

Meroë: the capital of Kush

▼ *In ancient times, gold for jewelry came from mines in the east. Incense and ebony came from trees that grew in the south and east. Traders found wild animals in central and southern Africa. These animals provided exotic hides, ivory, and eggs. Some animals such as monkeys, were probably kept as pets.*

? THINK ABOUT IT:

What makes a place a good center for trade?

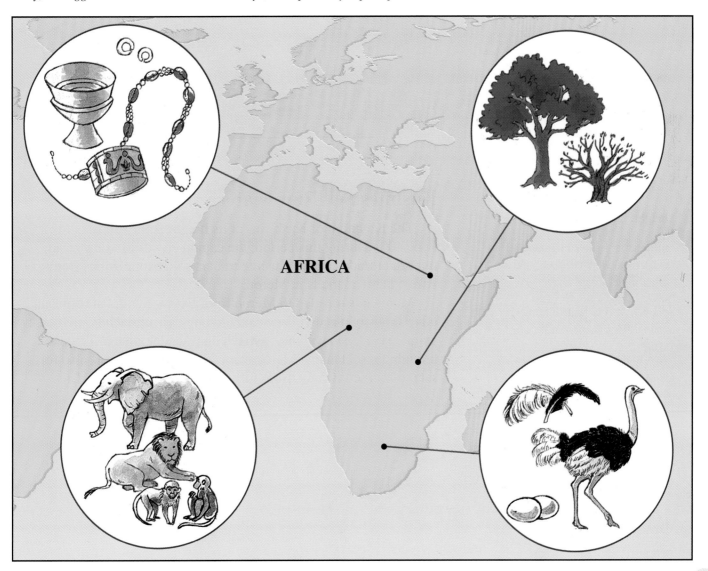

AFRICA

► *Merchants came from faraway places to buy exotic goods at the markets in Meroë.*

height: the highest point

mine: a large hole dug into the earth from which copper, gold, or other minerals are taken

ostrich: a very large bird that cannot fly, but can run very fast

raw materials: things such as animal skins, wood, or gold that can be used to make other things

? THINK ABOUT IT:

Have you ever been to an open market? What was it like? What kinds of items were for sale?

Kushites Sell Raw Materials

The Kingdom of Kush was at its **height** from 300 B.C. to A.D. 400. During this period, the capital city of Meroë was an important trade center. Kushite traders sold exotic goods from Africa at the markets in Meroë.

Merchants traveled to Meroë from Egypt, Syria, Palestine, and other faraway places. They came to buy **raw materials** such as animal skins, ebony, ivory, **ostrich** eggs, and feathers. Traders brought these items to Meroë from the south. Gold was also for sale in Meroë. It came from **mines** on the east coast of Africa.

Kushites Buy Manufactured Goods

Kushite merchants traded raw materials for **manufactured** goods from Egypt, Rome, and Greece. These were mostly luxury items such as glassware, jewelry, bronze lamps, and honey.

Kushites were very fond of Egyptian honey. Archaeologists have found empty **containers** that once probably held honey or other liquids. Archaeologists believe that Kushites also traded for perfumes, oils, and wine.

container: a can, bottle, jug, box, or anything else for holding something

manufactured: made in a factory or workshop

? THINK ABOUT IT:

How does trade help a nation?

▲ *This Egyptian wall painting shows some of the trade goods Kushites wanted. What goods do you see in this picture?*

▶ *This shows the remains of a Kushite tomb without its brick pyramid. In front of the burial chamber are the remains of the chapel and its stone offering table.*

▼ *The body of a warrior from Kush rests on a tanned ox hide.*

tanned: made into leather

Treasures of the Dead

Kushites treasured the luxury items they imported from Egypt and other places. People even took these items with them to the grave. Archaeologists have found tombs in Meroë full of imported goods such as furniture, glassware, and jewelry.

The graves in Meroë show Egypt's great influence on Kush. Like the Egyptians, Kushites believed in an afterlife. Kushites mummified their dead and buried them in tombs. They placed items needed in the next life, such as food, jewelry, horses, and slaves, in the tombs of rich people. The royal graves of leaders had an Egyptian-style brick pyramid on top. Nearby, there was an offering table and chapel.

Ordinary people were buried in simpler tombs. Their mummies were laid on **tanned** oxen hides. This method of burial began in Africa.

? THINK ABOUT IT:

How were graves in Kush like those in Egypt? How were they different?

A City Within a City

Meroë had a city within a city. Part of Meroë was completely surrounded by a wall. Archaeologists call this the Royal City. They believe that the kings and queens of Kush lived there.

We do not have much information about the rulers of Kush. We know that the leader was called king or queen. Like Egypt, one dynasty ruled at a time. Unlike Egypt, when a Kushite king died, the throne went to the son or daughter of the king's sister.

Beginning in A.D. 200, several queens ruled Kush. As a result, early historians thought that all Kushite rulers were women, but this was not true.

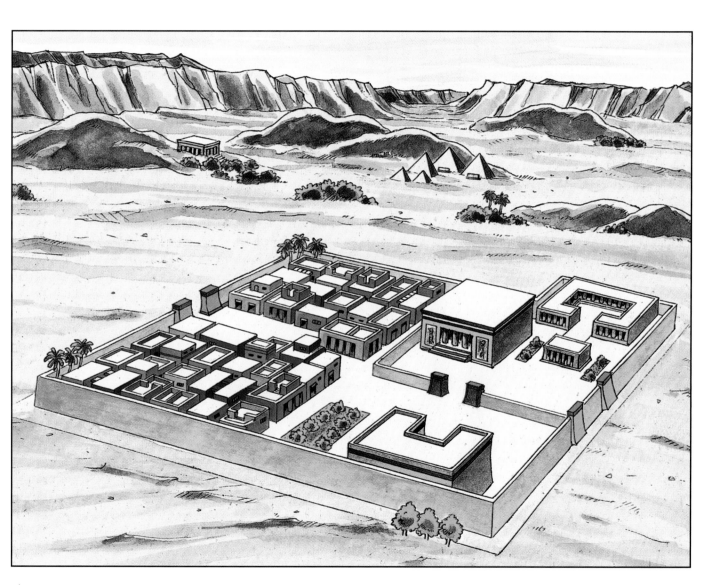

▲ *This shows the city of Meroë as it might have looked from 300 B.C. to A.D. 400. You can see the "city within the city" surrounded by a large wall.*

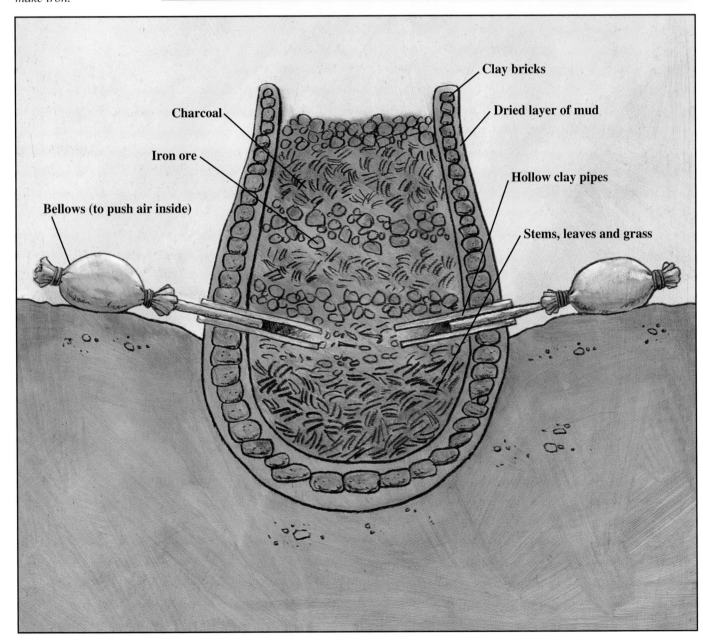

► *People from Kush traded iron tools and weapons such as the dagger in the picture, for cloth and glass.*

▼ *Iron makers in Meroë built furnaces like the one below to make iron.*

Clay bricks

Dried layer of mud

Charcoal

Iron ore

Hollow clay pipes

Bellows (to push air inside)

Stems, leaves and grass

Inside the Royal City

Inside the walls of the Royal City were many buildings, including royal palaces, meeting rooms, stores, and homes for the palace workers. During the height of the Kingdom of Kush, from 300 B.C. to A.D. 400, Egypt was controlled by leaders from Greece and Rome. They brought their building styles first to Egypt and then to Kush.

As proof of this **exchange** of ideas, archaeologists uncovered a structure within Meroë's Royal City that was like a Roman bath. It was a large brick-lined tank with water **channels** leading into it from a nearby well. The bath's design and decoration suggests it was a swimming bath, similar to the swimming pools of today.

Iron Making Outside the Royal City

It is difficult to know what life was like for those who lived outside the Royal City because archaeologists have not yet excavated the entire area. One thing is certain, there was an iron-making industry in Meroë. Archaeologists have found mounds and mounds of **slag** outside the Royal City.

Meroë was the perfect place for iron-making. There was plenty of wood for the **smelting furnaces** and plenty of iron **ore**. Factories in Kush turned the iron into all sorts of tools, including **hoe blades**, axes, scissors, and tweezers.

channel: a course through which water moves

exchange: a trade; giving back and forth

hoe blade: a tool used for cultivating, weeding, or loosening the earth around plants

ore: rock or earth that has iron, silver, copper, or other metals in it

slag: material left over when metal has been separated from ore

smelting furnace: a hot oven used to melt ore and separate it from slag

? THINK ABOUT IT:

How did the exchange of ideas from other places help the Kingdom of Kush? What could Kush give back in return?

? THINK ABOUT IT:

How did other cultures or places influence the art and architecture of the Kingdom of Kush?

Different Pots Made by Men and Women

Kushites also were known for their fine pots. Men usually made pots on a **potter's wheel**. These pots had especially thin walls. The thinness of the clay made the pottery **extraordinary**. The bowls, vases, and cups were all baked in brick **kilns** and painted with designs.

Women made pots by hand. These pots were usually black and intended for everyday use. They often looked like polished **gourds**.

Other Technology

Iron-making and pottery-making were not the only Kushite technologies. The people also used **mechanical** irrigation systems. Like the Egyptians and the Sumerians, Kushites used the shadoof. However, in some areas, the water was far below the level of the fields. Farmers needed a tool stronger than the shadoof. About A.D. 100, Kushites began using a **foreign** invention, a special kind of water wheel that was driven by oxen. It lifted water from the river to the fields. As the wheel turned, small clay pots dipped into the water and carried it up to a higher level.

▲ *This shows a close-up picture of the design on one of the pots.*

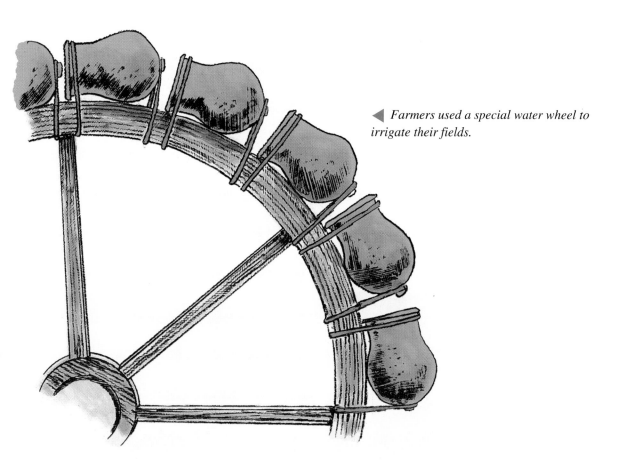

◀ *Farmers used a special water wheel to irrigate their fields.*

▲ *This shows several examples of Kushite pottery made on a potter's wheel. Some pots had vine-leaf or* **geometric** *patterns and were similar to Roman and Greek designs. Other pots had Egyptian symbols such as a* **lotus**.

Temples to the Gods

Meroë was a trading center, but it was also a place for people to worship gods and goddesses. There were temples to honor many gods and goddesses throughout the area. Kushites worshiped some of the same gods and goddesses as the Egyptians. The Kushites built a temple in honor of Amon next to the Royal City.

Kushites also worshiped gods that combined Egyptian and African traditions. The Kushite lion-god of war is one example. The lion-god was similar to the Egyptian goddess of war, who also was represented as a lion. In Meroë, only the god Amon was more important than the lion-god.

▶ *This fragment of a relief sculpture shows the lion-god at the Lion Temple at Meroë.*

▲ *The elephant statues stand guard at the Great Enclosure.*

Elephants and the Great Enclosure

Archaeologists believe that Kushites used elephants in religious ceremonies. This practice began in Africa.

Just south of Meroë is a set of buildings decorated with relief sculptures and statues of elephants. The largest of these buildings is called the Great **Enclosure**. It was built like a **maze**. One could get lost in all its passages, corridors, ramps, and rooms.

Some say the Great Enclosure was a major center for worship and religious festivals. Others say it was a palace. One archaeologist thinks it was a place to train elephants for war and for religious ceremonies. Most people agree that the purpose of the Great Enclosure was at least partly religious.

enclosure: an area surrounded by walls

maze: a puzzling set of paths or passageways

? THINK ABOUT IT:

Do you think there is enough evidence to decide how the Great Enclosure was used? What kind of information would be helpful?

*This is a **stele** with text written in Meroitic, the language of the Kingdom of Kush.*

bilingual: in two languages

decipher: to make out the meaning

stele: an upright stone or pillar, engraved with writing

text: a piece of writing

? THINK ABOUT IT:

Why do you think Kushites first used Egyptian hieroglyphics? Why do you think they developed their own written language?

The Mysteries of Kush

Much about the Kingdom of Kush remains a mystery because archaeologists have not been able to **decipher** the Kushite's written language. For part of their history, Kushites used Egyptian hieroglyphics. Later, they developed their own written language called Meroitic.

Archaeologists found a **bilingual text** written in both Egyptian and Meroitic hieroglyphics. From that text, archaeologists learned that the Meroitic alphabet had 23 letters. Unfortunately, the text was too short to decipher the Meroitic language. When archaeologists find a longer bilingual text, more secrets of the Kingdom of Kush may be revealed.

Chapter Summary—Power and Stability

The civilization of Kush reached its peak about A.D. 100. For the next 300 years, it slowly **declined**. Kushites stopped building large temples, palaces, and homes. The royal pyramids were not as **ornate** and did not contain as many valuables.

The main reason for the decline was the loss of trade with other countries. About A.D. 200, other countries began importing and selling goods from Africa. In addition, **alternate** trade routes were developed. Traders began using **camel caravans** to cross the Sahara Desert. There were also new trading ports on the Red Sea. Traders did not have to go through Kush anymore.

The Kingdom of Kush stayed strong and stable as long as it was the main trade route to Africa. Once it was no longer a center for trade, the Kingdom of Kush declined.

alternate: one that takes the place of another

camel caravan: a group of people on camels traveling across the desert together

decline: to lose strength or power

ornate: heavily decorated

? THINK ABOUT IT:

What things can make a city or a country strong and stable? What kinds of things can weaken a city or country?

▶ *When the Kingdom of Kush was at its peak, rulers had small pyramids built over their tombs.*

CHAPTER 8

The Indus Valley Civilization

3500 B.C.	3000 B.C.	2500 B.C.	2000 B.C.	1500 B.C.	1000 B.C.	500 B.C.	0	A.D. 500

Indus Valley Civilization (2500-1800 B.C.)

ERA: Early Civilizations
PLACE: The Indus Valley
PEOPLE: The people of Mohenjo-Daro and Harappa
THEME: Unity—the state of being one in goals, interests, and beliefs; and Diversity—the state of being different

CHAPTER FOCUS: The people of the Indus Valley developed a civilization that lasted for over 500 years.

◀ *This photograph shows what Mohenjo-Daro looks like today.*

LINK

In the last unit, you read about the Sumerians who built the world's first known civilization between the Tigris and Euphrates rivers. You also read about the Egyptians and Kushites and their great civilizations along the banks of the Nile River.

In this chapter, you will read about another ancient civilization near a river, this one in the Indus River Valley. As you read, think about how religious beliefs affect a society.

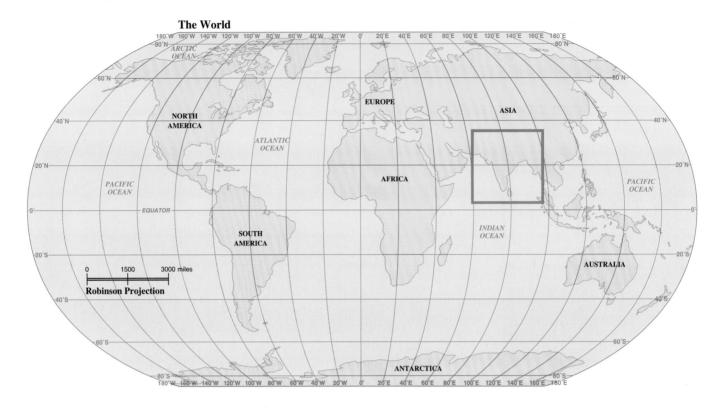
The World

▼ GEOGRAPHY IN FOCUS

subcontinent: *a large piece of land, somewhat separated but still part of a continent*

The Indus Valley is on the subcontinent of India.

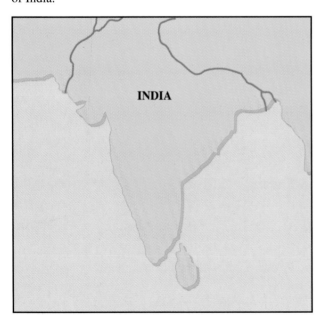

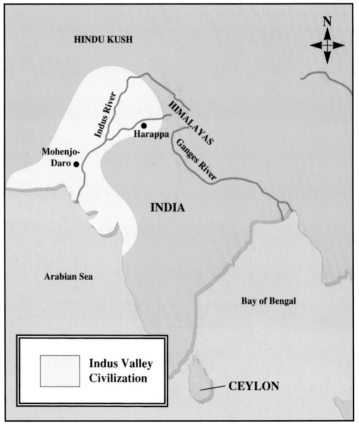

▲ *The Indus Valley civilization covered about 840,000 square miles of the subcontinent of India. It was larger in size than Sumer, Egypt, or Kush. Mohenjo-Daro and Harappa were almost 400 miles apart. The Indus Valley is now part of Pakistan.*

The Indus Valley

Along the banks of the Indus River is a plain. This area is part of the Indus Valley. Today it is hot and dry. In ancient times, this area may have been covered with fertile, grassy plains and forests of cedar, teak, and rosewood trees. No one knows for sure.

We do know that every spring the melting snow from the Himalayas caused the rivers to flood. Just like in Sumer and Egypt, the flood waters left a rich layer of fertile soil on the plain near the rivers.

Around 3500 B.C., nomadic herders began to come down from the hills to get away from the cold winters. Some of these families planted small gardens. In the summer they returned to the hills. In time, some of these families stayed on the plain all year. This was the beginning of agriculture in the Indus Valley.

? THINK ABOUT IT:

What are some possible reasons there are no longer forests in the Indus Valley?

▲ *This photograph shows the Indus Valley today. The Himalayas are in the background.*

▲ *This photograph of Mohenjo-Daro shows how the city looked in 1925 when it was being excavated.*

The Indus Valley Civilization

invade: to come in as an enemy

By about 2500 B.C., a great civilization had developed in the valley of the Indus River. Did the farmers from the hills build it or was it built by another group of people who **invaded** the valley? No one knows.

This Indus Valley civilization lasted until about 1750 B.C. During this time, cities and towns developed near the Indus River.

? THINK ABOUT IT:

What are some reasons we don't know who built the cities in the Indus Valley? Do you know who built the city in which you live? How can you find out?

Mystery in the Indus Valley

How did people live in these cities? What kinds of things were important to them? There are many questions we cannot answer about the Indus Valley civilization. No one has been able to find examples of their writing, except for short **inscriptions** on seals. So far, no one has been able to decipher this writing.

We do not know the name of even one ruler of this civilization. All we know about the people is from the things they have left behind.

> **inscription:** something engraved (carved) on stones or coins

? THINK ABOUT IT:

What are some things the people of the Indus Valley might have written?

▶ *These are seals carved from soft stones. Every important citizen had a seal. They used them to identify property and also carried them as amulets.*

<table>
<tr><td>

citadel: a walled place built on high ground to protect or defend a city

grid: a framework of parallel lines

public: for the use of all

twin: describing one of two persons or things that are very much alike

</td></tr>
</table>

Mohenjo-Daro and Harappa: Twin Cities of the Indus Valley

Archaeologists have found the ruins of many cities and towns in the valley of the Indus River. The two largest cities were Mohenjo-Daro and Harappa. Both cities were laid out according to the same plan. They are so much alike we might even call them **twin** cities.

Mohenjo-Daro and Harappa are very early examples of town planning. In each town there was a **citadel** beside the river. The citadel was built on a large platform to protect it from the flooding of the river. These early city planners built large, **public** buildings on the citadel and planned the rest of the city around it. They laid out the main streets in a **grid** pattern. The streets ran north to south and were straight and wide. Along the streets there were rows of small houses and also larger houses with two or three stories.

◀ *At Mohenjo-Daro there was a room to store grain, an assembly hall, and a large public bath on the citadel. The bath was probably used in religious rituals. The photograph shows how the bath looks now.*

? THINK ABOUT IT:

How do Mohenjo-Daro and Harappa compare to the towns and cities in Çatal Hüyük, Sumer, and Egypt? How do they compare to cities today?

▲ *This drawing shows how the bath might have looked around 2000 B.C.*

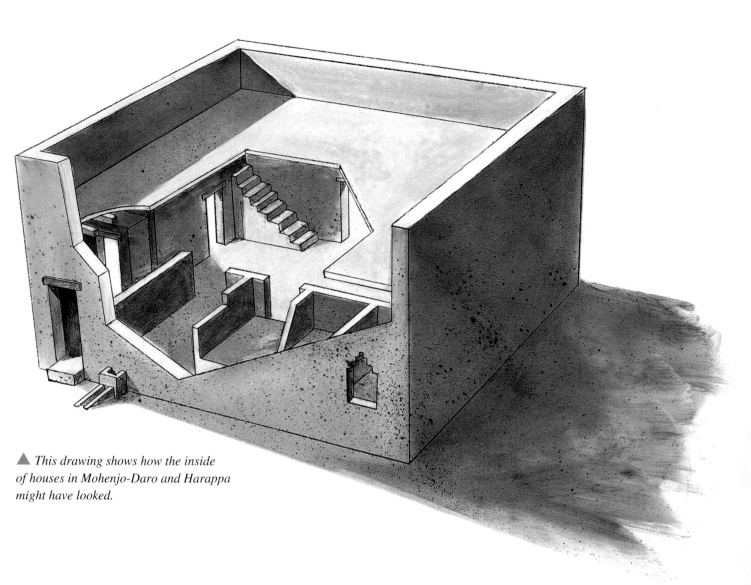

▲ *This drawing shows how the inside of houses in Mohenjo-Daro and Harappa might have looked.*

The Houses of Mohenjo-Daro and Harappa

The people of Mohenjo-Daro and Harappa built their houses out of brick. The houses and the other buildings were well built, but they were very simple. The building style stayed the same for over 500 years.

There may have been the danger of robbers because the houses were built without doors or windows on the street side. People went in and out through doors off small alleys.

Some houses had only two or three rooms, while others had 10, 20, or more. Almost all the houses were built around an inside courtyard. People cooked and ate their meals in the courtyard. They slept in small rooms that opened onto the courtyard.

The people there had one modern **convenience** that many people still do not have today, bathrooms. Most houses had a well in the bathroom. To take a shower, people filled buckets with water from the well and poured the water over themselves. The water then ran through a **drain** in the floor to drains in the street.

convenience: something useful; something that makes a person comfortable

drain: a pipe for carrying off water

? THINK ABOUT IT:

How are the houses of Mohenjo-Daro and Harappa like houses today? How are they different?

Trade in the Indus Valley

Some of the people of the Indus Valley were merchants. They traded with other merchants in the Indus Valley, Sumer, and other distant lands. Ships brought goods through the Persian Gulf. Donkey caravans carried trade goods over land. These traders were important in linking the cities and villages of the Indus Valley together.

The people of the Indus Valley exported peacocks, beads, cotton fabrics, **timber** (cedar and teak), ivory, seals, and spices to Sumer and other places.

They imported stones such as **steatite** and alabaster for seals and **figurines**. They also imported lapis lazuli and silver for jewelry.

figurine: a small figure that is carved or molded

steatite: a soft stone

timber: wood suitable for building houses or ships

? THINK ABOUT IT:

How did the merchants link the cities and villages of the Indus Valley together?

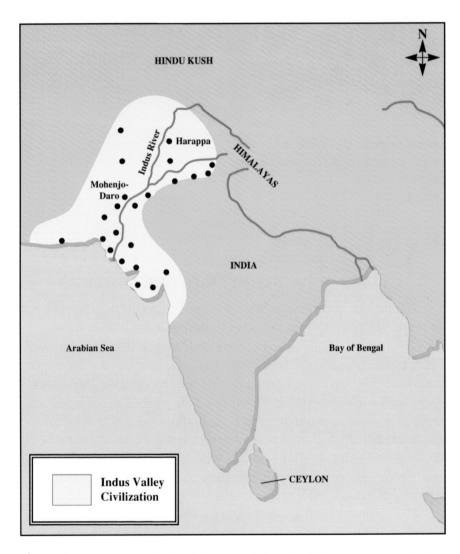

▲ Traders helped to unify the civilization of the Indus Valley as they traveled from place to place. The dots mark towns and cities of the Indus Valley that were linked by traders.

▲ *This family is planting seeds. The man is smoothing the soil with a harrow. The women are dropping seeds through the seed tubes. Farmers used tools like these at Mohenjo-Daro and Harappa around 2000 B.C.*

Farming in the Indus Valley

Most of the people in the Indus Valley were farmers. They grew cotton, wheat, barley, melons, and dates. They were probably the first people in the world to grow cotton. Just like in Sumer and Egypt, the soil near the rivers was fertile and easy to work.

The farmers built stone dams to control the flooding of the rivers. During rainy times, they could save water. Later, they could open the dam to allow the water to spread over the fields. These people did not build canals.

The Indus Valley farmers used **harrows** to help them plant seeds, but they did not use plows. Merchants who traveled to Sumer probably had seen plows and canals there, but they did not bring these ideas back to India.

harrow: a farm tool used to smooth the soil

? THINK ABOUT IT:

What are some possible reasons the merchants did not tell the farmers in the Indus Valley about the plows and canals in Sumer?

Government in the Indus Valley

What kind of government did these people have? Was there one strong, central government? Were there city-states? We do not have answers to these questions.

We do know, however, that there must have been good communication between the cities and **regions** because there was so much **uniformity**. For example, people all over the Indus Valley used the same kind of writing and the same system of weights and measures. The arts, crafts, and religion of these people were also the same. People in all the cities even used bricks of the same size to build their houses.

region: an area; a place

uniformity: always being the same; not changing

? THINK ABOUT IT:

What are some examples of uniformity in the Indus Valley? What are some examples of uniformity in the community where you live?

▶ *This statue from Mohenjo-Daro may represent a priest. Many people think the priests were also the rulers.*

▼ *Potters in the Indus Valley made pots like these on a potter's wheel.*

▲ *This toy cart was made from clay and hardened in the sun.*

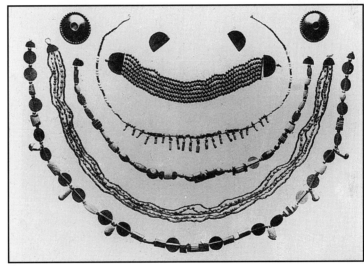

▶ *Artisans painted beads they made from clay. Then they used the beads to create beautiful jewelry.*

Crafts in Mohenjo-Daro and Harappa

Many toys and games have been found in the ruins of Mohenjo-Daro and Harappa. The people must have enjoyed playing games and making toys for their children. Children also made clay figurines of animals and people.

Artisans lived and worked in all the cities. Archaeologists have found fine jewelry made from ivory, silver, copper, bronze, and colorful stones. They also have found examples of excellent pottery. The jewelry and crafts were skillfully made, but artisans used the same patterns and styles over and over. It might have been more important to make things that were functional rather than to be **creative** and try new and different ideas.

> **creative:** inventive; able to make something new or different

> **? THINK ABOUT IT:**
>
> What are some possible reasons artisans used the same patterns over and over?

Religion in the Indus Valley

Archaeologists have found many clay figurines in the Indus Valley. Some of these may have represented a mother goddess. Every family probably had a figurine in a **niche** in the wall.

A few figures had the horns of a goat or bull. These figures represented other deities. Some of these figures sit with their legs close to their bodies and their heels touching. This position is still used today by people practicing **yoga**.

There are also figures of animals that represented gods in animal form. The people of the Indus Valley seemed to believe that certain animals were sacred or that the gods appeared in animal form.

> **niche:** a small hole or hollow place in a wall
>
> **yoga:** a system of concentration and exercise used in the Hindu religion

◄ *Archaeologists found this figurine of a woman at Mohenjo-Daro.*

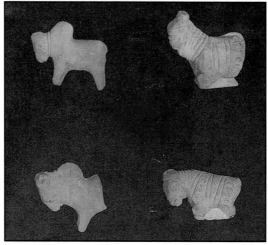

◄ *These clay figurines of animals also were found at Mohenjo-Daro.*

The Decline of the Twin Cities

Around 1900 B.C., the cities of Mohenjo-Daro and Harappa began to decline. Perhaps the rivers flooded and destroyed their crops. It is possible that a great earthquake caused the rivers to change their courses.

No one knows the reason, but the cities began to change and the new houses were not as well built as the older ones had been. The large rooms in older houses were divided into smaller rooms. Sometimes people added rooms onto the houses. Some of these rooms even stuck out into the street.

? THINK ABOUT IT:

What are some other possible reasons the cities began to decline?

◀ *This photograph shows how a narrow street in Mohenjo-Daro looked before the city's decline.*

Indo-European Migration, 2000 - 1500 B.C.

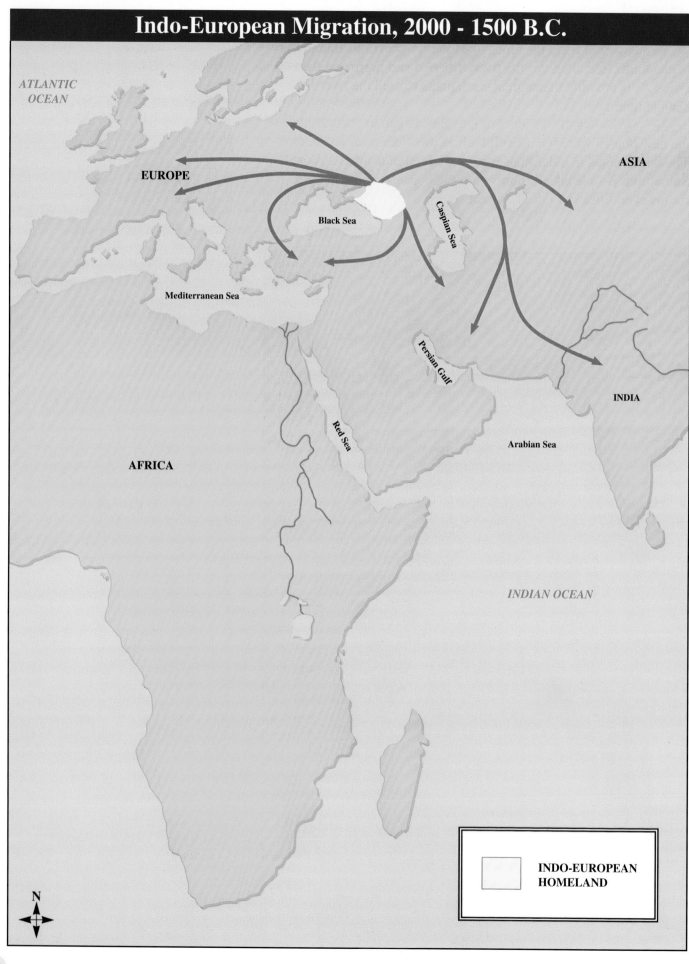

ATLANTIC
OCEAN

ASIA

EUROPE

Black Sea

Caspian Sea

Mediterranean Sea

Persian Gulf

INDIA

Red Sea

Arabian Sea

AFRICA

INDIAN OCEAN

N

INDO-EUROPEAN
HOMELAND

The Aryans

Also, about this same time, tribes of people called Aryans began to move into the Indus Valley. These Aryan people came from the area around the Caspian and the Black seas. The Aryans were forced to leave their homes, perhaps due to **drought**, **plague**, or overpopulation. The Aryan tribes went in many different directions. Eventually, some of them crossed the **Hindu Kush** mountains into India where they slowly spread over the subcontinent.

Chapter Summary—Unity

We have learned many things about the people of the Indus Valley by studying the artifacts they left behind. We know that the cities of Mohenjo-Daro and Harappa were connected to the other people of the Indus Valley by a network of trade. People throughout the land used the same systems of writing and measuring. They worshiped the same gods and goddesses. Artisans used the same designs on their pottery and on their seals. People even built their houses according to the same plans.

However, many questions remain unanswered. Archaeologists continue to study the ruins of the Indus Valley. Perhaps one day we will be able to decipher the writing on the inscriptions and find out more about the people who built this **remarkable** civilization in the Indus Valley.

drought: a long period of dry weather; lack of rain

Hindu Kush: a mountain range in Central Asia

migrate: to move from one place to settle in another place

plague: a disease that kills many people at one time

remarkable: unusual; extraordinary

? THINK ABOUT IT:

What kinds of information do we have about the Indus Valley civilization? What kind of information is missing? How does this compare with what we know about Sumer, Egypt, and Kush?

◀ *The Aryans left their homelands and* **migrated** *to India, Persia, southwestern Asia, and Europe.*

CHAPTER 9
The Aryan Age

ERA: Early Civilizations
PLACE: The Indus and the Ganges River Valleys
PEOPLE: The Aryans and Siddhartha Gautama, the Buddha
THEME: Unity—the state of being one in goals, interests, beliefs; and Diversity—the state of being different

CHAPTER FOCUS: The Aryans brought new ideas of religion and society to the Indus Valley. The Buddha offered an explanation for suffering and a way to escape it.

LINK

In the last chapter, you read about the cities of Mohenjo-Daro and Harappa with their straight streets and efficient system of drains. You also read that the Indus Valley civilization could have ended as a result of floods and earthquakes.

In this chapter, you will read about the Aryans and the 1,000 years of the Aryan Age in the Indus Valley and beyond. You will also read about one man, Siddhartha Gautama, and his search for the reasons for suffering and a way to avoid it. As you read, think about how religious beliefs affect a society.

00 B.C.	3000 B.C.	2500 B.C.	2000 B.C.	1500 B.C.	1000 B.C.	500 B.C.	0	A.D. 500

Aryan Age (1500-500 B.C.)   The Buddha's birth (c. 563 B.C.)

▲ *The Aryans traveled through the Hindu Kush Mountains into the Indus Valley.*

The World

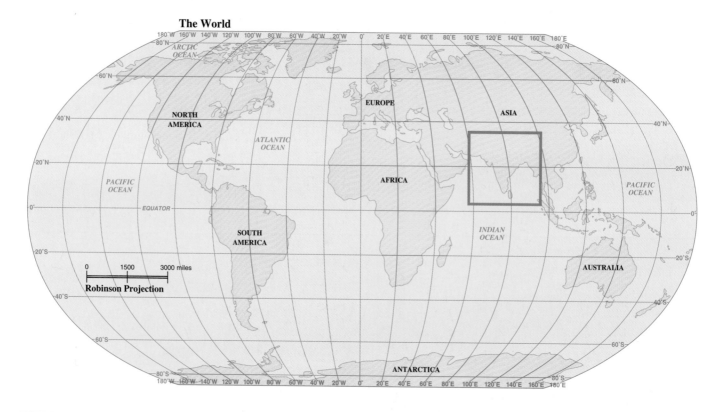

▼ GEOGRAPHY IN FOCUS

foothill: a low hill at the bottom of a mountain

Siddhartha Gautama, the Buddha, was born near a small town in the foothills of the Himalayas.

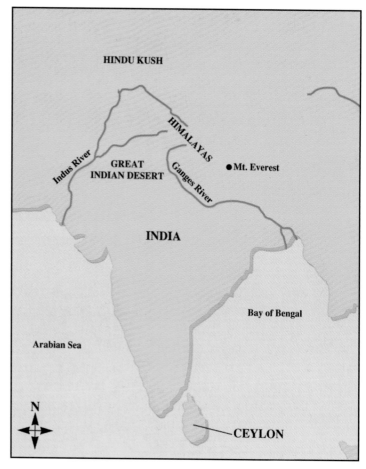

▲ *The Aryan culture spread slowly eastward from the Indus Valley across the Great Indian Desert. After nearly 1,000 years, it had reached the valley of the Ganges River.*

▲ *The Aryans measured their wealth by how many head of cattle they had.*

The Aryans in the Indus Valley

Aryan tribes continued to come into the Indus Valley. They came with chariots drawn by horses. They also brought their herds of cattle, sheep, goats, and horses. In time, they learned to grow grains such as barley and wheat. However, cattle were always important to the Aryans. They even used cattle as a kind of money.

At first, the Aryans were not city people. They didn't build cities. They usually didn't even live in the cities they conquered. They preferred to live in little villages. Their houses were made of wood and reeds.

? **THINK ABOUT IT:**

Why do you think the Aryans did not want to live in cities?

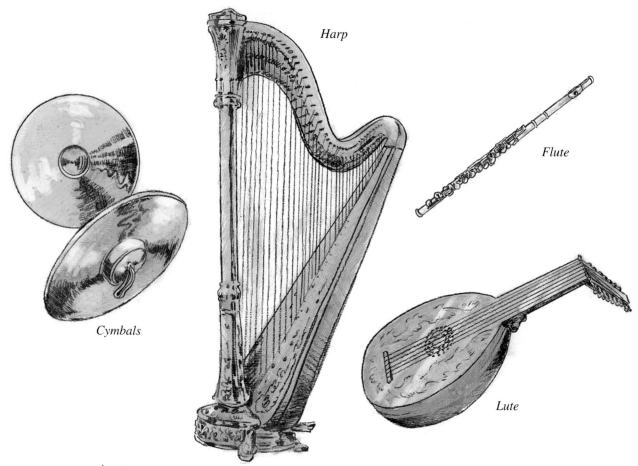

Harp

Flute

Cymbals

Lute

▲ *The Aryans loved music and played instruments like the modern ones pictured above.*

Aryan Culture

chant: to sing or say something without changing tone

compose: to make up; to create

hymn: a song in praise of a deity

memorize: to learn by heart

recite: to speak aloud from memory

sacrifice: an offering of the life of an animal or human

As far as we know, the Aryans did not carve statues, paint pictures, or create beautiful pottery. Archaeologists have not found any of these in the ruins of Aryan villages. However, the Aryans loved music. They played the flute, lute, and the harp, along with cymbals and drums. They also enjoyed dancing, drinking, gambling, and chariot racing.

Aryan priests **composed hymns** and poems in praise of their gods. Priests then **chanted** the hymns at **sacrifices**. Before the Aryans had a system of writing, the hymns were passed down by word of mouth. Priests had to **memorize** these long poems word for word.

One collection of over 1,000 hymns and poems is called the *Rig-Veda*. These hymns and poems are still part of the sacred writings of the Hindu religion. Even now they are **recited** at Hindu weddings and funerals.

? THINK ABOUT IT:

How would you describe the Aryans?

▲ *The chieftain and his warriors rode in chariots and shot arrows with metal tips.*

Aryan Social Classes

The Aryans were a proud and warlike people. They called themselves "the noble ones." The Aryan tribes constantly fought with each other and with the people of the Indus Valley who were there before them.

When they arrived in the Indus Valley, each Aryan tribe was headed by a chieftain. Their society was divided into three groups or classes: 1) the chieftains and warriors; 2) the priests; and 3) the landowners and merchants.

Each group had certain duties or jobs. The warriors protected people. The chieftains came from this class. The priests studied, taught, and made sacrifices. The landowners and merchants took care of cattle, farmed the land, and bought and sold goods.

The Class System

Because the Aryans wanted to be separate from the local inhabitants of the Indus Valley, they added another class. This fourth class was made up of **servants**. No Aryan wanted to be a servant. The servants were the lowest class. Their duty was to serve the three higher classes.

Only the top three classes, the warriors, the priests, and the landowners, were considered true Aryans. They were the only ones allowed to take part in religious services and to be educated.

Later, the Aryans added another group. The people in this group were even lower than the servants. They performed jobs that were so strange or "unclean" that even the servants did not want to touch them.

Butchers and **tanners** were part of this group. They were considered "untouchables." They were not even allowed to live in Aryan villages.

▶ *This man was part of the servant class. He must have been a native of the Indus Valley because no Aryans wanted to be servants.*

servant: a person who works in or around the home of someone else

tanner: someone who works with animal hides to make leather

? THINK ABOUT IT:

How does this division of society into classes compare with the way your society is organized?

◄ *In Aryan times, there was a hearth or altar in each home where the priest sacrificed sheep and goats. Today, Hindus still perform rituals such as the one shown in this photograph.*

The Aryan Religion

The Aryans worshiped nature gods. Their gods represented such things as the earth, the sky, storms, and lightning. Their most important god was Indra. He was both a war god and a storm god.

To keep the gods happy and to keep nature in **balance**, priests had to make sacrifices to the gods. People paid priests, or Brahmans, to make these sacrifices. As time went on, the priests made up more and more rules about the sacrifices.

Because of the importance of the sacrifices and other rituals, the priests became more important than the chieftains. The priests even told people that they were more powerful than the gods. They demanded that people respect and even worship them.

> **balance:** equal in value or weight; being in harmony

? THINK ABOUT IT:

What do you think people were afraid might happen if nature got out of balance?

The Power of the Priests Questioned

In time, people began to question the power of the priests. Sometimes there was a flood or a drought even after the priests had offered sacrifices. Some people began to think it was wasteful to sacrifice so many animals. They began to wonder if the **rituals** the priests performed did any good.

Some priests also began to wonder about their roles. Priests and other people began to leave their homes and jobs to wander through the countryside **seeking** answers to life's difficult questions. One of these people was named Siddhartha Gautama.

beg: to ask for something as a kindness or favor

meditation: the act of thinking about spiritual things; in Buddhism, calming the mind

ritual: a set form of religious rites

seek: to try to find; look for

▼ *Some men left their families and possessions to spend time in **meditation**. They wandered from place to place, **begging**.*

▲ *This ivory carving shows Siddhartha Gautama as the Buddha seated on a lion throne. He is shown wearing a crown and jewels.*

Siddhartha Gautama Is Born

Siddhartha Gautama was born around 563 B.C. in the foothills of the Himalayas. According to **legend**, the wise men said that Siddhartha would become a great ruler. However, one wise man said that Siddhartha would become a **spiritual** ruler, not the ruler of a kingdom. He said Siddhartha would see four signs. These signs would show him the **misery** of the world. As a result, Siddhartha would leave his palace to try to find a way to overcome suffering.

This upset Siddhartha's father. He wanted Siddhartha to follow him as ruler of his kingdom. He did not want him to be a spiritual ruler. Siddhartha's father decided to keep the young prince from seeing any kind of suffering. No one who was old or sick or in pain was allowed to be near Siddhartha.

legend: a story handed down through generations; a myth

misery: a condition of great pain; suffering

spiritual: having to do with things of the spirit

▲ *The Buddha is pictured preaching his first sermon.*

? THINK ABOUT IT:

Do you think there is anyone who has never seen suffering? Why or why not?

Siddhartha Sees the Four Signs

However, one day Siddhartha was riding in his chariot and saw an old man. Siddhartha asked his **charioteer** who this was. The charioteer told him that it was an old man and explained that all men grow old. This was the first sign. Another day, Siddhartha saw a very sick man. This was the second sign. Later, he saw the third sign—a dead man being carried to his funeral. Siddhartha was very upset to see this suffering.

Then Siddhartha saw a wandering holy man, the fourth sign. This man had nothing, but he seemed to be calm and peaceful. Siddhartha wondered why the man was so happy when he had nothing. Siddhartha decided that he wanted to know what was important in life. In the middle of the night, Siddhartha left the palace to begin his search.

Siddhartha Becomes the Buddha

Siddhartha began to wander in the forest with five other men who were also seeking the truth. He searched for six years and **fasted** until he became very weak, but he did not find the answers he was looking for. Then he decided to sit under a tree and meditate until he knew the truth.

As he sat under the tree, evil spirits offered him all kinds of pleasures and powers. He turned them all down. After seven weeks he had his answer. He understood the reason for suffering and what people must do to overcome it. When other people heard of his experience they called him the Buddha—the "enlightened one."

The legend tells us he found the five wanderers again and preached his first **sermon** to them. These men became his **disciples**. Soon more men joined him. The Buddha organized the men into a group of **monks**. They wanted to leave behind all things important to them. They shaved their heads, wore yellow robes, and went barefoot.

disciple: a student of a religious teacher

fast: to stop eating for a period of time

monk: a man who joins a religious group and lives away from the rest of society

sermon: a speech giving instruction in religion

▶ *The Buddha is shown stopping an*
elephant that had gone mad.

moderation: avoiding extremes

starvation: becoming weak from
hunger

The Teachings of the Buddha

When the Buddha spoke, his followers tried to memorize his teachings. Later, after he died, these teachings were written down and called "sutras" or scripture. These sutras teach the "Middle Way," the "Four Noble Truths," and the "Eightfold Path."

In the "Middle Way," the Buddha taught people to enjoy life's pleasures in **moderation**. Others taught that **starvation** led to spiritual insights, but the Buddha said that it was all right to have enough food to eat, to have clothing, and to have shelter, but that people should not be greedy. This was called the "Middle Way."

The Four Noble Truths

In the "Four Noble Truths," the Buddha taught:

1. Life is full of suffering and sorrow.
2. The desire for things and for power causes suffering.
3. Suffering and sorrow can be overcome when people give up their greedy desires.
4. People can overcome their desires by following the Eightfold Path.

The Goal of Enlightenment

The Buddha taught that people should search for enlightenment. He said enlightenment or nirvana is seeing things as they really are. Nirvana means the end of wanting things or power.

According to the Buddha, if a person dies and has not reached nirvana, the person goes through **reincarnation**. In the next life, the person tries to reach nirvana again. This **cycle** goes on until the person reaches nirvana.

According to the Buddha, when the person finally finds enlightenment or nirvana, the person escapes from suffering in this life and also breaks the cycle of reincarnation.

cycle: a period of time in which certain regular events occur

reincarnation: rebirth of the soul in another body

? THINK ABOUT IT:

How are nirvana and heaven alike? How are they different?

The Eightfold Path

The "Eightfold Path" guided the Buddha's followers.

1. *Right views* means knowing the truth.
2. *Right resolve* means intending to resist evil.
3. *Right speech* means saying nothing to hurt others; not lying or gossiping.
4. *Right conduct* means respecting life, morality, and property; not killing or stealing.
5. *Right livelihood* means holding a job that does not hurt others.
6. *Right effort* means trying to free one's mind of evil.
7. *Right mindfulness* means being aware of the world.
8. *Right meditation* means practicing proper forms of concentration.

▲ *Prajnaparmata, the goddess of wisdom, represents the teachings of the Buddha.*

? THINK ABOUT IT:

How did the Buddha help people avoid suffering?

What do you think the Buddha thought about the division of society into classes?

The Death of the Buddha

Around the year 483 B.C., the Buddha became sick and died. His followers gave him a great funeral. They also continued to preach about the "Four Noble Truths" and the "Eightfold Path."

Many people were attracted to Buddhism. The Buddha's followers believed that if they followed the standards of behavior set out in the "Eightfold Path," they would escape the suffering of human life. People of all classes became followers of Buddhism. The Buddha did not intend to start a religion, but after his death people began to worship him.

▶ *This is a close-up picture of the scroll shown above.*

Chapter Summary—Unity and Diversity

As the Aryan tribes slowly moved across the subcontinent, their society and religion changed. The rules for the social classes and for religion became much stricter. By the year 500 B.C., many people were unhappy. Siddhartha Gautama, the Buddha, offered hope to the people by giving them an explanation for suffering and showing them a way to avoid it.

However, not everyone followed the Buddha. Many Aryans still practiced the religion of the Brahmans. Peasants in the villages worshiped the gods of the Indus Valley civilization. There were other differences as well. In the huge subcontinent of India there were people of different cultures, languages, religions, and customs. The social classes of the Aryans gave everyone a place in society. They gave unity to this huge area with its different religions and cultures.

? THINK ABOUT IT:

How did the social classes of the Aryans bring unity to ancient India? How was this good and bad?

Chieftain/Warrior

Priest

Merchant

Servant

▲ *This picture shows an example of each of the social classes of ancient India (chieftains and warriors, priests, merchants, and servants).*

Chapter 9   131

CHAPTER 10
India's Golden Ages

ERA: Early Civilizations
PLACE: The Indian Subcontinent
PEOPLE: Asoka, Chandra Gupta II, and the people of India
THEME: Unity—the state of being one in goals, interests, and beliefs; and Diversity—the state of being different

CHAPTER FOCUS: Two emperors, who lived 500 years apart in time, brought unity to the Indian subcontinent.

3500 B.C.	3000 B.C.	2500 B.C.	2000 B.C.	1500 B.C.	1000 B.C.	500 B.C.	0	A.D. 500
						Mauryan Empire (324-183 B.C.)		Gupta Empire (A.D. 320-467)

▼ *Indian armies used elephants trained for war.*

In the last chapter, you read about the Aryans who came into the Indus Valley and brought their own ideas about religion and society. You also read about the Buddha, who taught people reasons for suffering and showed a way to avoid it.

In this chapter, you will read about an emperor who unified most of India with the Buddha's ideas of peace, compassion, and non-violence. This emperor's reign was followed by 500 years of political chaos. Then you will read about another emperor who brought unity to India again, by conquering most of the north and restoring the class system. As you read, think about how religious beliefs affect a society.

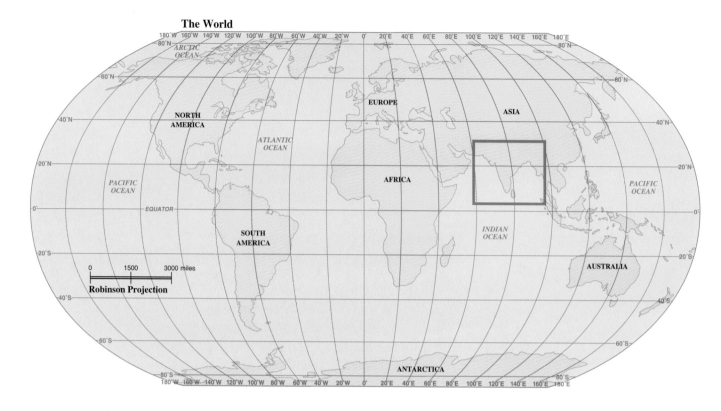

The World

▼ GEOGRAPHY IN FOCUS

river basin: *the area drained by a river and its branches*

The Mauryan Empire covered both the Ganges and Indus river basins as well as all of central India.

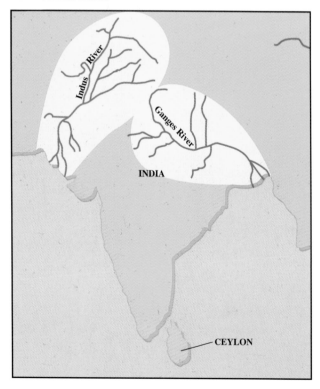

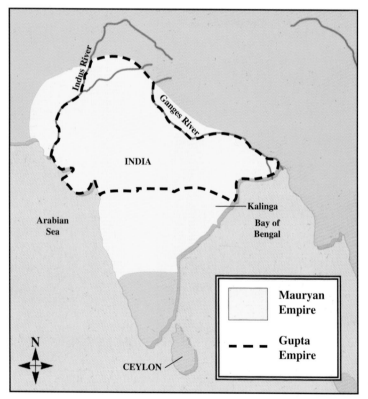

▲ *In 232 B.C., the Mauryan Empire covered more of India than any other empire until modern times. The Gupta Empire controlled part of northern India in A.D. 375.*

Asoka—Mauryan Emperor

More than 200 years after the Buddha died, one of India's first emperors helped to spread Buddhism in India and many other places. This emperor was Asoka (ah-SHOH-kuh). Asoka became the third ruler of the **Mauryan** Empire in 269 B.C. For the first eight years of his reign, Asoka followed in the footsteps of his father and grandfather and conquered one tribal kingdom after another. He and his soldiers were **ruthless** warriors. When he conquered the kingdom of Kalinga, 100,000 soldiers died and 150,000 people were taken prisoner.

Asoka felt great **remorse** after this battle, and it was the last war he ever fought. Soon after this, Asoka became a follower of Buddhism. He began to preach goodness, gentleness, and nonviolence. He also tried to make the class system less important. Asoka taught that all living things are sacred. He encouraged people to give up hunting and sacrificing animals. He also encouraged them to eat less meat.

▼ *Asoka built this shrine to* **honor** *the Buddha. Asoka built 84,000 of these shrines called "stupas." They are built of solid stone.*

> **honor:** to show great respect for
>
> **Mauryan:** name of a line of conquering kings
>
> **remorse:** a deep sense of guilt; regret
>
> **ruthless:** without pity

? THINK ABOUT IT:

What do you think caused Asoka to stop fighting wars?

Asoka had Buddhist beliefs carved on pillars. He also had rest stops built for travelers.

Asoka Brings Unity to India

Asoka wanted to bring unity to India with all its different cultures, languages, religions, and traditions. He hoped that Buddhism would help do this, so he had Buddhist beliefs carved into rocks and pillars from one end of his kingdom to the other.

Asoka did many things to make life better for the people and the animals of his empire. He had trees planted for shade and for fruit. He had wells dug, rest houses built for travelers, and watering places made for animals. He even had **medicinal** herbs planted to help people and their animals. Asoka also established one official language to help unify his empire.

medicinal: healing

? THINK ABOUT IT:

What are some of the beliefs of Buddhism that might bring unity?

Asoka Sends out Buddhist Monks

Asoka wanted people in faraway places to know about Buddhist beliefs. He **encouraged** Buddhist monks to follow the trade routes to Egypt, Greece, and the Middle East to tell people about Buddhism. However, Buddhism never became popular in these places.

He also sent monks to **Ceylon** to tell them about the beliefs of Buddhism. Buddhism became an important religion there. It also spread to Southeast Asia, China, and Japan.

Ceylon: an island to the south of India now called Sri Lanka

encourage: to urge someone to do something

missionary: a person sent to tell other people about a religion

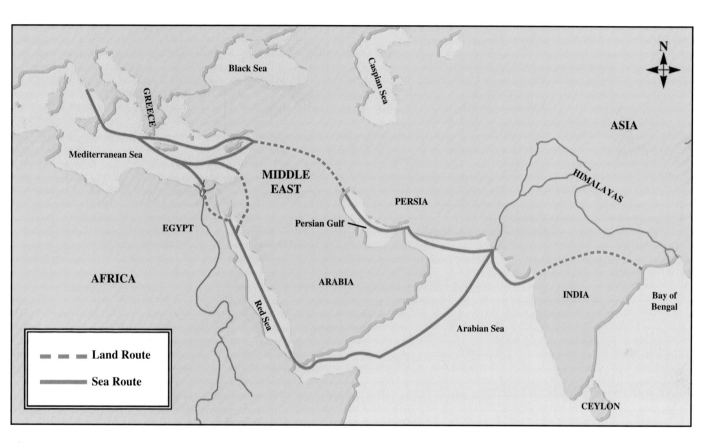

▲ Asoka's **missionaries** *followed trade routes to Egypt, Greece, and the area of southwestern Asia that today is often called the Middle East.*

? THINK ABOUT IT:

What are some ways people spread their religious beliefs today?

Asoka—Emperor of Peace

Asoka called the people of the empire his children. He said he wanted for them, "every kind of welfare and happiness both in this world and the next."

Asoka has been called the "emperor of peace." Some people think he was the greatest and **noblest** ruler India has ever had. Some believe he was one of the great emperors of the world. While he was emperor, the Mauryan Empire reached its golden age, its peak of power and glory.

Many of Asoka's beliefs are still important in India today. **Jawaharlal Nehru** (juh-wah-her-LAHL NAY-roo), a modern-day ruler of India, said that Asoka's actions and ideas "still speak to us in a language we can understand and appreciate. And we can still learn much from them."

Political Chaos

After Asoka died, the regions of his empire became more and more independent, and his empire began to fall apart. About 50 years after Asoka's death, the last Mauryan emperor was killed.

This began a time of political **chaos** in India that lasted several hundred years. Instead of an empire, there were many independent kingdoms constantly at war with one another. There were **riots**. Groups of people went from place to place stealing money and property. At the same time, more invaders came into northern India **raiding** the villages. People in the villages were afraid.

chaos: great confusion and disorder

Jawaharlal Nehru: prime minister of India from 1947 to 1964

noble: having high moral qualities or ideals

raid: to make a sudden, hostile attack

riot: wild or violent disorder of a group of people

? THINK ABOUT IT:

What makes a good ruler?

◀ *Asoka traveled around his empire to be sure that the people were happy.*

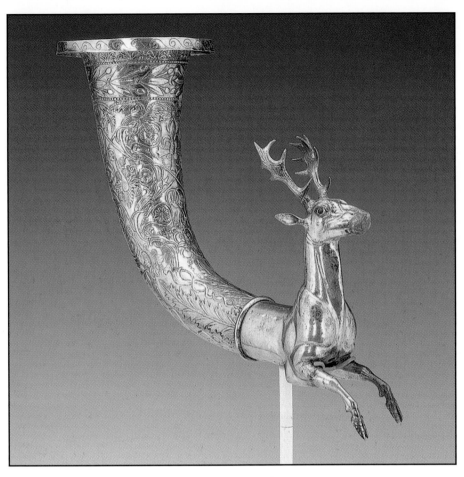

▲ *These treasures were found at a city on the overland trade route.*

Economic Growth

Even though there was political chaos, the economy was improving. Each group of invaders stayed and made contributions to the growth and **economic** development of India. One group built up trade over land with central Asia. Another group developed trade with Egypt, Africa, **Persia**, and **Arabia** by way of the Persian Gulf.

New cities grew up at the caravan stops. Merchants became wealthy from the profits of their trade. This increased trade caused a demand for luxuries. People wanted beautiful glassware and gold objects like the ones pictured above. They also wanted **plaques** and other decorative items. There was also an exchange of ideas with people in Greece and China.

Arabia: a peninsula in southwestern Asia surrounded by the Red Sea, the Arabian Sea, and the Persian Gulf

economic: having to do with the production, distribution, and use of wealth and resources

Persia: a country in western Asia now known as Iran

plaque: a thin, flat piece of wood, metal, glass, or clay used for ornamentation

The Guptas

In A.D. 320, a man named Chandra Gupta I began to rule a small kingdom in the northern part of the subcontinent. This was the same place where the Mauryan Empire began. It was Chandra Gupta's goal to conquer the whole subcontinent and bring cultural and **political** unity to India.

Just like the Mauryan emperors, he conquered many small kingdoms. Chandra Gupta I began the Gupta Empire, but he did not reach his goal of unifying all of India.

political: having to do with government

> **? THINK ABOUT IT:**

What are the advantages of political and cultural unity? What are the disadvantages?

▲ *The emperors of the Gupta Empire lived in beautiful palaces and had many servants.*

▲ *These Hindus and their water buffaloes are bathing in the sacred waters of the Ganges River.*

cult: a system of religious worship or ritual

? THINK ABOUT IT:

How do these changes in religious beliefs reflect the diversity of India?

The Rise of Hinduism

In A.D. 375, Chandra Gupta's grandson, Chandra Gupta II, became emperor. Chandra Gupta II also hoped to find a way to bring unity to the subcontinent of India. Just like Asoka, Chandra Gupta II decided to use religious beliefs to accomplish his goal.

By the time Chandra Gupta II became emperor, the religions of India had changed. Buddhism was not as popular as it had been. The old religion of the Aryans with its class system had blended with the **cults** of the earliest inhabitants of the Indus Valley and Buddhism. This blending became another religion known as Hinduism.

Chandra Gupta II supported both Buddhism and Hinduism. However, he gave his strongest support to Hinduism. He hoped that its system of classes would help to unify India.

Hinduism and the Caste System

Hinduism recognized the four classes of the Aryans: 1) the priests; 2) the kings and warriors; 3) the merchants and landowners; and 4) the servants, poorer farmers, and tradespeople.

In addition to the four classes, Hindus believed that people were born into a **caste**. A person's caste could never change. The caste determined what **occupation** a person would have, and it also determined many other details of life. For instance, if you were born into the spice **vendor's** caste, you would live in a certain part of the village, dress in a certain way, and eat certain foods. You would even have to marry someone from the spice vendor's caste.

caste: a hereditary social class

occupation: job

vendor: a person who sells things

? THINK ABOUT IT:

If we had a caste system, would your life be different? How?

◄ *This spice vendor is a member of the third class, which included landowners and merchants.*

Hindu Temples and Deities

There are many gods in Hinduism, but most Hindus worship just one. The Guptas worshiped the god Vishnu. Many other people worshiped Shiva. Both Vishnu and Shiva had been **minor** deities of the Aryans.

Hindus built temples as homes for their deities. Priests took care of the statues of the gods just as if they were human. They bathed and dressed them and gave them food and water. They entertained them with music and dancing. People went to the temple to worship whenever they wanted, not just on a certain day.

The first Indian temples were in caves. Hindu temples during the time of Chandra Gupta II were made to look like mountains on the outside and caves on the inside.

▼ *This cave temple was carved during the time of the Gupta Empire.*

▼ *This statue shows the god Shiva as King of Dancers.*

minor: less important than others

? THINK ABOUT IT:

How is Hinduism like other religions? How is it different?

▲ *While Chandra Gupta II was emperor, astronomers studied the stars and taught students from all over the world. Can you find the Big Dipper in this photograph of the night sky?*

India's Golden Age

While Chandra Gupta II was emperor, the Gupta Empire came to the peak of its power and glory. He invited the greatest artists, **scholars**, writers, and scientists of his time to visit his palace. Great **universities** were built where students from all over the world came to study.

At this time, India was the most advanced country in the world. Indian **astronomers** at the universities knew that the earth was round. Mathematicians developed the idea and symbol for zero and the system of numbers we use today, called Arabic numerals.

Chandra Gupta II also brought India its greatest era of peace. While he was emperor, a Buddhist monk from China named Faxian (fah-shee-ANH) traveled in India. He wrote in his journal that the country was peaceful and that people enjoyed religious **tolerance** and personal freedom.

Faxian also wrote that the hospitals he saw were free to "the poor of all countries, the destitute, crippled, and diseased."

astronomer: a person who studies stars and other heavenly bodies

scholar: an advanced student; an educated person who may teach or do research

tolerance: respect for the beliefs of others

university: a place of higher education; a group of colleges

▶ *Camel caravans followed a trade route called the "Silk Road."*

▼ *Traders followed the Silk Road as trade among China, India, and Rome increased.*

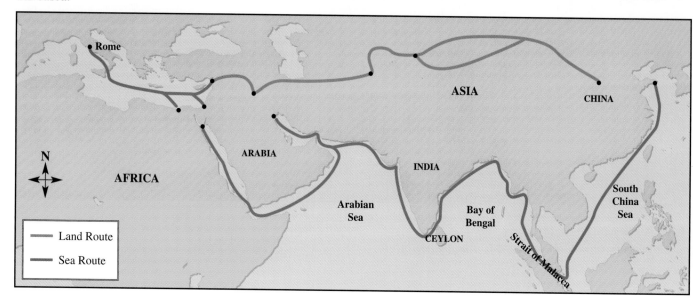

balance of trade: the difference in value between all the imports and all the exports of a country

musk: an oil from an animal used in making perfumes

tung: an oil from a tree used in paint to give a shiny finish that is water-resistant

? THINK ABOUT IT:

What are some of the advantages of trade?

Trade in the Gupta Empire

The Chinese monk Faxian was one of many to visit India during this time. While Chandra Gupta II was emperor, trade with both China and Rome grew. Camel caravans carried cotton, ivory, brassware, monkeys, and parrots over the silk trade route to China. They brought back silk, **musk** and **tung** oil, and a gemstone called amber from China. Some traders used the sea routes that went to Ceylon and then east through the Strait of Malacca.

People in Egypt, Greece, and Rome eagerly bought India's jewels, ivory, perfume, woods, spices, and cloth as well as silk and other items from China. India imported Arabian horses, copper, tin, and lead from the west. However, the **balance of trade** was in India's favor. Some Romans were unhappy that so much Roman gold was going to India.

Chapter Summary—Unity and Diversity

The Indian subcontinent has always been a place of great diversity. This huge region is inhabited by people of different cultures, religions, and languages.

In ancient times, two empires, the Mauryan and Gupta, brought unity to part of the subcontinent. Two men brought their empires to golden ages: Asoka, to the Mauryan Empire; and Chandra Gupta II, to the Gupta Empire.

Asoka established unity through the beliefs of Buddhism. Chandra Gupta II achieved unity by encouraging the caste system of Hinduism. Both men ruled over their empires during times of great achievement in art, architecture, literature, and science.

However, unity did not last. Soon after these men died, their empires fell apart. Instead of one empire, there were many small kingdoms again. In India, there has always been a **tension** between the desire for unity and the diversity of its people.

local: of a certain place

tension: a pull from two different directions; a strain

unique: different from all others

? THINK ABOUT IT:

What things help unify a country?

▲ *For thousands of years, groups of people invaded the Indian subcontinent. Each group brought its own ideas of religion and society. These ideas blended with **local** traditions to make the **unique** culture of India.*

UNIT 4: ANCIENT CHINA
CHAPTER 11
China's Bronze Age

ERA: Early Civilizations
PLACE: Northern China
PEOPLE: The people of the Shang and Zhou dynasties
THEME: Continuity—an unbroken line; and Uniformity—the state of being the same, not changing

CHAPTER FOCUS: The nobles of the Shang and Zhou dynasties used their powerful bronze weapons to control the peasants and nearby tribes.

LINK

In the last unit, you read about the beginning of civilization in the subcontinent of India. You also read about the efforts of different rulers to unify India's many different cultures, religions, and languages.

In this chapter, you will be introduced to the Shang (shawng) and Zhou (joh) dynasties. These dynasties mark the beginning of the written history of Chinese civilization. You will read about nobles who loved to hunt and go to war with bells ringing and banners flying. As you read, think about how having tools, weapons, and trade leads to new classes in society.

3500 B.C.	3000 B.C.	2500 B.C.	2000 B.C.	1500 B.C.	1000 B.C.	500 B.C.	0	A.D. 500

Shang Dynasty
(1523-1027 B.C.)

Zhou Dynasty
(1027-256 B.C.)

▲ *Hunting was a favorite sport of the nobles of the Shang Dynasty.*

The World

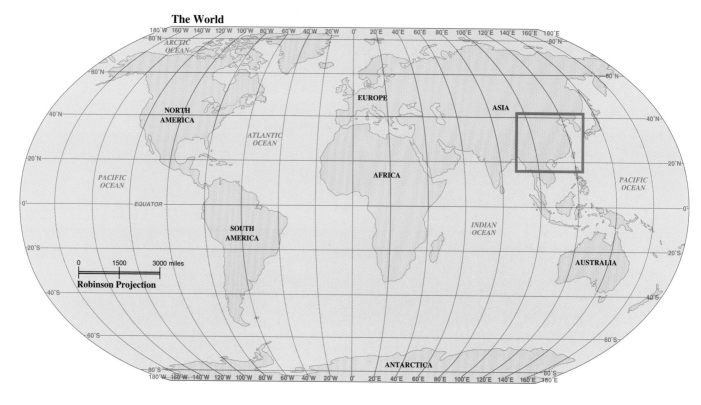

China has many natural boundaries that keep it separated from other countries. On the east and south there is ocean. On the north and west are deserts and high mountains. The Shang and Zhou dynasties controlled most of northern China between the Yellow River and the Yangtze River. Tribes of nomads lived to the north. Other tribes lived to the south.

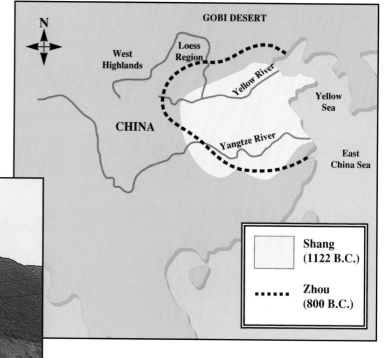

◀ GEOGRAPHY IN FOCUS

loess (LOH-es) *highlands: a high area above the North China Plain covered by deep layers of windblown yellow soil called loess*

The Yellow River carries loess down from the highlands to the valleys and plains.

The Yellow River

Just like the civilizations in Sumer, Egypt, and the Indus Valley, the first civilization in China developed in a river valley. And like the Euphrates, the Nile, and the Indus rivers, the Huang He (hwahng hay), or Yellow River, overflowed its banks almost every year. Each time it overflowed, it brought fertile yellow soil to the valley.

The Yellow River still overflows its banks. This flooding is both good and bad. It is good because the flood brings with it fertile soil that makes the crops grow better. It is dangerous because when it floods, houses and crops are destroyed and people are killed. So many people have been killed by the river it has been called "China's Sorrow."

silt: soil or sand left behind by water

? THINK ABOUT IT:

What are some of the things people can do to protect themselves from flooding?

▲ Huang He *means "yellow river" in Chinese. The river was given this name because of the yellow* **silt** *it carries down from the highlands. This modern photograph shows a city skyline along the Yellow River.*

▲ *The nobles of the Shang Dynasty used bronze weapons to **subdue** the peasants and nearby nomads.*

The Beginning of the Shang Dynasty

The first civilization in China developed along the Yellow River. Around the year 1500 B.C., the first ruler of the Shang Dynasty came to power. His name was Tang.

King Tang and his **nobles** had something that gave them a great advantage over their farming neighbors—they had weapons made of bronze. King Tang used his power to claim all the land for himself. He gave some land to his brothers, sons, and other relatives and forced the peasants to work on the land for them. Because of this, there were just two classes of people in Shang society, the nobles and the peasants.

noble: a person who is a member of the ruling family

subdue: to conquer

? THINK ABOUT IT:

How does Shang society compare with other societies you have studied?

Nobles and Peasants of the "Middle Kingdom"

King Tang and the nobles lived inside walled palace-cities in large houses of wood and earth. They lived a life of luxury and privilege. They spent their time hunting, going to war, and conducting religious rituals.

Most of the peasants lived outside the cities in pits dug into the ground. They worked for the nobles and lived in poverty. Most of them were farmers, but some were artisans who made luxury goods for the nobles. Many of the peasant women raised silkworms and wove silk cloth for the king and the nobles.

The Shang nobles called themselves the "Middle Kingdom" because they thought they were in the center of the world. They thought they were better than the nomads and other peoples who lived around them.

? THINK ABOUT IT:

Do you think the nomads and people of other tribes agreed that the Shang nobles were better than them? Why or why not?

▲ *Peasant women are gathering leaves from mulberry trees to feed silkworms.*

▲ *Communicating with their ancestors was so important to Shang nobles that they offered sacrifices almost* **continually**.

Worship and Sacrifice

The Shang king was a kind of high priest. People thought he had a special gift for communicating with the gods. Only the king was allowed to sacrifice to their most important gods, the gods of heaven and earth. The other nobles sacrificed to the gods of the soil and grain. People believed that the gods demanded sacrifices so that there would be rains at the right time and good harvests. They sacrificed both animals and humans.

The nobles also worshiped their ancestors. They believed that their prayers helped the souls of their ancestors get to heaven. They also believed that their ancestors in heaven could guide them and help them. Nobles and peasants had different religious practices. Peasants did not have **surnames** and did not keep track of their family lines. They did not worship their ancestors.

continually: over and over; without interruption

surname: last name; family name

? THINK ABOUT IT:

How does the religion of the Shang Dynasty compare with the religions of other societies you have studied?

Responsibilities of the King

One of the most important responsibilities of the king was to lead religious ceremonies. The king and his nobles used beautiful bronze vases and weapons in ceremonies for their ancestors. Creative artisans made beautiful objects of carved jade, ivory, antlers, and bone decorated with **turquoise**. The bronze **vessels** that were made during the Shang Dynasty are among the best in the world. Bronze was hard to get, so they probably used these bronze vessels only for religious ceremonies. They used pottery for everyday activities.

The king had a special responsibility to keep an **accurate** calendar. Mathematicians and astronomers in the royal court created a calendar with 29-day and 30-day months. They kept records of **eclipses** and recognized the summer and winter **solstices**. They used the calendar to predict the seasons and the positions of the stars and **planets**.

accurate: free from mistakes

cast: to form into a shape by pouring into a mold

eclipse: partial or complete darkening of the moon when the earth's shadow falls on it; or darkening of the sun when the moon comes between it and the earth

mold: a hollow form used to give shape to something poured into it

planet: a heavenly body that shines by reflected sunlight and revolves around the sun

solstice: the point at which the sun is farthest north or south of the equator

turquoise: a blue to blue-green substance found in rocks, used to make jewelry

vessel: a container such as a vase, bowl, or pitcher, used for holding something

? THINK ABOUT IT:

Do you think the Shang Dynasty learned things from other people of the world? Why or why not?

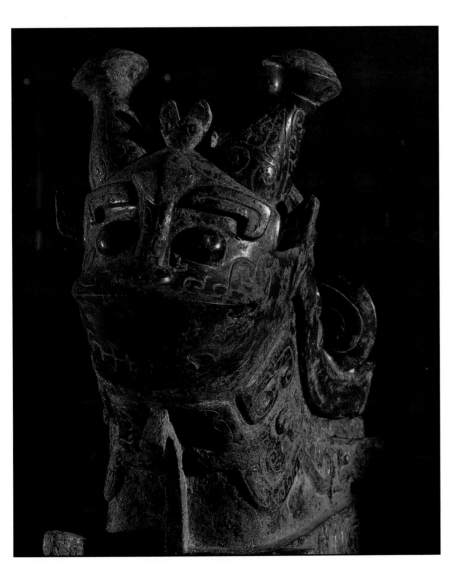

▲ *Animals were common subjects in Shang art. Some of the same designs were popular for almost 1,000 years. Artisans used **molds** of clay to **cast** bronze objects that weighed as much as 1,500 pounds.*

? THINK ABOUT IT:

What are some things historians can learn
from these oracle bones?

The Oracle Bones

Nobles did not do anything important without **consulting** their ancestors. The king and men called **diviners** heated the bones of animals and tortoise shells until they cracked. These were called **oracle** bones. The diviners then interpreted the cracks in these bones to help the king make decisions. For example, one diviner asked the question, "Should we hunt in Kuei, and would we have success with our traps?" The answer must have been "yes" because the diviner later wrote on the bone, "That day, we caught one tiger, 40 deer, 164 wolves, 159 fawns, and some foxes which were rather small."

Over 100,000 of these oracle bones have been found near the cities of the Shang Dynasty. Historians have learned many things about the Shang Dynasty from these bones.

▲ *Shang nobles used oracle bones such as this to help them make decisions.*

▲ *During the Shang Dynasty, many animals lived in the Yellow River Valley, including the tiger, wild boar, and water buffalo. Most of these animals no longer live in the Yellow River Valley. Many people believe that the climate was wetter and there were forests and swamps in this area during the time of the Shang Dynasty.*

The Royal Hunt

Hunting was a popular sport with the king and nobles. The Shang used the same weapons for both warfare and hunting. In fact, they used hunting as a way to train soldiers for war.

The Shang had special hunting grounds where they hunted wild boar, buffalo, deer, elephant, rhinoceros, and tiger. Shang nobles often killed hundreds of animals at a time. The inscription on one bronze vase tells that 348 deer were killed on one hunt. Eating meat was a special privilege of the nobles.

? THINK ABOUT IT:

What are some possible reasons the climate has changed in the Yellow River Valley?

WRITING IN ANCIENT CHINA WENT THROUGH STAGES

1 The first symbols, used before the Shang Dynasty, were pictographs.	"sun" ⊖ "tree"
2 The Shang combined symbols to form **ideographs**.	"sun" + "tree" = "the east"
3 The Shang used the same symbol for words that sounded the same. In ancient Chinese, the word *corn* sounded like the word for *come*, so they used the same pictograph for *corn* and *come*.	"corn" "come"

decay: to rot

dialect: the different sounds or words used by a group of people in a certain place that others using the same language do not understand

ideograph: a symbol representing an idea

Writing

Shang nobles needed a way to keep track of their family lines for ancestor worship. They developed a system of writing that is very similar to the writing system still used in China today. Even though people in China speak different **dialects**, they can all read the same writing.

We have examples of Shang writing on bronze vessels and on the oracle bones, but no other written records have survived. The Shang wrote with ink and writing brushes on strips of wood or bamboo. Most of these writings **decayed** long ago.

? THINK ABOUT IT:

What symbols can people of different languages all read today?

◀ *Workers dug huge pits, sometimes 40-feet deep and covering 5,000 square feet, for burial pits.*

▼ *This dagger-ax is made of bronze. It was used in human sacrifices.*

Luxury and Violence

The Shang kings and nobles built large tombs for themselves. They filled the tombs with bronze bells and vases, weapons, pottery, and sometimes even horse-drawn chariots.

Inside these tombs, archaeologists have found the skeletons of people who were sacrificed with the king or queen. Inside one tomb, and nearby, there were 300 human skeletons. These people may have been killed to be servants to the king in the **afterworld**. Kings sometimes went to war just to get prisoners to kill and bury with the nobles and kings when they died.

? THINK ABOUT IT:

What are some reasons why ancient people put things in the tombs with people who died?

> **afterworld:** a world thought to exist after death

? THINK ABOUT IT:

Ancient Chinese rulers studied **astrology** to learn about the future. What kinds of questions do you think they wanted to answer?

The End of the Shang Dynasty

King Tang and his descendants ruled over northern China for about 500 years. Then the kings began to live in even greater luxury. They raised taxes and spent the money on huge parties, sacrifices, and funerals. A Chinese **sage** who lived in a later time wrote on a **scroll**: "Enjoying ease from their birth, they did not know the painful toil of sowing and reaping. They sought for nothing but excessive pleasure."

By the year 1027 B.C., the Shang Dynasty had become weak. The Zhou, a group of people from the west highlands, led a revolt against the Shang Dynasty and conquered it. The Zhou built their own cities, and a Zhou king ruled the land. Eventually the Shang cities were destroyed by floods and buried deep in silt.

The Zhou—Tradition and Moderation

The lives of the peasants did not change much when the Zhou took over. The peasants still lived in poverty. The king and the nobles still controlled the land. The peasants had to pay the nobles so that they could farm the land. The peasants also gave the nobles part of the **produce** from their farms.

The nobles gave some of this produce to the king. The nobles also sent soldiers to help the king in times of war. The nobles and the king protected the peasants from attack by invaders. This system is called feudalism.

Some things did change, however. Instead of luxury and violence, the Zhou nobles valued tradition and moderation. They lived by a set of rules called "li" (lee). According to li, a noble must:

- be loyal to the king.
- come to the king's aid when the **beacon** fires burned on the mountain tops.
- respect the gods and the ancestors.
- be **chivalrous**, even in war.

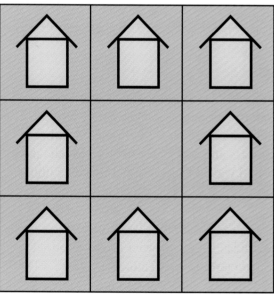

▲ The Zhou divided farmland into 40-acre sections. Then they divided each section into nine parts. Eight peasant families lived and worked on the outside pieces of land. All the families cultivated the land in the center for the noble.

▲ The picture at the top of this page shows the way the farmland may have really looked. This diagram shows the ideal or perfect model of the system.

▶ *Warfare was a way of life for the Zhou nobles. The Zhou kings lit the beacon fires to call the nobles and their armies to help in times of war. Three men rode in each chariot—a driver, the king or a nobleman, and an **archer** or **lancer**. Each man wore a bronze helmet, and the tips of their arrows and spears were made of bronze.*

archer: a person who shoots with a bow and arrows

lancer: a soldier who carries a lance, a long wooden weapon with a sharp metal tip

sportsmanlike: losing without complaining, winning without bragging, and treating others with fairness

tournament: contest in a sport

? THINK ABOUT IT:

What are some other societies for whom warfare was a way of life? Why did they fight?

The Ritual of War

The Zhou developed a kind of warfare that was almost like a **tournament**. Nobles went to war in chariots drawn by horses. The nobles were accompanied by soldiers on foot. Sometimes these soldiers carried wooden spears and bows and arrows. Musicians played bells, beat drums, and waved flags. Sometimes one noble ruler fought with another noble, and other times they went to war against tribes of nomads.

The goal of their warfare was to capture slaves, artisans, animals, and precious goods. The nobles followed strict rules of courtesy. They did not think it was **sportsmanlike** to attack a warrior who had been thrown from his chariot. They waited until he could get back in or get another chariot. Most wars lasted only a day.

> *There is a legend that a Zhou king made a big mistake. He decided to light the mountain beacon fires over and over just to make the women in his **court** laugh. Each time, the nobles from all around jumped in their chariots and came to help the king. When they arrived, they found out it was just a joke.*
>
> *Soon after, the king was attacked by a group of nomads and nobles. The king lit the mountain beacon fires, but no one came to help him.*

▲ *Whether the story above is true or not, the fact is that the king was killed, the capital was destroyed, and the Zhou had to move to a new capital in the East. A new Zhou king was named, but he did not have much power. His main job was to perform religious ceremonies.*

Chapter Summary—Continuity and Uniformity

The people of the Shang and Zhou dynasties developed a system of writing and ways of living that continued to be part of life in China up to modern times. However, there were many changes to come. In the next chapter, you will read about a metal that changed people's lives and new ideas that began to take the place of tradition and moderation.

court: the family, advisors, and attendants of a king or queen

? THINK ABOUT IT:

Does the legend of the Zhou king and the beacon fires remind you of a story you have heard? What lesson can you learn from this story?

CHAPTER 12

The End of Feudalism

3500 B.C.	3000 B.C.	2500 B.C.	2000 B.C.	1500 B.C.	1000 B.C.	500 B.C.	0	A.D. 500

Zhou Dynasty (1027-256 B.C.)   Confucius (551-479 B.C.)

ERA: Early Civilizations
PLACE: China
PEOPLE: Confucius and the people of the Zhou Dynasty
THEME: Continuity—an unbroken line; and Uniformity—the state of being the same, not changing

CHAPTER FOCUS: Political unrest and new developments in warfare and agriculture caused changes in society.

In the last chapter, you read about the Shang and Zhou dynasties and the beginning of China's written history. You read about nobles who fought with bronze weapons and lived by the rules of "li," or chivalry and moderation.

In this chapter, you will read about a society that was in disorder as the Zhou kings lost their power and a new metal came into use. You will also read about a philosopher named Confucius who looked for ways to bring back order to society. As you read, think about how having tools, weapons, and trade leads to new classes in society.

◀ *Chinese armies are defending themselves against invaders along the northern border. Ancient Chinese rulers built short sections of walls to protect themselves from invaders. Later dynasties connected the walls to make the Great Wall.*

The World

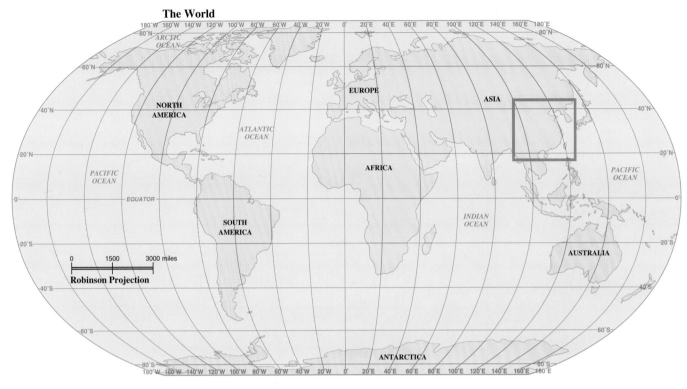

▶ *In 770 B.C., the Zhou moved their capital to Luoyang when nomads destroyed their first capital in Changan (CHAHNG-ahng).*

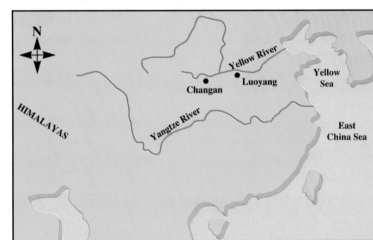

▼ **GEOGRAPHY IN FOCUS**

steppe: a plain with few or no trees

Tribes of nomads lived in the steppes to the north of the Zhou kingdom.

The End of War According to the Rules of Li

After the Zhou king lost his power, the rulers of all the states began to fight with one another. For several hundred years the states made **alliances** with each other, broke them, and fought with one another. Generals of the armies began to push the nobles from their thrones and make themselves rulers.

Sometimes one ruler would gain control over all the states for a while, until he was overthrown by another ruler. Larger states swallowed up the smaller states. The states in the central part of China valued the old traditional ways. The outlying states were influenced by the nomads around them and were more **aggressive**. Each state wanted to be the most powerful.

aggressive: starting fights or quarrels

alliance: close association for a common purpose

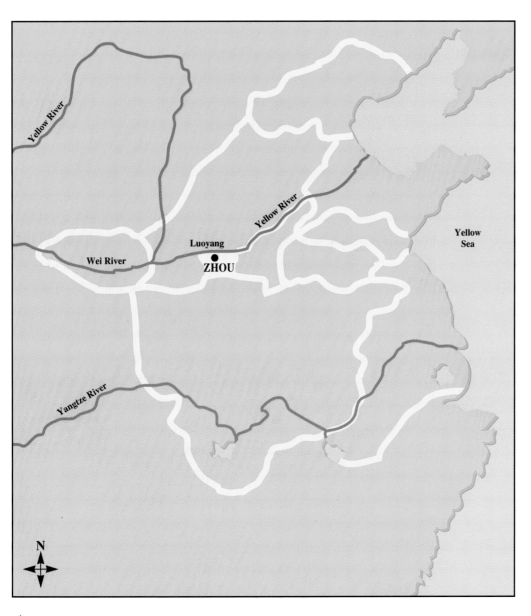

▲ *All that was left of the Zhou kingdom was a small area around Luoyang. The other states (whose boundaries are shown by yellow lines) around the Zhou kingdom fought with each other and with the Zhou.*

Confucius and the Importance of Ritual

The traditional order of society had broken down. It was a time of change and chaos in China. Many people began to look for ways to bring peace and security to society. There were so many **philosophers** talking about their new ideas that historians have called this the time of "The Hundred Schools." The most well-known of these philosophers was Confucius.

Confucius was born in 551 B.C. He believed that the chaos would be replaced by order if people returned to the rules of li and the traditions and rituals of the first kings of the Zhou Dynasty. He believed that the Zhou kings were models people should follow. Confucius went from place to place teaching people how to restore order in society.

philosopher: a person who thinks about and studies the basic questions of life

rubbing: a picture made by placing a paper over the surface to be copied and moving a crayon or pencil back and forth

? THINK ABOUT IT:

How could the rules of li help to restore order in society?

▶ *This is a* **rubbing** *of a stone engraving of Confucius.*

How to Live Honorably

Confucius taught the importance of self-discipline and tolerance. His ideal man was a "gentleman." He believed that a gentleman must have the qualities of **integrity**, fairness, loyalty, and concern for others.

Confucius also believed that a gentleman should be educated and trained in good manners. He taught the basic principle, "Never do to others what you would not like them to do to you."

Confucius's followers began to call him Master, but they did not think he was a god. Confucius did not consider himself a god or expect to be worshiped. Confucianism is not a religion. It is a **moral** code, a way of living.

integrity: honesty; sincerity

moral: having to do with principles of right and wrong

? THINK ABOUT IT:

Do you think people in America admire the same qualities that Confucius admired? Who are your heroes? What qualities do they demonstrate?

▶ *This rubbing shows Confucius with some of his disciples. It was taken from a stone stele.*

A Place for Everyone in Society

Confucius taught that parents were **superior** to children, men were superior to women, and rulers were superior to their subjects. He taught that the person of lower **rank** owed complete **obedience** to the person of higher rank. However, he also believed that the higher-ranking person was responsible for the lower-ranking person.

Just like the caste system in ancient India, this philosophy gave each person a place in society. Everyone, even the poorest beggar, could be an accepted member of society. Confucius believed that the important thing was to behave properly. He believed that if everyone performed his or her role, there would be order in society. He also believed that a stable family meant a stable society. His goal was to set a standard of behavior for the world to follow.

PLAN FOR RIGHT LIVING

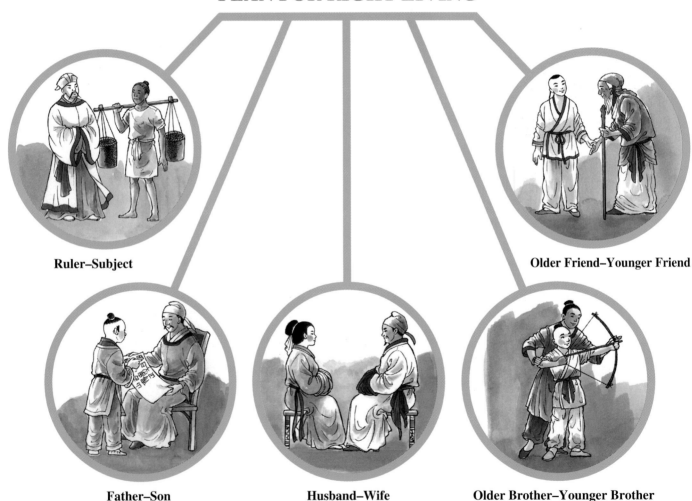

Ruler–Subject

Older Friend–Younger Friend

Father–Son

Husband–Wife

Older Brother–Younger Brother

▲ *The family has always been important in Chinese society. Of the five relationships that Confucius taught, three of them have to do with the family.*

▲ *Confucius studied ancient Chinese* **literature** *as a young man. Books were written on strips of bamboo and held together with* **hemp** *tape.*

Education and the Bureaucracy

As a result of Confucius's teachings, people began to think education was important. They believed it was important to prepare people for their place in society. After Confucius died, the government set up schools to teach Confucian ideas. People went to these schools to prepare to hold government jobs.

Administrators who had been trained in these schools began to take the places of nobles who had held their positions because of their relationship to the king. This was the beginning of a **bureaucracy** in China.

bureaucracy: government through departments and officials

hemp: a tall plant with tough fibers

literature: stories, poetry, and other writings

From Chivalry to Violence

After Confucius died, the chaos in Chinese society continued. In fact, there were so many wars that this is called the period of the warring states. Wars became more violent and many people were killed.

War was no longer just a **pastime** for nobles. Now the object of war was to conquer the enemy and gain new land. Each state wanted to control all the others and create an empire. Instead of small armies fighting according to the rules of li, there were now large armies of 500,000 soldiers. Wars and **sieges** against cities often lasted months.

However, ritual was still an important part of war. Diviners asked for guidance and offered prayers before a battle. Generals presented reports and the **booty** of war, including enemy heads, at the altars of their ancestors.

New Weapons Change Warfare

Some of the changes in warfare were caused by the use of new weapons. Around 500 B.C., the Chinese invented the crossbow. This bow was much more powerful and accurate than the bow they had been using.

Peasants also began carrying iron swords and wearing iron armor. Because of these iron weapons and armor, peasants began to play a more important part in warfare. Before this time, only nobles carried weapons with metal tips because bronze was scarce.

Then, in 307 B.C., one of the kings of the warring states decided to copy the nomads and use men on horseback in battles. Soon this **cavalry** took the place of chariots.

booty: goods taken from the enemy

cavalry: troops on horseback

pastime: a way of spending spare time; hobby; anything done for amusement or recreation

siege: a type of warfare in which an army camps around a town and fights to destroy it

? THINK ABOUT IT:

How was this new warfare different from war according to the rules of li?

▶ *Horseback riders copied the nomads from the steppes and began to wear trousers or pants. Cavalry soldiers carried a new, stronger weapon called the crossbow.*

New Tools Change Farming

During this time of change in government and warfare, other important changes were happening as well. One of the most important of these was the beginning of the use of iron for tools.

Around 500 B.C., the Chinese people began to use iron tools for farming. As a result, many things began to change quickly. With strong iron tools, farmers were able to clear much more land. Soon this land was drained and cultivated. Then rulers forced large numbers of people to build canals to irrigate these lands.

Because of this increase in land being farmed and because of the new, stronger tools, farmers were able to grow more food. As a result, the population grew rapidly. At this time, it was an advantage to have more people.

? THINK ABOUT IT:

What new "tool" has changed our modern society?

▲ *Strong, cheap, iron tools like the one this woman is using changed farming methods in China.*

▲ *At first, the Shang used shells as money. Around 600 B.C., the Zhou began making official coins in the shape of knives and spades. By 500 B.C., they were using a round copper coin with a hole in the center. This allowed them to string many coins together. Round copper coins were used in China for 2,000 years.*

Changes in Trade

Trade was also changing. In earlier times, traders supplied luxury goods such as silk, pearls, and jade for the kings. As food production and the population increased, merchants began to trade a wider variety of goods, including grain, salt, metal, fur, and leather.

Earlier traders used shells, silk fabric, and **ingots** of precious metals for exchange in trade. During this time, they also began to use coins. This made trading much easier.

Trade also became easier as merchants followed roads made by the armies. Traders loaded their goods onto carts and followed the new roads to distant regions. Traders also transported goods on river boats.

ingot: metal cast into a bar

? THINK ABOUT IT:

What is the connection between iron plows and increased trade?

How do coins make trading easier?

Trade Leads to Growth of Towns

Towns and cities developed along the trade routes. Business people built factories to manufacture goods for trade. There were textile factories to weave fabric and factories to make pottery and vessels of bronze and iron.

This trade led to an increase in **wealth**. Now it was not only the nobles who had money. Many families became wealthy because they were successful in **commerce** or owned land. Some of the merchants were becoming wealthier than the nobles. This did not please the nobles.

commerce: the buying and selling of goods

wealth: much money or property; riches

? THINK ABOUT IT:

How did the use of iron also lead to the growth of cities?

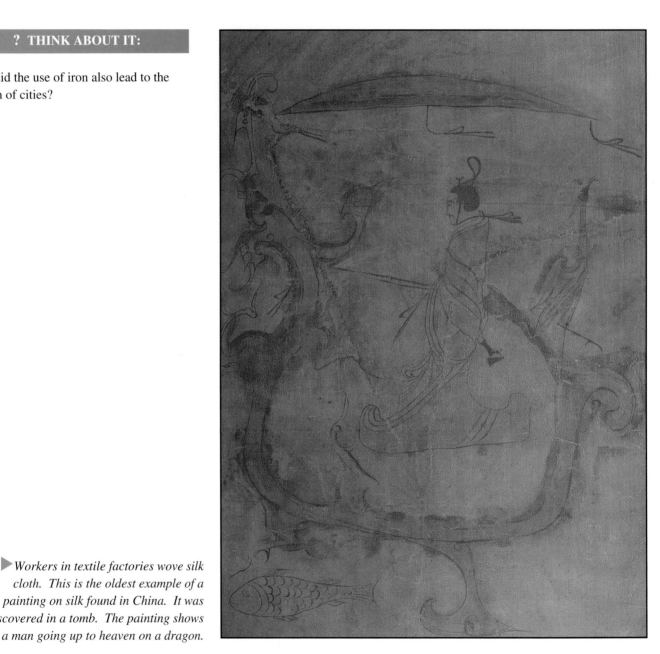

▶ *Workers in textile factories wove silk cloth. This is the oldest example of a painting on silk found in China. It was discovered in a tomb. The painting shows a man going up to heaven on a dragon.*

▲ *This is a photograph of a Chinese merchant today. Merchants have used carts in China for thousands of years. During the time of the warring states, trade made merchants wealthy.*

Changes in Society

In the feudal society there were just two classes of people—nobles and peasants. Everyone respected the traditional order of society. Because of all the changes, two more classes were added—artisans and merchants. The nobles were especially afraid of the merchants because they were becoming wealthy.

To keep the merchants from getting too much power, the nobles set up a new order of the classes. They put the warriors and administrators at the top level of society. The peasants were next because they produced the basic necessities of life. The artisans were third because they created beautiful and useful objects. The merchants were last because the nobles did not think they had any value. The nobles thought merchants were **parasites** who lived off the peasants. For the next 2,000 years, merchants were not highly respected in China.

parasite: a person who lives at the expense of another without making a contribution

? THINK ABOUT IT:

How did the nobles decide the new order of the classes? Do you agree with their decisions? Why or why not?

Culture Flourishes

Even while there was great political unrest, the arts **flourished**. Writers composed poems, songs, hymns, and kept historical records. One book, the *Spring and Autumn Annals*, covers the history of one state in Zhou from about 722 B.C. to 481 B.C. Some people think this record was **compiled** by Confucius.

During the warring states period, artisans carved beautiful objects of jade. Wealthy people used the jade in rituals and had these objects placed in their tombs. Other artists made objects of bronze. These were often used as containers for wine. However, the most important artistic work was done in lacquer. Many artifacts of lacquer have been found in tombs from the warring states period.

annals: yearly written account of events

compile: to gather and put together

flourish: to grow vigorously; to be at the peak of development

▶ *Artisans mixed sap from the laq tree with color to make lacquer. They painted thin layers of lacquer on wooden or leather objects to give them a hard, smooth, shiny finish.*

> *R*iches and honor are what men desire; if not obtained in the right way, they do not last.

▲ *After Confucius died, some of his students wrote down his ideas and teachings in a book called* Analects. *The quotation above is taken from that book.*

Chapter Summary—Uniformity and Continuity

The later period of the Zhou Dynasty was a time of disorder, growth, and development. The rulers of the noble class lost their power to generals and bureaucrats. Warfare became more violent. People no longer valued the old rules of chivalry. However, new developments, including the use of iron, led to advances in agriculture and trade. All of these changes caused disorder in society.

Philosophers such as Confucius looked for ways to bring back order. Confucius taught people to return to the traditions of the first Zhou kings. He also introduced the idea of training government workers for their jobs. This was the beginning of bureaucracy in China.

At the beginning of this period, there were over 100 states. By the end, there were only seven powerful states. In the next chapter, you will read about one state that conquered all the other states and unified China into the first Chinese empire.

? THINK ABOUT IT:

Is disorder always a bad thing? Why or why not?

CHAPTER 13
The Chinese Empire

ERA: Early Civilizations
PLACE: China
PEOPLE: The First Emperor of the Qin Dynasty, Emperor Wudi of the Han Dynasty, and the people of China
THEME: Continuity—an unbroken line; and Uniformity—the state of being the same, not changing

CHAPTER FOCUS: A strong ruler conquered the warring states and created the first Chinese empire.

3500 B.C.	3000 B.C.	2500 B.C.	2000 B.C.	1500 B.C.	1000 B.C.	500 B.C.	0	A.D. 500

The Qin Dynasty
(221-206 B.C.)

The Han Dynasty
(204 B.C.-A.D. 2

▼ *In 1974 these clay soldiers were discovered in the tomb of the First Emperor of China.*

LINK

In the last chapter, you read about the period of the warring states—a time of political disorder, but also a time of economic growth and development in the arts.

In this chapter, you will read about a harsh ruler who conquered all his rivals and became the first emperor of China. After a time of disorder, another dynasty reunited China with a government based on the teachings of Confucius. As you read, think about how having tools, weapons, and trade leads to new classes in society.

The World

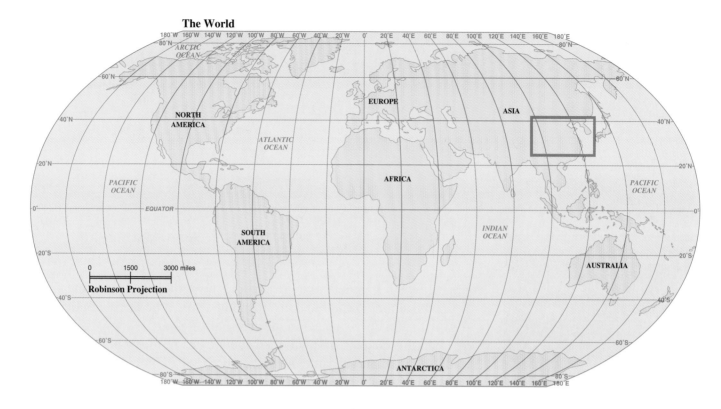

▶ *The Qin (chin) Dynasty controlled most of northern China. The Han (hahn) Dynasty added territory to the north, south, and west.*

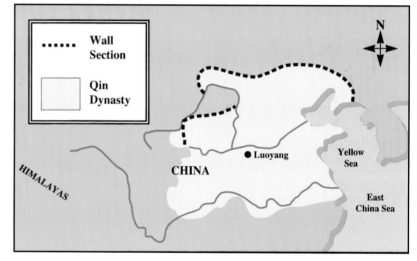

▼ GEOGRAPHY IN FOCUS

frontier: *the part of a country that borders another country or an undeveloped region*

Rulers of China built walls along the frontier to keep out invading nomads. At first, these walls were not connected to each other. The First Emperor, Shi Huangdi, ordered the walls to be connected in order to form a protective barrier.

The First Emperor

The state of Qin was a **rugged** land surrounded by mountains. Some people thought the people of Qin were as rough as the land. A noble of a rival kingdom said, "Qin has the heart of a tiger or a wolf. … It knows nothing about etiquette, proper relationships, and virtuous conduct."

For 35 years after the last Zhou king died, the states fought among themselves. During this time, a young boy became king of the state of Qin. He was a cruel ruler. Historians wrote that he was an **impetuous tyrant** and that he ruled by **terror** and **whim**.

In 221 B.C., this king of Qin conquered the last of the other states and proclaimed himself emperor. He took the name Shi Huangdi (shee HWAHNG-dee), First Emperor, because he thought his empire would last 1,000 generations.

impetuous: acting suddenly with little thought

rugged: rough; severe; harsh

terrace: an area of flat land, one above the other, on a hillside

terror: intense fear

tyrant: a cruel ruler

whim: sudden fancy or desire

▲ *Qin farmers built* **terraces** *to make the best use of their rugged, mountainous land.*

A Strong Central Government

The First Emperor and his chief minister were disciples of a philosophy called legalism. They believed the central government should have **absolute** power. They also believed in strict laws and severe punishment. To break the power of the conquered states, the emperor forced all the nobles to move to the capital where he could keep his eye on them. He **confiscated** their lands and gave the land to the peasants. He took the people's weapons and had them melted down and made into statues.

Next, the First Emperor divided the empire into 36 regional **provinces**. He appointed three officials to rule each province. Under his rule, five to 10 families were grouped together. Everyone in the group was held equally responsible. If anyone broke a law, everyone in the group was punished. As a result, crime decreased. It was possible to leave valuables out in the open without having them stolen.

absolute: unlimited

confiscate: to take private property for the government

province: territory; region

? THINK ABOUT IT:

Would you be willing to accept a system like the First Emperor's system to control crime? Why or why not?

◀ *The First Emperor ruthlessly killed his enemies in order to gain absolute power.*

◄ *This picture shows government officials burning books and throwing Confucian scholars into a pit. Some people say they buried 460 scholars alive.*

Books Burned

Both the First Emperor and his chief minister were against the ideas of Confucius and the Confucians' emphasis on education. When some Confucian scholars complained, the chief minister began to burn all books on philosophy, history, art, and music, except the ones in the government libraries. He only allowed people to keep books on what he called useful subjects such as agriculture, medicine, and **divination**.

The First Emperor and his chief minister **transformed** China into an orderly state with a strong central government. They expected all the people to work hard, pay their taxes, and obey the laws of the government.

divination: the practice of trying to foretell the future

transform: to change

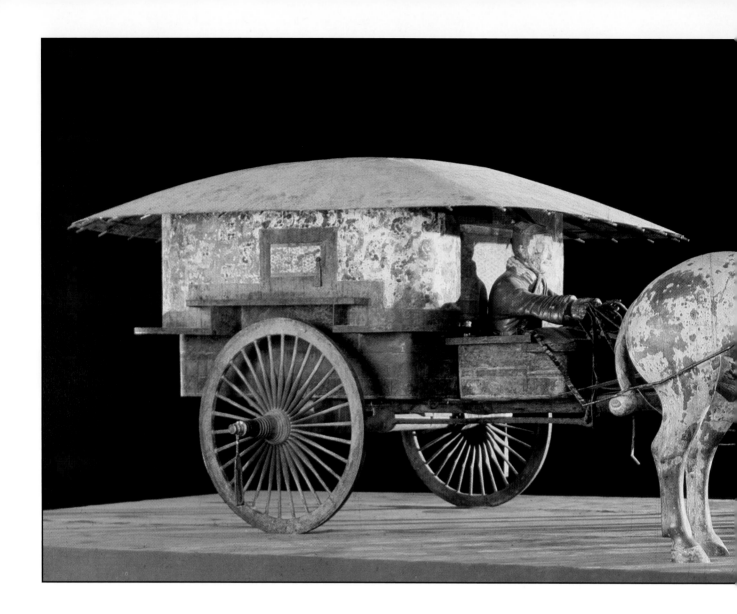

? **THINK ABOUT IT:**

There were 7,500 clay statues in the First
Emperor's tomb. How many students are
there at your school? How much space
would it take if they all stood up together?

Clay Soldiers and a Tomb

When he became ruler, the First Emperor immediately ordered
work to begin on his tomb. Hundreds of thousands of farmers,
prisoners of war, and slaves spent 36 years building it.

In 1974, workers digging a well discovered the tomb. Inside the
tomb they found four pits filled with life-size statues. There were
7,500 statues of warriors made from terra cotta, a type of clay.
There were statues of archers, soldiers, and officers, all armed with
bronze weapons and lined up in battle formation. The face of each
statue was molded individually. Originally they were painted red,
green, lavender, and blue. No two were alike.

These clay soldiers were put there to protect the emperor. They
took the place of the human sacrifices of the Shang and Zhou
dynasties.

Copies of the buildings of the royal palace and major rivers and
mountains were also built in the tomb. The tomb was protected
against robbers by crossbows set to go off if they were touched.
The entire tomb was covered by an earth mound 140-feet high.

◄ *There were real chariots and horses of clay along with the clay soldiers in the First Emperor's tomb. After he died, he became known as Qin Shi Huangdi.*

The End of the Qin Dynasty

The First Emperor did many things to unify the empire. During his reign, thousands of peasants built over 4,000 miles of highways and canals. The First Emperor began a government postal service to send communications along the new highways. He also made it a rule that everyone had to use the same written **script**. He even sent out word lists around the empire so that everyone would write words the same way.

Although he was successful at unifying the empire, the First Emperor worked the people until they were **exhausted**. He also overtaxed them until they could no longer take care of their families.

In 210 B.C., on a tour around his empire, the First Emperor became sick and died. After his death, the peasants began to revolt. His son, the Second Emperor, was not able to maintain order. Three years after the First Emperor died, **rebel** armies burned the capital and the palace. It was the end of the Qin Dynasty. Historians recorded that "they reaped what they had sown."

exhausted: very tired

rebel: a person who openly resists authority

script: written words

? THINK ABOUT IT:

What do you think historians meant when they said, "They reaped what they had sown"?

Why was it important for people to write words the same way?

▲ *Liu Bang, the first ruler of the Han Dynasty, marches to the capital to be crowned emperor.*

intrigue: a plot in secret

Korea: a country east of China

martial: having to do with war

Vietnam: a country south of China

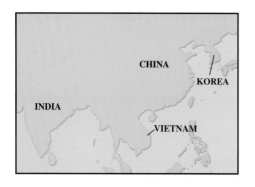

The Beginning of the Han Dynasty

After the Qin empire collapsed, there was a time of rebellion, violence, and **intrigue** as several people tried to take over the government. About 200 B.C., one man was victorious. His name was Liu Bang (LEE-oh bahng), and he established the Han empire. China was united again into one empire. Under the Han emperors, China began a new period of stability and prosperity.

In 141 B.C., Han Wudi (WOO-tee) became emperor. He is called the **Martial** Emperor because he sent out large armies to expand China's territory. In the north, his soldiers fought tribes of nomads. In the south, they conquered territory that is now part of **Vietnam** and added it to the empire. His armies also conquered land that is now **Korea** and started colonies there. Although he fought wars with neighboring peoples, the country was at peace at home. Both the wealthy and the common people gave him their support.

The Teachings of Confucius Become Official

Emperor Wudi combined the legalist ideas of the First Emperor and the ideas of Confucius. He believed the ruler had absolute power. However, he also wanted **efficient** Confucian scholars as advisors and **civil service** administrators.

The emperor made the teachings of Confucius official. To train men to be government officials, Emperor Wudi started a school at the capital. This "Imperial University" soon had 3,000 students.

The emperor also encouraged education throughout the country. Students studied the Confucian collections of writings on history, rituals, and folk songs. They also studied such subjects as mathematics and astronomy.

civil service: all the people who work for the government except people in the military, the people who make laws, and the judges

comet: an object that looks like a star and travels along a definite path around the sun

efficient: able; capable

▲ *Emperor Wudi encouraged education. This manuscript on silk describes the movements of the planets and **comets**.*

? THINK ABOUT IT:

"If a man is paid 40 coins for carrying two measures of salt for a distance of 100 li, how much will he be paid for carrying 1.73 measures for a distance of 80 li?" Can you solve this mathematics problem from the Han Dynasty?

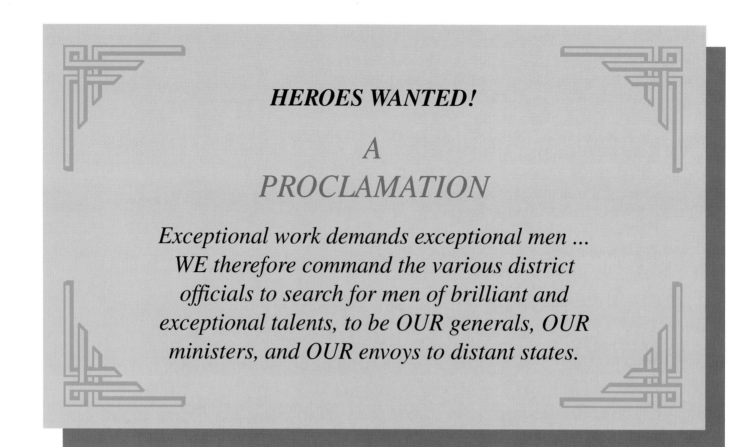

HEROES WANTED!

A
PROCLAMATION

*Exceptional work demands exceptional men ...
WE therefore command the various district
officials to search for men of brilliant and
exceptional talents, to be OUR generals, OUR
ministers, and OUR envoys to distant states.*

▲ *Emperor Wudi announced that he wanted capable men for government jobs.*

? THINK ABOUT IT:

How are government employees chosen in the United States? How does this compare with the way they were chosen under Emperor Wudi?

Heroes Wanted!

Many of the officials Emperor Wudi appointed for the government and the military were Confucian scholars. The emperor also asked for recommendations to fill government positions. He sent out announcements around the empire asking government officials to search for capable men.

After the men were recommended, they were given an examination at court. The grand master of ceremonies graded their papers. The emperor himself chose the men who would get the jobs.

China's First Written History

Sima Qian (SOO-muh CHEE-yehn), Emperor Wudi's court historian, wrote China's first official history. His book tells China's story from the earliest times.

Sima Qian and other Chinese writers collected classics of literature from earlier times. They tried to piece together what had been lost when the books were burned during the Qin Dynasty.

? THINK ABOUT IT:

Where do you think Sima Qian got the information to write his history book?

◀ *Sima Qian was China's greatest historian. He was also the court astrologer.*

The Silk Road

Emperor Wudi sent one of his **diplomats** to the northwest frontier to try to make an alliance with a tribe of nomads. This diplomat wasn't able to make an alliance, but he returned with animal and plant **specimens**. He also brought stories of people who rode elephants and lived in lands of great wealth.

People became interested in his stories of the lands to the west. More and more traders began to follow the Silk Road all the way to India and Rome. Traders carried silk cloth and **raw** silk, gold, cinnamon, and furs to the West. They brought back wine, linen, horses, and woolen goods. Soon there were rugs from Persia in the emperor's palace, and people in Rome were wearing clothes made of Chinese silk.

diplomat: a representative of a government who conducts relations with another country

loom: a machine for weaving thread into cloth

raw: in its natural, unchanged condition

specimen: a sample or an example

? THINK ABOUT IT:

Who was ruling in India at this time? How did government in India compare with China?

▲ *Chinese weavers used **looms** to weave complicated designs such as this one.*

▼ *Traders followed the Silk Road to India and Rome.*

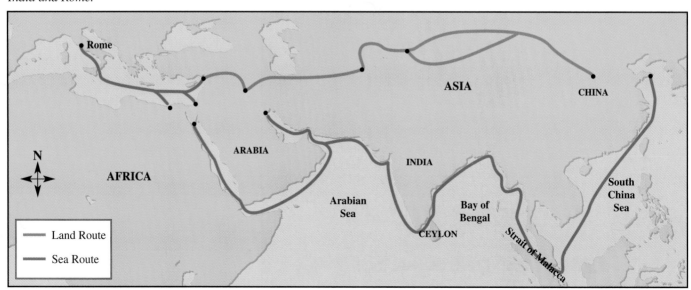

▲ *This relief shows nobles watching acrobats and dancers.*

Economic Prosperity

The first part of the reign of Emperor Wudi was a time of prosperity for China, even for the peasants. In fact, China was the greatest empire on earth. The capital city of Changan was perhaps the largest city in the world with a population of 300,000 to 650,000. The city had streets 150-feet wide and beautiful royal parks.

Emperor Wudi loved luxury. He had beautiful gardens with exotic plants and animals at his palace. The gardens were filled with orchids, sweetly scented trees, peacocks, monkeys, and **pheasants**. He had the walls of public buildings painted with murals showing scenes from China's history.

Everyone in the empire seemed to enjoy music and dancing. However, wealthy people had different types of entertainment than people in the rest of society. The wealthy people listened to orchestras with drums, bells, flutes, harps, and lutes. They also enjoyed tiger fights, performing animals, **jugglers**, and **acrobats**. The poor people enjoyed seasonal festivals, **cockfights**, and horse races.

acrobat: a performer who does tumbling or tricks on the trapeze or tightrope

cockfight: a fight between birds trained to fight

juggler: a person who performs tricks with balls

pheasant: a bird with a long, sweeping tail and brightly colored feathers

? THINK ABOUT IT:

What is the population of the town or city where you live? How wide are the streets? What are different forms of entertainment today?

▶ *This is a clay model of the kind of watchtowers that were built along the frontier.*

The End of Emperor Wudi

Although the empire prospered during the first part of Emperor Wudi's reign, in time the empire began to weaken. The emperor taxed the people to build palaces, roads, canals, and walls. Military posts were too spread out and too expensive to keep up. The ruling class began to demand more and more luxuries.

After Emperor Wudi died in 87 B.C., the empire continued to decline. The next rulers were weak. As the rulers became weaker, the landowners and palace officials began to become more powerful.

This was not the end of the Han Dynasty, however. In time, strong rulers came to power again and China entered a new period of creativity.

Chapter Summary—Uniformity and Continuity

From the time of the warring states, there was a struggle between the nobles who inherited their power and a central administration that selected leaders because of their ability. However, the Han Dynasty established a pattern of bureaucratic government that lasted over 2,000 years.

The Qin and Han dynasties united China into an empire. Even though there were times when the empire crumbled, the ideal was always a united China. Three things helped to unify China: its written language; the importance of the family; and its bureaucratic government. In spite of the struggles, there was more uniformity in China than in any other ancient culture.

? THINK ABOUT IT:

Why would it be expensive to keep up military posts far from the capital?

CHAPTER 14
The Ancient Israelites

ERA: Early Civilizations
PLACE: Egypt and the Sinai Desert
PEOPLE: Moses and the Israelites
THEME: Ethics—standards of conduct based on right and wrong; and Religion—a belief in God or in many gods

CHAPTER FOCUS: The Israelites escaped from slavery in Egypt and made an agreement with God.

3500 B.C.	3000 B.C.	2500 B.C.	2000 B.C.	1500 B.C.	1000 B.C.	500 B.C.	0	A.D. 500

Moses and the Israelites leave Egypt (1290 B.C.)

In the last unit, you read about ancient China and its different religions and philosophies. In this chapter, you will learn about the Israelites, who founded Judaism, a religion based on a belief in one God. As you read, think about how religion and literature influence society.

◀ *Moses hit a large rock with his staff to get water for the Israelites in the Sinai Desert.*

The World

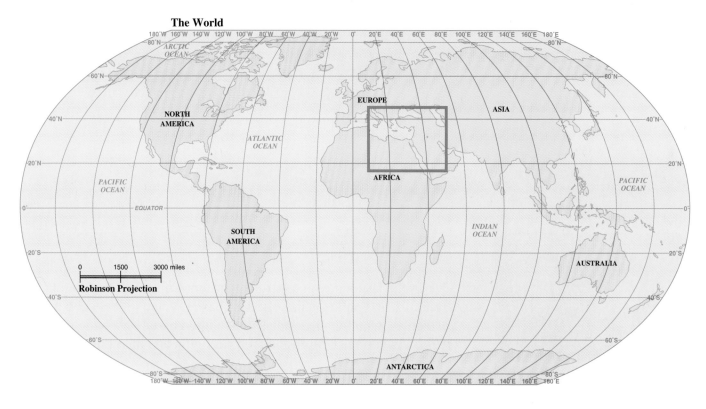

▼ GEOGRAPHY IN FOCUS

desert: *a body of dry, sandy land with almost no water and few plants or trees*

The Israelites crossed the Sinai Desert to reach the land of Canaan.

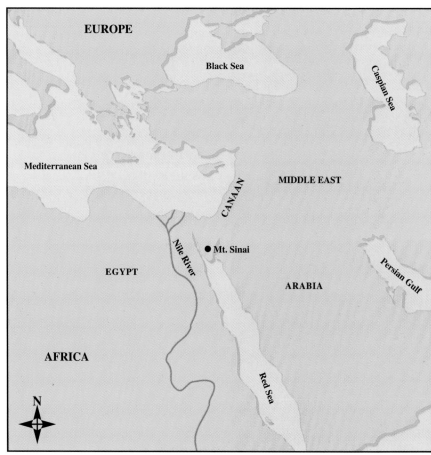

▲ *Moses led the Israelites out of slavery in Egypt and into the Sinai Desert. The Israelites escaped from Egypt by crossing the Red Sea. Their destination was Canaan.*

The Call of Abraham

In **Genesis**, the first book of the **Bible**, a story is told of a man called Abraham. Abraham lived in the city of Ur in Sumer. According to this account, God told Abraham to leave his home and go to a faraway land. Around 1900 B.C., Abraham obeyed God and went to the land of Canaan. He took with him his wife Sarah, his nephew Lot, and their servants. He also took their **flocks** of sheep and goats.

After Abraham's family had been in Canaan for about 200 years, there was a terrible **famine**. They were no longer able to grow enough food to feed themselves. The famine lasted so long that finally Abraham's grandson Jacob, and Jacob's sons and their families, went to Egypt to live.

▲ *The* **Torah** *is the central Jewish text. The word* torah *comes from a word meaning "direction" or "teaching."*

? THINK ABOUT IT:

What do you know about life in Ur and Egypt around 2000 B.C.? What can you find out about the land of Canaan? How did it compare with Ur and Egypt?

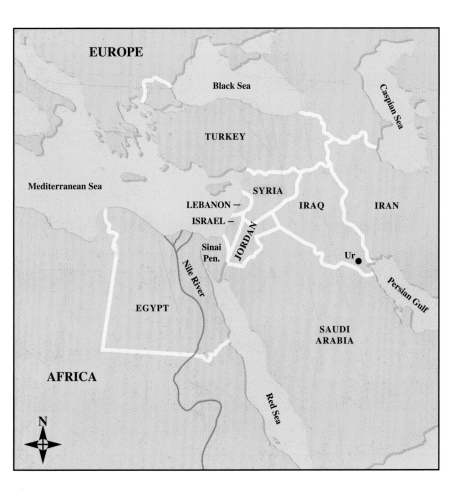

▲ *The lands where Abraham traveled are now known by new names: Israel, Lebanon, Jordan, Syria, Saudi Arabia, and Iraq.*

Bible: in Judaism, the holy scriptures contained in the Torah; in Christianity, the Old and New Testament; the Jewish Bible is identical to the Christian Old Testament

famine: hunger caused by a widespread lack of food

flock: small numbers of animals

genesis: the beginning; origin; creation

Torah: the sacred history and laws of the Israelites

The Israelites in Egypt

When Jacob and his sons first came to Egypt, they were shepherds. They **tended** flocks of sheep, goats, and donkeys.

In time, however, many Israelites began to work as servants and in other occupations. This story is in the book of Exodus in the Bible. The Israelites worked hard and became very important to Egypt's way of life. After the Israelites had been in Egypt about 400 years, there was a new ruler. This pharaoh was afraid that the number of Israelites in his country was growing too fast. He believed there would soon be more Israelites than there were Egyptians.

tend: to look after

? THINK ABOUT IT:

Why was the Israelites' work important to the Egyptians?

Why would the pharaoh be afraid of too many Israelites in his country?

▲ *Shepherds tend sheep today in the land where Abraham and his family once brought their sheep and goats to feed.*

▲ *Workers made mortar and bricks for the pharaoh.*

Israelites Became Slaves

The pharaoh could have killed the Israelites or driven them out of Egypt, but he needed them as workers. So instead of killing them or making them leave, he made them **slaves**.

Egyptian guards with whips forced Israelite workers to carry heavy loads of bricks and **mortar** for building. The harder the Israelites worked, the harder their **overseers** drove them. The overseers severely beat the Israelite workers who became tired or who were slow.

To make sure the number of Israelites did not increase, the pharaoh ordered all newborn Israelite **males** killed.

male: boy or man

mortar: dry powder that hardens when mixed with water

overseer: a person in charge of others; a supervisor

slave: a person who is owned by others and must work for and obey them

? THINK ABOUT IT:

How could the pharaoh make the Israelites slaves?

How did slavery change the lives of the Israelites?

▲ *The pharaoh's daughter pulled the baby Moses from the river.*

? THINK ABOUT IT:

How did being found by the pharaoh's daughter change Moses's life?

Moses Is Born

According to a story in the Bible, about 1370 B.C., a child was born to Israelite parents. The parents hid the child so that the pharaoh's soldiers would not kill him. When the child was three months old, his parents put him on the Nile River in a basket made of reeds. They hoped he would be found and cared for by someone who did not know that he was an Israelite.

While the pharaoh's daughter was bathing in the river, she found the child. When she saw that it was a male baby, she **suspected** he was an Israelite. She remembered her father's order to **execute** such children. To protect the child, she decided to raise him as her own. She chose a woman to take care of him until he was old enough to live with her at the palace. The pharaoh's daughter named the little boy Moses and raised him as her son, a prince of Egypt.

Moses Flees Egypt

As he grew, Moses learned of his Israelite **heritage**. One day he went to watch some Israelites working. He saw how harshly the Egyptians were treating them. When he saw one Egyptian guard beat a slave, Moses became very angry and killed the guard.

The next day, Moses went out again among the Israelites. This time he saw two Israelites fighting each other. When he tried to stop them, one said angrily: "Who made you a ruler and a judge over us? Are you thinking of killing me as you killed the Egyptian?"

Moses thought no one saw him kill the Egyptian. Now he realized that was not so. Moses was afraid he might be turned in and **punished** for what he had done, so he decided to **flee** Egypt.

flee: to run away or escape from danger

heritage: a person's culture and traditions passed down by one's parents

punish: to cause pain or suffering

? THINK ABOUT IT:

Why do you think Moses was angry when he saw Egyptian guards beating slaves?

▲ *When Moses fled Egypt, he went into the Sinai Desert.*

The Burning Bush

After he left Egypt, Moses became a shepherd. One day while he was tending his flock, he **encountered** something almost beyond belief.

This **miracle** is described in the Bible as a bush flaming bright with fire, yet not destroyed by the blaze. Moses heard a voice coming from the burning bush that said, "I am the God of your father, the God of Abraham, the God of Isaac, and the God of Jacob."

The voice **commanded** Moses to **deliver** the Israelite people from slavery: "I am sending you to pharaoh to bring my people, the Israelites, out of Egypt."

During this time, most people believed that there were many gods. The belief in many gods is called "polytheism." Moses, however, like Abraham before him, believed there was only one god. The belief in one god is known as "monotheism."

---

command: to order that something be done

deliver: to set free or rescue

encounter: to meet or come upon

miracle: something almost beyond belief; an event or action that seems to go against scientific laws and is thought to have a supernatural cause

---

? THINK ABOUT IT:

Do most religions today teach polytheism or monotheism?

▲ *Moses was surprised to hear a voice coming from a burning bush.*

▲ *Artists have pictured God in many ways. This painting shows God separating the earth from the sea.*

Moses Accepts His Charge

According to the Bible, when God told him to free the Israelites, Moses said he could not do it. He asked, "Who am I that I should go to pharaoh and bring the Israelites out of Egypt? I do not know how I shall do it." Although he was well-educated, Moses was uncomfortable speaking before people. He also was afraid the Egyptians might **imprison** him for murder.

However, the voice that came from the burning bush **insisted** Moses do as he was told. Moses gave in and returned to Egypt.

imprison: to put in prison or jail

insist: to continue to ask or demand

? THINK ABOUT IT:

Why do you think Moses finally agreed to return to Egypt?

The Israelites appeared before the pharaoh to seek his favors.

gnat: a small insect that flies

hail: frozen raindrops; pieces of ice that sometimes fall during thunderstorms

locust: a type of grasshopper

refuse: to not do as asked

? THINK ABOUT IT:

What effect did the plagues have on the Egyptians? Why would the pharaoh continue to refuse to free the Israelites from slavery?

The 10 Plagues

Moses went to the pharaoh and said, "Let my people go." The pharaoh refused. The Bible records that soon the first of 10 terrible plagues struck the Egyptian people. The water in the Nile River turned to blood. Then the Egyptians were overrun by frogs, **gnats**, and flies. Sickness struck their livestock and the people themselves. **Hail** and **locusts** destroyed their crops and darkness covered the land.

After each plague the pharaoh said he would let the Israelites go, but each time he changed his mind. The plagues continued one after the other. Still the pharaoh **refused** to let the Israelites go. Finally, God told Moses, "About midnight I will go throughout Egypt. Every firstborn son in Egypt will die … " God said the firstborn of the Israelites would be spared if they put the blood of a lamb around their doors. The Israelites believed this would identify them as Israelites and that God would "pass over" their homes.

The Israelites obeyed their God and their children were spared, but the firstborn sons of the Egyptians were killed. After this last plague, the pharaoh let Moses and the Israelite people go. Jews continue to remember this entire event in the Passover celebration.

The Parting of the Sea

After Moses and his people had fled Egypt, the pharaoh changed his mind again and wanted them to stay in Egypt. He ordered soldiers to **pursue** Moses and the Israelites. The soldiers chased them toward the Red Sea.

According to the Bible, when the Israelites reached the edge of the Red Sea, "Moses stretched out his hand over the sea and all that night the Lord drove the sea back with a strong east wind and turned it into dry land." The Israelites walked on dry land between the parted water to get to the other side. However, when the Egyptian soldiers arrived and drove their chariots onto the land between the waters, the Red Sea closed in and they were **drowned**.

drown: to sink into water, become unable to breathe, and die

pursue: to chase or go after

▲ The Bible tells how Moses and his followers crossed safely on land, and the Red Sea swallowed up the Egyptian army.

? THINK ABOUT IT:

How do you think the Israelites felt when the Red Sea closed in on the Egyptians?

▲ *Palm trees and water are a welcome sight for desert travelers. A place in the desert that provides travelers with shade and water is called an oasis.*

Promised Land: Canaan, in the Bible, the land promised by God to Abraham and his descendants

? THINK ABOUT IT:

What are some dangers of traveling in the desert?

The Exodus from Egypt

According to the Bible, Moses and his followers began a 40-year journey into the desert toward the **Promised Land** in Canaan. This journey is called the Exodus.

The desert was hot and stretched many miles. The Israelites had little food and water. The people became exhausted. "If only we had died by the Lord's hand in the land of Egypt," they cried.

Nevertheless, Moses insisted they keep going. When they found food and drink, they believed it to be a miracle provided by God. At last, they reached Mt. Sinai near where Moses had seen the burning bush and heard God's voice.

The Ten Commandments

The Bible says that God made a **covenant** with the Israelite people at Mt. Sinai. God said, "I will be your God and you will be my people." God promised to love and protect them and the people promised to love God and obey God's **commandments**.

Moses climbed Mt. Sinai alone to talk with God. When he came back down, he brought with him the Ten Commandments. They were written on tablets of stone:

> I am the Lord, your God, who brought you out of the land of Egypt, out of the house of **bondage**.
>
> 1. You shall have no other gods before me.
> 2. You shall not make for yourself an **idol**.
> 3. You shall not misuse the name of the Lord your God.
> 4. Remember the **Sabbath** day by keeping it holy.
> 5. Honor your father and your mother.
> 6. You shall not murder.
> 7. You shall not **commit adultery**.
> 8. You shall not steal.
> 9. You shall not give false **testimony** about your neighbor.
> 10. You shall not **covet** your neighbor's house; you shall not covet your neighbor's wife . . . nor anything that belongs to your neighbor.

Moses had done as God commanded. God spoke to Moses, and Moses spoke to the people. Moses was God's spokesperson.

adultery: the act of being unfaithful to a wife or husband

bondage: slavery

commandment: a law or order

commit: to do or be guilty of

covenant: a sacred agreement or promise

covet: to want what another person has

idol: a picture or likeness of a false god

Sabbath: a day set aside for worship; Saturday in the Jewish religion; Sunday in the Christian religion

testimony: statement or evidence

? THINK ABOUT IT:

Why would the Israelites obey God's Ten Commandments? How many of the Ten Commandments are laws today?

◀ *Moses returned from the top of Mt. Sinai with the Ten Commandments.*

Principles to Live By

The Ten Commandments outlined how the people should relate to God and how people should relate to each other. The Ten Commandments **prohibited** murder, theft, lying, and certain other acts. They taught the importance of respect for family and neighbors. Moses's followers now had standards of right and wrong to guide them.

The laws of other ancient societies, such as Sumer, named specific crimes and their punishments. The Ten Commandments, however, offered both moral and **legal principles**. The first four commandments concerned a person's relationship with God. The last six commandments gave principles for people's relationships with each other.

Chapter Summary—Ethics and Religion

The Israelites looked for a better life in Egypt, but the pharaoh made them slaves. After 400 years of suffering, Moses helped them escape. According to the Bible, at Mt. Sinai, Moses received the Ten Commandments from God and gave them to the people. After years of wandering, the Israelites finally settled in Canaan. They continued to raise sheep and goats, but they also planted crops and built towns and cities. Today this land is called Israel.

For over 3,000 years, the Ten Commandments have provided them with a set of principles, or ethics, by which to live their daily lives. Their ideas about law and ethics have spread to other places. Many legal ideas of the Western world are based on the Ten Commandments. Some people say that the Ten Commandments "**shaped**" the **conscience**" of Western civilization.

conscience: a person's sense of right or wrong

legal: something that is right under the law

principle: a law upon which other laws are based

prohibit: to not allow

shape: to give a form or direction to

? THINK ABOUT IT:

What was one of the laws of King Ur-Nammu of Sumer? How is that law different from the Ten Commandments?

Where can the descendants of Israelites find a history of their ancient times?

◀ *This is Mt. Sinai today, the place where the Bible says God gave the Ten Commandments to Moses.*

CHAPTER 15
The Ancient Greeks

ERA: Early Civilizations
PLACE: Greece
PEOPLE: Homer, the Minoans, and the
Mycenaeans
THEME: Ethics—standards of conduct based on
right and wrong; and Religion—a belief in God or
in many gods

CHAPTER FOCUS: The history of ancient
Greece was kept alive through myths and legends.

LINK

In the last chapter, you read about the Israelites. They escaped
from slavery in Egypt and began a new nation based on a belief in
one God. Out of this nation came two important religions in the
Western world: Judaism and Christianity.

In this chapter, you will read about two great ancient
civilizations, the Minoans (mih-NOH-uhnz) and the Mycenaeans
(my-suh-NEE-uhnz). These civilizations laid the foundation for
another new nation, ancient Greece. Western civilization has gotten
many of its ideas about art, literature, and government from ancient
Greece. As you read, think about how religion and literature
influence society.

3500 B.C.	3000 B.C.	2500 B.C.	2000 B.C.	1500 B.C.	1000 B.C.	500 B.C.	0	A.D. 500

Minoans in Crete (2000-1450 B.C.)   Mycenaean civilization in Greece (1450-1100 B.C.)

▲ *Minoan ships were loaded with goods for trade with other Mediterranean countries.*

The World

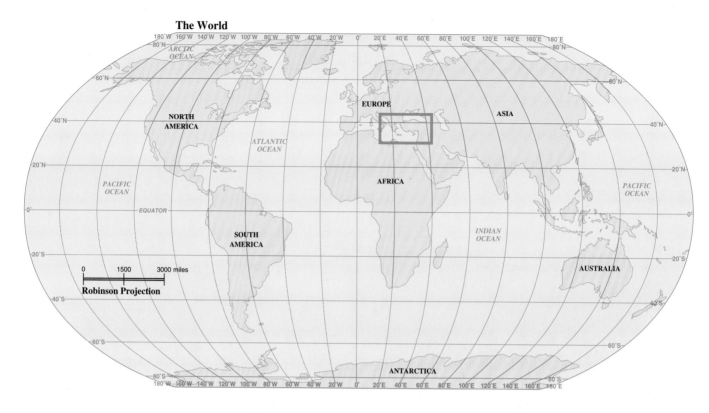

▼ GEOGRAPHY IN FOCUS

island: a piece of land completely surrounded by water

peninsula: a land area almost entirely surrounded by water

The Minoans lived on the island of Crete. The Mycenaeans lived on the Peloponnesian Peninsula.

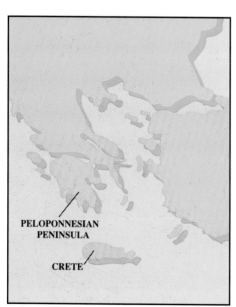

PELOPONNESIAN PENINSULA

CRETE

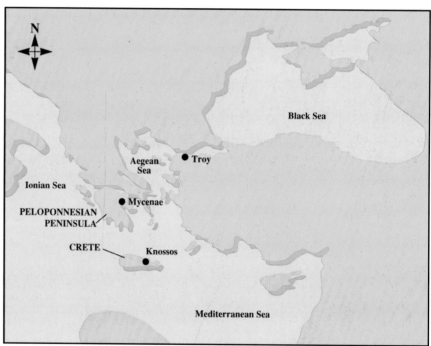

▲ *The Minoans built their civilization on the island of Crete. The Mycenaeans built their civilization on the Peloponnesian Peninsula.*

The Minoans in Crete

Around 2000 B.C., a group of people called the Minoans began to develop a civilization on the island of Crete. The Minoan kings built huge **palaces** and covered the walls with colorful pictures. There were pictures of **dolphins**, monkeys, flowers, and scenes of life in the palace. The palace had beautiful stairs and columns. It even had running water and a **plumbing** system similar to what we have today.

The Minoans were peaceful and fun-loving. Both men and women enjoyed dancing and taking part in sports. The Minoans also were hardworking. They raised olive trees so they could make olive oil. Artisans made swords, daggers, and beautiful jewelry. Minoan traders took these and other items to Egypt, Sumer, and other places around the Mediterranean Sea.

dolphin: a mammal from the whale family that lives in the ocean

palace: a very large building in which kings, queens, and their families live

plumbing: a system of pipes through which water passes in and out of a building

▲ *This picture on the wall of a palace shows Minoan athletes, both men and women, jumping over charging bulls.*

? THINK ABOUT IT:

What other ancient civilization had a plumbing system? What does a system of plumbing tell us about a civilization?

▶ *The Minoan palace at Knossos covered 4½ acres of land. This photograph shows only part of one room.*

erupt: to spill over or explode suddenly

tidal wave: a giant wall of water called a tsunami caused by a storm in the ocean, an earthquake, or volcanic eruption

? **THINK ABOUT IT:**

What other societies have you studied that were invaded? Where did the invaders come from?

The Mycenaeans Conquer the Minoans

About 1600 B.C., a large earthquake destroyed the Minoan palace and other buildings. Later, a volcano **erupted**. This eruption caused a huge **tidal wave** that killed thousands of people and destroyed ships and towns. At the same time, some people began to rebel against the king. All these events weakened the Minoan society.

For almost 1,000 years, invaders had been coming into the Peloponnesian Peninsula from around the Black Sea. One group built a city called Mycenae (my-SEE-nee). For many years these Mycenaeans wanted to take over the Minoans. When they realized the Minoan society was weak, they attacked the island of Crete and conquered the Minoans.

The Mycenaean Culture

The Mycenaeans copied much of the Minoan culture. Just like the Minoans, they built great palaces. The Mycenaeans also made excellent pottery. Greek artisans who lived in later times used the same **decorative** designs.

Mycenaean trading ships carried pottery, hides, timber, wine, and olive oil to other lands around the Mediterranean Sea. These ships came back filled with gold, silver, tin, copper, ivory, linen, **papyrus**, and rope.

The Mycenaeans also had a form of writing, but it was only good enough to keep records of sales.

decorative: artistic; pleasing to the eye

papyrus: a plant from which people of ancient civilizations made a paper-like material to write on

? THINK ABOUT IT:

How were the Mycenaeans like other invaders? How were they different?

▲ *The Mycenaean palace was the home of the king and his family. It was also headquarters for the military and the government and was used as a place for manufacturing and storing goods.*

▲ *Dorian invaders destroyed the beautiful Mycenaean palaces.*

disaster: a sudden event that causes great damage, loss, or destruction

handicraft: an art piece made by hand

wreck: to tear apart, destroy, or ruin

? THINK ABOUT IT:

How were the Dorian invaders different from the Mycenaeans?

The Dark Age

Then, just as it happened with the Minoans, earthquakes and other natural **disasters** hit the land of the Mycenaeans. Next, invaders came from the northern part of Greece. They were Dorians who did not appreciate the culture of the Mycenaeans. The Dorians **wrecked** the great palaces and burned the cities to the ground.

The Mycenaeans ran from their homes into the mountains and valleys. Artisans no longer made beautiful pottery and other **handicrafts**. People no longer used writing. This period is now remembered as the Dark Age of Greece. It lasted nearly 400 years.

Myths and Legends

During the Dark Age, each family had to take care of itself. The outside world seemed filled with enemies and unknown **terrors**.

The small groups of people were separated by miles of valleys and mountains. However, they still spoke the same language. Slowly, groups began to communicate with each other. These Greek people shared stories of the great civilizations of the Minoans and the Mycenaeans. Some stories were about historical events. Others were about heroes and gods and goddesses. These kinds of stories are called myths and legends.

terrors: things that make one afraid

? THINK ABOUT IT:

How does a common history and language bring people together?

▲ *This is the top of Mt. Olympus. The Greeks believed their most important gods and goddesses lived here.*

Homer, a Poet

People who had special skills in storytelling began to tell the stories of gods, goddesses, and heroes. These people were called poets. They did not actually write down their poems. Instead, they sang them.

A man named Homer became the most famous of the poets. Homer is credited with writing two great poems, the *Iliad* and the *Odyssey*. Almost nothing is known of Homer as a person. Some historians think parts of the stories may have been told by others over the years and collected by Homer. Nevertheless, the two poems are great works of literature. They are full of beauty, **drama**, and history.

The *Iliad*

The *Iliad* tells the story of a war between the city of Troy and the Mycenaeans. This war is called the Trojan War. Troy was across the Aegean Sea from Greece. According to the legend, a king of Troy **kidnapped** Helen, the beautiful wife of a Mycenaean king's brother. In 1200 B.C., the Mycenaean king took a **fleet** of hundreds of ships and sailed to Troy to rescue Helen. The Mycenaeans and Trojans fought for 10 years.

Finally, the Mycenaeans won the war by tricking the people of Troy. They offered the soldiers of Troy a wooden horse as a gift. The Trojans took it inside the city, not knowing that soldiers were hiding inside the horse. At night, while the Trojan soldiers slept, the Mycenaeans slipped out and opened the city's gates so that their army could rush inside. The legend says the idea for the wooden horse came from a Mycenaean warrior named Odysseus. He is the subject of the other famous poem by Homer called the *Odyssey*.

▶ *According to a Greek legend, Mycenaean warriors jumped out of a wooden horse to surprise the soldiers of Troy and win the Trojan War.*

The *Odyssey*

adventure: exciting travel or event

endurance: the ability to keep trying to do something though it is difficult

obstacle: something in the way that makes it hard to do what a person is trying to do

survive: to live through

The *Odyssey* tells of the **adventures** of Odysseus after the Trojan War ended. Odysseus started home, but the trip took him 10 years. During that time, he visited strange lands and met very strange people. He also lost all his possessions. Odysseus finally reached home, pretending to be a beggar.

The story of Odysseus shows how one person used intelligence, courage, and **endurance** to **survive** dangers and **obstacles** to return to his home and family.

? THINK ABOUT IT:

What stories have you read that are similar to the *Odyssey?* Why do you think people like to read adventure stories?

▲ *Odysseus, dressed as an old beggar, returns to his wife and son after traveling for 10 years.*

▲ *This sculpture tells the story of Selene, the Greek goddess of the moon.*

The Greek Gods and Goddesses

Homer and other Greek poets also told stories, called myths, about gods. The Greeks believed in many gods and goddesses. There was Zeus, god of weather, and king of all the other gods; Apollo, god of the sun; Selene, goddess of the moon; and many others.

The Greeks believed that the gods and goddesses were sometimes **vain** and **jealous**, just like people. They also believed that the gods and goddesses did not always agree and that they sometimes took opposite sides in human **disputes**. The Greeks believed that sometimes the gods and goddesses disguised themselves in wind, water, or animals. To win their favor, Greeks conducted rituals and made sacrifices.

dispute: an argument or fight

jealous: afraid of losing what one has or wishing for what another person has

vain: to greatly admire one's own looks, possessions, or abilities

? THINK ABOUT IT:

How does the religion of the Greeks compare with the religion of the Israelites?

▲ *Grapes grew well in the rocky soil of Greece.*

The Daily Life of Greeks

Homer wrote about an earlier time in Greek history. He wrote about gods, goddesses, and heroes. During Homer's lifetime, life was very difficult for the Greeks. People worked hard to grow crops and raise animals in wooded **swamps** and rocky mountains. Wild animals and **roaming** bands of warriors attacked them.

The poor people ate fish, grain, and sometimes vegetables. Only rich people and warriors ate meat. Rich farmers raised cattle, sheep, pigs, goats, and horses.

There were no schools in Greece during the Dark Age. Boys learned from their fathers. Girls learned from their mothers. Most people did not know how to read or write.

Everyone wore simple clothes made from woolen cloth. The cloth was draped and fastened with a rope or pin.

The ancient Greeks had no coins for money. They used iron, bronze, gold, or livestock to trade for the goods and services they needed.

The *Iliad* and the *Odyssey*—A Link to the Past

By 600 B.C., the Greeks were coming out of the long Dark Age. The *Iliad* and the *Odyssey* were important to the Greek people because these poems were a link to their past. The poems kept their heroes alive in their minds and this inspired them.

These stories **glorify** the history of Greece. Even today, part of what we know about the ancient Greeks comes from the poems handed down from Homer.

glorify: to surround with praise

? THINK ABOUT IT:

Can you think of a story that inspired you?

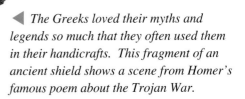

◄ *The Greeks loved their myths and legends so much that they often used them in their handicrafts. This fragment of an ancient shield shows a scene from Homer's famous poem about the Trojan War.*

A New Civilization

honesty: truthfulness

loyalty: being true to a friend, a country, or a cause

Homer's stories show good winning over evil. They also teach lessons about qualities such as **honesty** and **loyalty**. These stories try to explain things that happen in nature, such as floods and earthquakes.

The Greeks began to build a new civilization based on these ideas. By the end of the Dark Age, the Greeks had improved their alphabet and made it into a more useful set of letters. With the new alphabet, Greeks could now write down their poems. They also could write down their ideas about science, mathematics, and government.

? THINK ABOUT IT:

How could writing help people develop ideas about science, mathematics, and government?

▲ *This shows a record of a sale, written using the Greek alphabet, carved in marble.*

▲ *This carved stone relief sculpture shows gods fighting giants.*

◄ *This is a close-up view of the battle scene shown above.*

Chapter Summary—Ethics and Ideas

The Minoans and the Mycenaeans developed great civilizations in Greece. These civilizations were later destroyed. However, during the Dark Age, people remembered these earlier civilizations in myths and legends about gods, goddesses, and heroes.

These myths and legends taught lessons about right and wrong. They also brought hope and new ideas to the people.

In the next chapter, you will read about the new civilization in Greece that developed from these ideas.

? THINK ABOUT IT:

How did Homer's poems help the Greek people?

CHAPTER 16

The Rise of the Greek City-States

3500 B.C.	3000 B.C.	2500 B.C.	2000 B.C.	1500 B.C.	1000 B.C.	500 B.C.	0	A.D. 500

Sparta defeats Athens (404 B.C.) | Alexander the Great spreads Greek culture (338-323 B.C.)

ERA: Early Civilizations
PLACE: Greece
PEOPLE: Alexander the Great and the people of Greece
THEME: Ethics—standards of conduct based on right and wrong; and Religion—a belief in God or in many gods

CHAPTER FOCUS: Small kingdoms grew into city-states, and Alexander the Great spread Greek culture all the way to India.

▲ *Alexander the Great, on the left, defeated King Darius III of Persia in battle.*

In the last chapter, you read about the beginnings of Greek civilization with the Minoan and Mycenaean cultures. In this chapter, you will learn how the Greeks formed city-states and developed a system of government called democracy. You will also read about how one man spread Greek culture as he conquered one nation after another. As you read, think about how religion and literature influence society.

The World

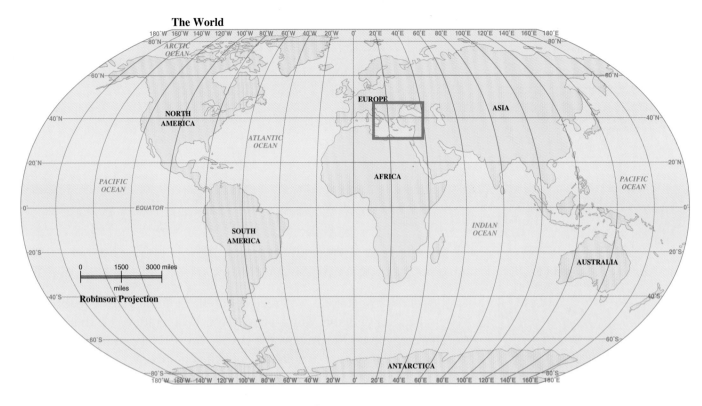

▼ GEOGRAPHY IN FOCUS

shore: *the land bordering a large body of water*

Ancient Greece controlled much of the land along the shores of the Mediterranean and Aegean seas.

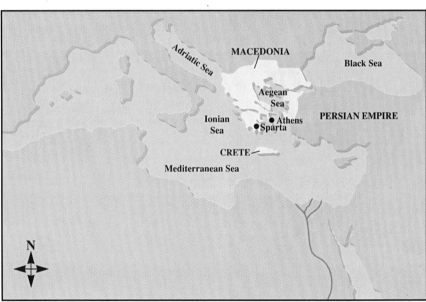

▲ *Around 500 B.C., Greece held territories on the Aegean, Adriatic, Ionian, Mediterranean, and Black seas.*

A Changing Society

Good farmland was scarce in Greece. Toward the end of the Dark Age, families began fighting each other over land **boundaries**. Many people were killed or injured. It was such a dangerous time that people even carried weapons when they worked.

The people grew tired of this, and families began to gather in small groups. Leaders ruled small areas and settled disputes. These leaders called themselves kings.

By 800 B.C., there were dozens of these small kingdoms. Each king had a **council** made up of large landowners. These council members helped the king make important decisions. Kings also called an **assembly** of all citizens to get their opinions about these decisions.

assembly: a group of people who meet together

boundary: a line or place that is the end or beginning of someone's land

council: a group of people who advise or govern

? THINK ABOUT IT:

Do people in your community have problems like those of families in ancient Greece? How are these disputes settled?

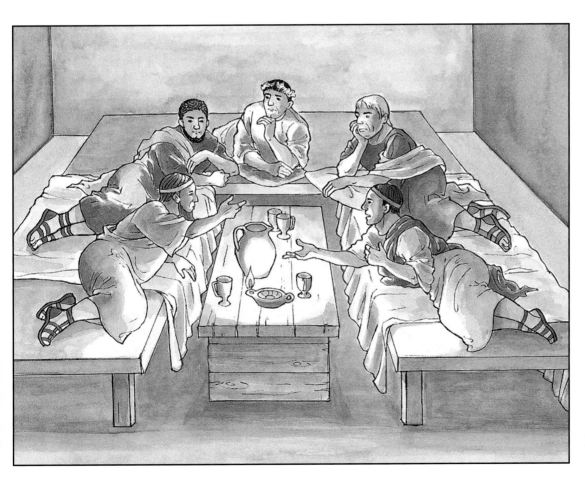

◀ *The king and his council met to settle disputes during Greece's Dark Age.*

▲ *This is the Eurotas Valley today.*

Athenian: one who lives in Athens

fortress: a structure or place that protects from an attack

military: people or places having to do with an army or navy

port: a city or town with a harbor where ships can load and unload goods

Two Great Cities

In time, the small kingdoms grew together into a few large city-states. The two most important city-states were Sparta and Athens. Each city-state, called a polis, was independent.

Sparta was located in the Eurotas Valley. The Dorians invaded Sparta and turned it into a **military** camp. Athens was surrounded by high mountains that provided a natural **fortress**. The **Athenians** were able to fight off the Dorians. Athens was located near the coast and was near the **port** city of Piraeus.

In the years that followed the Dark Age, Athens and Sparta developed in different ways.

? THINK ABOUT IT:

What other ancient civilizations had city-states? Did any of them let all citizens have a voice in running the government? Explain your answer.

Government in Sparta

After the Dorians invaded Sparta, there were three classes of people: citizens, slaves, and free men. Only Dorian men were citizens. The Dorians were called Spartans. The earlier inhabitants of the area became the slaves of the Spartans. Some slaves escaped and lived as free men in other city-states.

Women, slaves, small farmers, and most merchants did not have any political rights and could not be citizens. This meant that only about 10 percent of the people of Sparta were citizens.

All Spartan citizens belonged to an assembly. The assembly elected the senators and the ephors (EE-forz). They also voted on laws written by the senate or the ephors. However, the senators and ephors often ignored their vote. The real power of the government was in the hands of a few important senators and ephors.

? **THINK ABOUT IT:**

Since only about 10 percent of the people could vote, how do you think this influenced the laws in Sparta?

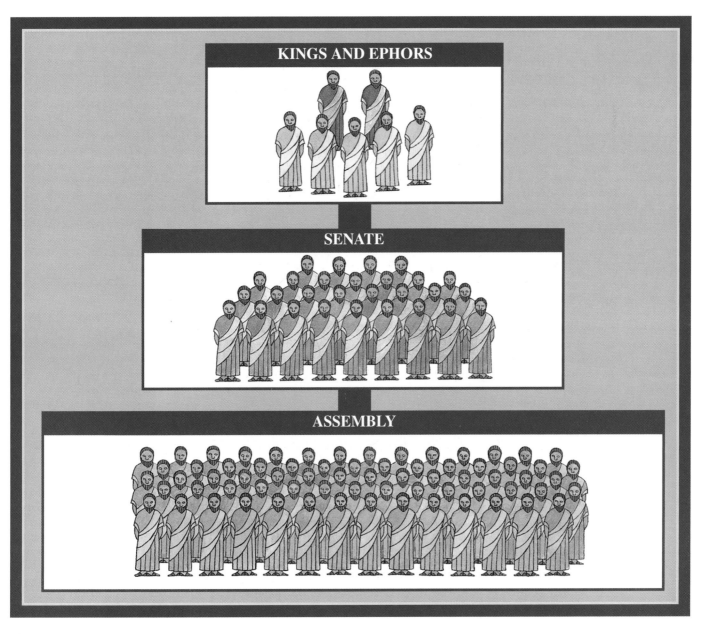

▲ *Sparta was ruled by two kings, five officials called ephors, a senate, and an assembly.*

▲ *Spartan boys began learning to be soldiers at the age of seven.*

? **THINK ABOUT IT:**

What kinds of things do you think were important to Spartan men?

Do young men have to become soldiers in the United States today?

Sparta—A Military Camp

The Spartans spent most of their time training for war. All Spartan men were soldiers. They were not even allowed to have other occupations. Men who were not citizens did all the other work.

Spartan boys had to leave their homes when they were seven years old. They lived with other boys in army buildings called barracks. The boys learned to read and write. However, they spent most of their time learning physical skills such as boxing, wrestling, and running. They trained to be soldiers.

Discipline at the barracks was very strict. Boys had little to eat and slept on the bare ground. Sometimes they were beaten just to make them better soldiers.

Women in Sparta

Spartan girls stayed at home, but they had physical training, too. They ran, wrestled, and learned to throw the **discus**. This was to make them strong and healthy mothers.

Although they could not vote or hold public office, women in Sparta had more freedom than other women of Greece. They ran their households and took part in business. Many of them became wealthy.

Young Spartan women were very physically fit. Because they were good at **disciplining** children, Athenian parents sometimes hired women from Sparta to take care of their children.

discipline: strict control to make people obey rules

discus: a heavy, round piece of metal thrown for distance as a test of strength and skill

? THINK ABOUT IT:

How do women's lives in the United States differ from those of the women of ancient Greece?

How is your life different from the lives of young people in Sparta?

▲ *This is a bronze figure of a Spartan girl running.*

Democracy in Athens

content: happy with what one has; satisfied

democracy: rule of the people

inherit: to receive something as the result of another's death

Athenians believed that each individual man was important. Every free man over 18, born in Athens, was a citizen. All citizens were members of the assembly and could vote. The assembly met every nine or 10 days to vote on laws. We call this system of government a **democracy**.

Athenian women did not have the same rights as men. A woman could not vote, hold a public office, make contracts, or **inherit** her husband's property.

? THINK ABOUT IT:

How does this system of government compare with our government in the United States?

How does the way men and women were treated in Athens compare with our society in the United States?

▲ *Athenian women were expected to be* **content** *in the home, as shown in this picture of a grandmother and her grandchild.*

▲ *This shoemaker might have been a metic—someone who came to Athens to live and work.*

Workers in Athens

Each Athenian man served two years in the military. Then, if he came from a wealthy family, he might become a poet, scholar, philosopher, or writer. If he came from a poor family, however, he would have to work in other jobs.

Poor farmers worked hard to grow food in the dry land around Athens. Even so, there was not enough grain. Only olives, grapes, and figs grew well. Most animals were used for wool, milk, or transportation, but not for meat.

Some slaves worked in the mines and did construction work. Other slaves worked for families or were merchants, tradespeople, artists, and craftspeople. Many foreigners came to Athens to live. They were called metics and were not citizens. The metics did many of the same jobs as slaves.

? THINK ABOUT IT:

Did Athenian society make the best use of each person's talents or abilities? Why or why not?

▲ *Greeks built a temple called the Parthenon more than 2,400 years ago. The ruins of the Parthenon still stand on a hill in the middle of Athens.*

admire: to like; look upon with pleasure

imitate: to copy

? THINK ABOUT IT:

Are there any buildings in your city built in the Greek style? How would you describe Greek architecture?

The Golden Age of Athens

Because wealthy Athenians did not work, they had time to study medicine, mathematics, music, astronomy, and philosophy.

The Athenians **admired** beauty in the human form. In their art they tried to show perfect people and animals. The Athenians also tried to design buildings that were perfect in form.

Athenians wrote plays and poetry that people still read and enjoy today. They built great buildings. Athens became such a beautiful city that it was **imitated** throughout Greece. Even today people visit ruins of Greek theaters, stadiums, and temples. Many buildings around the world have been built to look like those in ancient Greece.

The Lives of Young People in Athens

Athenian boys went to school at the age of six to learn to read and write. They studied music, poetry, and arithmetic. Girls stayed home with their mothers. They learned to become wives, cooks, and housekeepers.

Because they loved stories of the physical **feats** of gods and heroes, Athenians and people from other Greek city-states started contests for young people. One of these contests was called the Olympic Games. At the first Olympic Game, held in 776 B.C., there was just a foot race. In time, more contests were added, including wrestling, boxing, jumping, chariot races, and other events. Only men and boys were allowed to compete in the races and other events. This was the beginning of the Olympic Games.

feat: a great deed or act

? **THINK ABOUT IT:**

What other events are included in the Olympic Games today? Do you think people in the United States admire athletic ability as much as the Greeks? Why or why not?

◀ *Men and boys from Athens and other city-states competed in atheletic contests. This was the beginning of the Olympic Games. The discus throw is still an event of the Olympic Games today. Greeks admired gods and heroes with athletic ability.*

Athens and Sparta at War

As Athens and Sparta grew, Athens built a great navy and army. Athenian ships carried goods to and from other countries. Athenians were welcomed in many lands. Many other countries imitated their culture.

Sparta was very different. Spartans saw people in the world around them as enemies. Sparta **isolated** itself from all but a handful of other city-states. As Athens grew in power, Sparta became **envious** and **suspicious**.

Still, Athens and Sparta tried to avoid conflict by signing a treaty respecting each other's rights. However, both broke the treaty, and in 431 B.C., they went to war.

This fight, known as the Peloponnesian War, went on for nearly 27 years. In 404 B.C., Athens **surrendered** to Sparta.

envious: to want what another has

isolate: to stay apart; avoid others

surrender: to give in or accept defeat

suspicious: to have no trust in

? THINK ABOUT IT:

What were the important differences between Athens and Sparta? How were Athens and Sparta influenced by their geographical locations?

▶ *Spartan soldiers defeated the forces of Athens.*

▲ *Alexander the Great led his soldiers against the Persians after he and his father captured Greece.*

New Rulers of Greece

Even after Athens surrendered to Sparta, the two city-states continued to disagree. The other city-states of Greece also fought among themselves. All the Greek city-states were so weak from fighting each other that they were not able to defend themselves when people from **Macedonia** attacked.

Macedonia was north of Greece. Its king, Philip II, wanted to control Greece and Persia. In 338 B.C., Philip's army **defeated** the armies of Greece.

Although he conquered their armies, Philip admired Greek culture. He wanted to spread it throughout the lands under his power. Philip was soon **murdered**, however, and his son, Alexander, became king of Macedonia and Greece.

defeat: to beat; win out over

Macedonia: an ancient kingdom north of Greece

murder: to kill

? THINK ABOUT IT:

Why would other nations admire Greece?

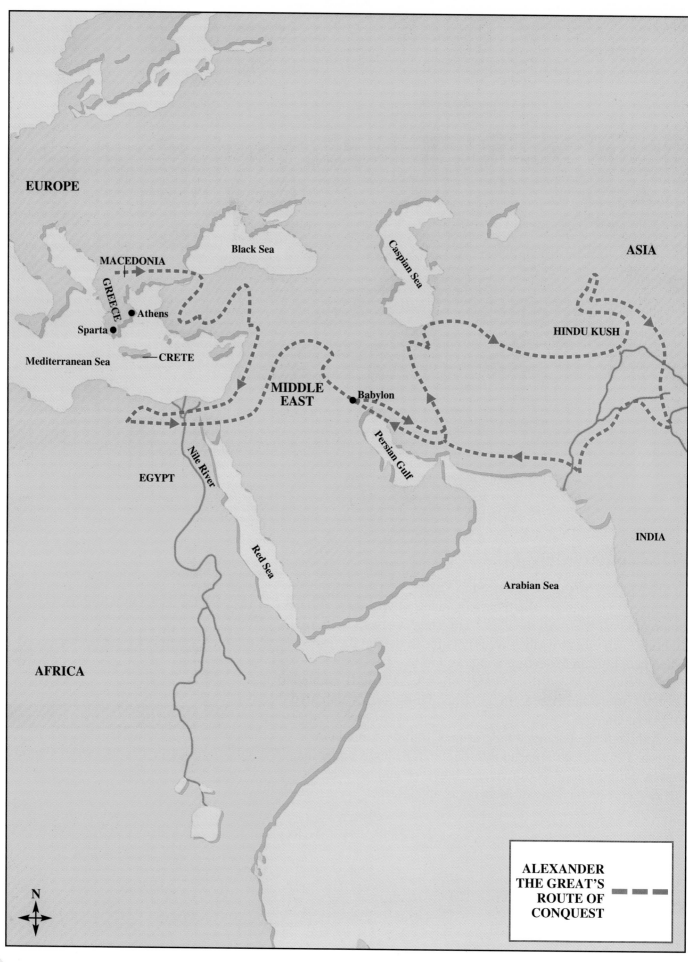

EUROPE

MACEDONIA

GREECE

Athens

Sparta

Black Sea

CRETE

Mediterranean Sea

Caspian Sea

ASIA

HINDU KUSH

MIDDLE
EAST

Babylon

Persian Gulf

EGYPT

Nile River

Red Sea

INDIA

Arabian Sea

AFRICA

N

**ALEXANDER
THE GREAT'S
ROUTE OF
CONQUEST**

Alexander the Great

Alexander admired Greece and believed in its **legendary** heroes. Like his father, he wanted to share Greek culture in the lands he conquered.

Alexander became one of the greatest generals in history. He took his army into Asia, conquered Persia, and spread Greek culture to Egypt, the **Near East**, and parts of India. During his travels Alexander established libraries and many cities. While he was in **Babylon**, Alexander became sick and died. By then, however, Alexander had spread Greek ideas through much of the world. Almost 100 years later, Rome defeated Macedonia and freed the Greek city-states. But the Greek city-states still fought with each other and with Rome. Finally, Rome grew angry and conquered Greece. Even so, Greek ideas lived on.

> **adopt:** to take or use as one's own
>
> **Babylon:** an ancient city on the Euphrates River
>
> **legendary:** famous
>
> **Near East:** the countries near or east of the eastern Mediterranean Sea

Chapter Summary—Ethics and Ideas

The scattered families of Greek-speaking people slowly gathered into villages and then city-states. These city-states had citizen-assemblies that voted on laws and leaders. This put more power into the hands of the people. It was the beginning of democracy.

The Greeks studied architecture, art, science, and literature. They wrote plays and poems, and played music. This was especially true in Athens, which became a center of culture. Other nations conquered Greece, but the conquerors **adopted** Greek ideas and culture. The ideas of Greece lived on and shaped the future of Western civilization. Many of our ideas about government, beauty, art, architecture, and the world around us have come from Greece.

? THINK ABOUT IT:

How might Western history be different if Alexander the Great had not taken his armies and Greek culture to much of the world?

What are some possible reasons why the people of Greece developed a democratic form of government?

◄ *Alexander's conquest of most of the known world of 300 B.C. took him all the way to India.*

CHAPTER 17

The Founding of Rome and the Roman Republic

ERA: Early Civilizations
PLACE: Rome
PEOPLE: Julius Caesar and the Romans
THEME: Law—a rule that tells people what they can or cannot do; and Government—a system for ruling a country

CHAPTER FOCUS: Rome grew from a small settlement to a powerful empire.

LINK

In the last unit, you read about the Greeks and their contributions to the art, literature, and government of Western civilization. In this chapter, you will learn about the Romans, a group of people who founded a new kind of government called a republic. As you read, think about how civilizations borrow ideas from earlier cultures.

▲ *Julius Caesar was a powerful leader of Rome. He was not the first ruler of Rome, but he was one of the most famous ones.*

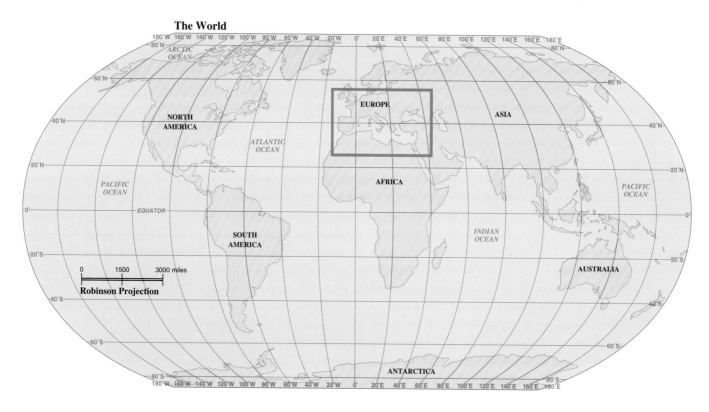

The World

▼ GEOGRAPHY IN FOCUS

sea: *a large body of water, usually salt water*

Italy is surrounded by the Adriatic, the Mediterranean, and the Tyrrhenian (ty-REH-nee-uhn) seas.

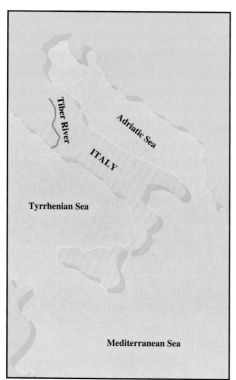

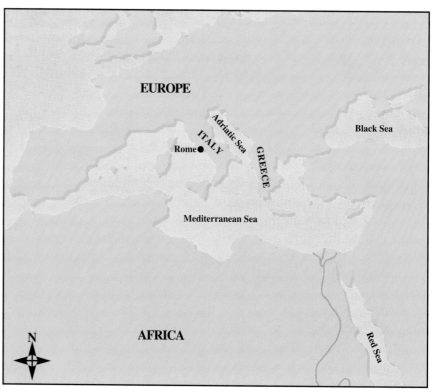

▲ *Rome began as a small village along the Tiber River in what is now Italy.*

How Rome Began

There is a legend that Rome was founded by Romulus in 753 B.C. According to the legend, Romulus and his twin brother, Remus, were cared for by a wolf after being separated from their mother. Later the brothers fought over where to build a city. According to the legend, Romulus killed his twin and then built the city and named it after himself.

This is probably just a story, but we do know that Rome began as a very small settlement along the Tiber River. Farmers lived in mud huts with straw roofs. They worked the fertile land and kept sheep and cattle. It was easy to cross the Tiber River from the settlement. Because of this, the settlement soon drew merchants from all over western Italy.

? THINK ABOUT IT:

Why did ancient cities often grow up near rivers?

▲ *This photograph shows the hills of Rome.*

▲ *The Etruscans lived north of Rome. Their civilization was older and more advanced than that of Rome's farmers.*

The Etruscans' Rule

Etruria (ih-TROOR-ee-uh) was on the Tiber River opposite Rome. The people who lived in Etruria were called Etruscans.

Merchants and traders from Etruria came to the young settlement of Rome. Many of them moved in among the Romans. They brought with them the art, architecture, **engineering**, and religion of their civilization.

In time, Etruscan kings began to rule over the people of Rome. By 509 B.C., however, the Romans decided they no longer wanted Etruscan rulers. They forced the Etruscan king to leave and then fought off angry Etruscan soldiers. The Etruscans gave up and went back across the Tiber River.

engineering: the planning, design, and construction of things such as roads, bridges, or large buildings

---

? THINK ABOUT IT:

Why might the people of Rome not want an Etruscan king?

The Republic Begins

By the time the Etruscans left, Rome had spread out into several villages. There were now two social classes in Rome. One group was called the patricians (puh-TRISH-unz). The patricians were wealthy landowners and military leaders. The other group was the plebeians (plih-BEE-unz). The poor traders, artisans, small farmers, and freed slaves were all plebeians. Most of the people of Rome were plebeians.

When the Etruscans left, the Romans needed a government. They knew they did not want another king. Instead they chose to become a **republic**. They wanted to be able to choose their own leaders.

The patricians met together and called themselves the "assembly." The assembly elected two of its members as **consuls** to head the Roman Republic.

Other patricians served as advisors to the consuls. The advisors were called senators. The consuls and the senators made the Roman Republic's important decisions. The consuls served for one year. The senators served as long as they wished.

consul: a government official with power to administer the law

republic: a government in which people elect their leaders

? THINK ABOUT IT:

What bodies of government do we have in the United States today?

▲ *Rome's most important ruling body was the Senate. Its members argued for or against new laws.*

The Plebeians as Second-Class Citizens

There were great differences in how the people of Rome lived. The rich patricians lived in **mansions** and owned other houses in the country. Most plebeians lived in apartments or **tenements**. Poorer plebeians sometimes had to **scrounge** for food. Most plebeian farmers did not own much land. They could not grow enough food to feed their families.

The plebeians were citizens of Rome, but they were **second-class** citizens. They had to pay taxes and serve in the Roman army, but they could not hold public offices. They could not marry a patrician or perform certain religious rituals.

Plebeians Gain New Rights

Over time, some plebeians became wealthy merchants. These newly wealthy people wanted to have more power in the government. They encouraged the poor plebeians to protest and demand more **rights**. The wealthy plebeians banded together with the poor plebeians, promising to protect and support each other.

The plebeians started a council and demanded that the patricians recognize it. They said they would not work unless they were allowed to choose their own leaders. The patricians needed the plebeians to grow food and help fight wars, so they decided to give plebeians some new rights.

---

mansion: a large, impressive house

right: something a person has a just claim to, such as the right of free speech

scrounge: to try to find as best one can

second-class: considered inferior; lower in value

tenement: apartments that are run-down and overcrowded

? THINK ABOUT IT:

How is ancient Rome like the United States today? How is it different?

Why did the wealthy plebeians need the poor people? The plebeians could have taken other actions against the patricians. Why do you think they started a council?

◀ *The poor people of Rome often had to scrounge for food in the dark and dangerous streets of the city.*

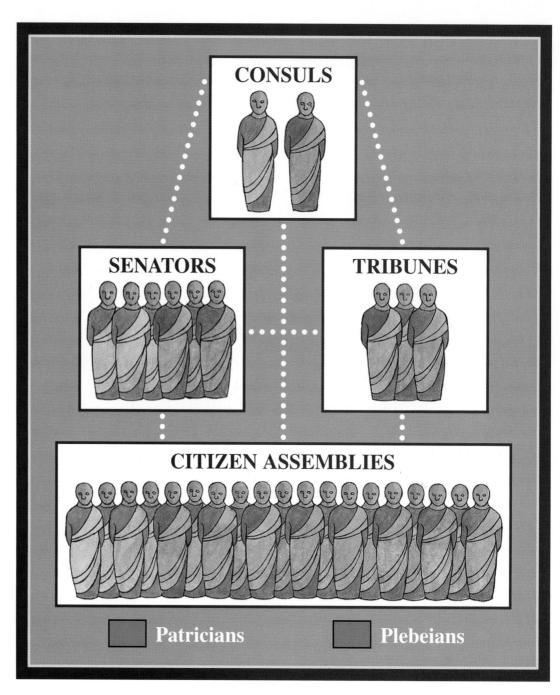

CONSULS

SENATORS

TRIBUNES

CITIZEN ASSEMBLIES

Patricians   Plebeians

▲ *The Roman Republic was ruled by both patricians and plebeians.*

tribune: a Roman official appointed to protect the rights of the plebeians

? THINK ABOUT IT:

How did the plebeians and the patricians become more alike?

"I Forbid!"

The leaders of the council of plebeians were called **tribunes**. These plebeian tribunes had the power to block any law proposed by the Senate. They did so simply by shouting out a word that meant "I forbid!" The word was "veto."

In time, the Roman government made other changes in the treatment of plebeians as well. Plebeians were allowed to marry patricians, and they could hold the office of consul. As Rome grew, there were fewer differences between the patricians and the plebeians.

Expansion of the Republic

While the plebeians were demanding their rights, Roman armies continued to take over nearby settlements. By 300 B.C., Rome controlled all of central Italy. Even the Etruscans were conquered by the Romans as the Roman Republic **expanded**.

The Romans took many conquered people as slaves, but they also knew how to make **allies**. They gave citizenship or other privileges to some of their new **subjects**. The Romans hoped the conquered people would become loyal Romans.

The Roman government, however, had problems governing the conquered lands. Many Roman officials were **corrupt**. They took **bribes** and became wealthy. This was true both in the city of Rome and in the **territories**.

ally: a friend, friendly nation, or group

bribe: money or favors given in order to get something done unlawfully

corrupt: willing to do wrong for money or other gain

expand: to grow, spread out, or get larger in size

subject: a person under the authority or control of a group

territory: land or country

? THINK ABOUT IT:

Do modern governments face some of the same problems as ancient Rome?

▲ *The Romans built the most powerful army in the world.*

The Triumvirate

triumvirate: government by three
people

Problems continued to grow in Rome and its new territories. Various groups began to struggle over control of the Republic.

In 60 B.C., three powerful generals made a secret agreement to help each other gain power. Their names were Pompey, Crassus, and Julius Caesar. These men did not try to overthrow the government. They only used their powers to influence the government.

All three men were elected to positions of power in Rome. Even though each wanted more power for himself, they agreed on how to share their duties. In order to expand the Republic, Caesar and Pompey led their armies in victories outside of Rome. Crassus kept his army in Rome to defend the Republic. The three men were called the **Triumvirate**.

? THINK ABOUT IT:

What are some possible problems of having three rulers?

▲ *This statue shows Julius Caesar, one of Rome's powerful generals.*

▲ *This drawing shows Roman soldiers leading rebellious slaves away in chains.*

Slaves Revolt

During this time, Rome's slaves were becoming a problem. Rome made slaves of many of the people it conquered in battle. Romans also bought slaves from slave ships. These slaves had no legal rights. They could not marry or own property. They worked in all kinds of jobs. The Romans trained some of the slaves as **gladiators**. These gladiators had to fight **brutal** battles in public for the pleasure of the people of Rome.

Slaves began to **revolt** in the outlying territories. Soon, these revolts spread to Rome. A gladiator named Spartacus became the leader of 70,000 rebellious slaves. These slaves **terrorized** Rome for three years.

brutal: harsh; violent

gladiator: an armed fighter who battles another person or a wild animal as public entertainment

revolt: to turn or fight against

terrorize: to cause fear by act or threat of violence

? THINK ABOUT IT:

Do you think the slaves had a right to revolt? Why or why not? Why do you think they did not try to form a council of their own?

Julius Caesar Returns to Rome

civil war: war between two groups in the same country or group

crucify: to kill a person by nailing their hands and feet to a cross made of wood

disband: to break up; dismiss from military service

triumphantly: with pride in winning or being a winner

Crassus's army in Rome eventually stopped the slave revolt. The soldiers **crucified** 6,000 slaves on crosses that stretched along a road for 130 miles. The Romans did this to make the slaves afraid to revolt again.

Some time later, Crassus was killed in battle when his army tried to invade another country. Now there were only two leaders—Pompey and Julius Caesar. These two men began to compete for power. Pompey never really liked Caesar, and he persuaded the Senate to order Caesar to **disband** his army. Caesar refused and a **civil war** began. Caesar's soldiers defeated Pompey's army and marched **triumphantly** into the city. Pompey fled.

? THINK ABOUT IT:

After Caesar became the only leader, how do you think the Senate treated him?

▲ *Julius Caesar and his army marched triumphantly into the city of Rome.*

▲ *In Roman cities the most important buildings were in a public square called the forum. These are the ruins of a temple. Other buildings in the forum were for business or government.*

Julius Caesar as a Ruler

The senators named Caesar **dictator** for 10 years. Julius Caesar was not the first dictator of Rome, but he was one of the most famous. As dictator, Caesar did many things that were good for Rome. He provided work for the poor people, planned roads, and added new laws to stop crime. He increased the number of government officials in order to make the nation's business run better. He did not allow waste or corruption in government.

dictator: a ruler who has total power in government

? THINK ABOUT IT:

Which of Julius Caesar's reforms would help our country today? Why do you think the senators gave Julius Caesar total power?

The Death of Julius Caesar

In 44 B.C., two years after Julius Caesar began his rule, the Senate decided to name him dictator for life. Still, there were men who were afraid of his power and **ambition**. Some of them were Julius Caesar's own trusted friends and admirers. A group of these men, both friends and enemies, decided to **assassinate** him.

On March 15, 44 B.C., Julius Caesar prepared to attend a Senate meeting. His wife asked him not to go because she had a dream that something bad would happen to him. One of the men involved in the assassination plan persuaded Julius Caesar to attend the meeting anyway. When he arrived, a group of attackers surrounded him and stabbed him to death.

Chapter Summary—Law and Government

Rome began as a small settlement of huts and farms and grew into a city. In time, Rome conquered all the surrounding settlements.

The Romans decided to make their government a republic. As Rome grew, however, it began to have problems. These problems **resulted** in attempts to overthrow the government. One man finally rose to lead Rome. His name was Julius Caesar. He passed laws giving equal rights to citizens. He was **popular** with the people, but other leaders in government were afraid of him. They thought he wanted to become a king. They did not want a king to rule Rome. This led to his assassination.

The time of the Roman Republic was almost over. But the era of the Roman Empire was about to begin.

ambition: the desire to do or achieve something

assassinate: to murder a politically important person by surprise attack

popular: liked by people

result: to cause to happen; to effect

? THINK ABOUT IT:

Do you know of other leaders who were assassinated? Why do you think people wanted to kill them?

Why was Julius Caesar popular with the people of Rome? Who are popular political leaders today? Why are they popular?

◀ *The Romans loved powerful leaders, but also feared them. Julius Caesar was assassinated as he attended a Senate meeting.*

CHAPTER 18

The Roman Empire

3500 B.C.	3000 B.C.	2500 B.C.	2000 B.C.	1500 B.C.	1000 B.C.	500 B.C.	0	A.D. 500

Octavian becomes Emperor Augustus (27 B.C.) | The birth of Jesus (c. A.D. 4)

ERA: Early Civilizations
PLACE: The Roman Empire
PEOPLE: Augustus and the people of the Roman Empire
THEME: Law—a rule that tells people what they can and cannot do; and Government—a system for ruling a country

CHAPTER FOCUS: Over time, the Roman Republic developed into a vast empire.

Rome's main offices of government were in the Roman Forum.

LINK

In the last chapter, you read about how Rome began. Romans drove the Etruscan kings out and set up their own form of government called a republic. They became strong and took over other territories. In this chapter, you will read about Augustus, the first emperor of Rome. Augustus brought Rome a time of peace called the Pax Romana. As you read, think about how civilizations borrow ideas from earlier cultures.

The World

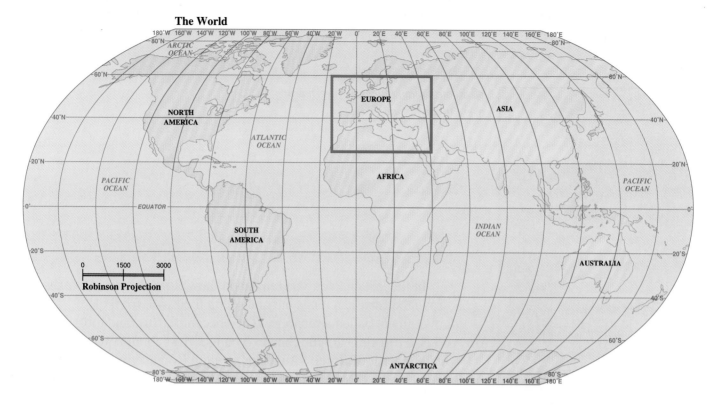

▼ GEOGRAPHY IN FOCUS

mountain range: *a group of mountains forming a line*

The Apennine and Alps mountain ranges protected Rome.

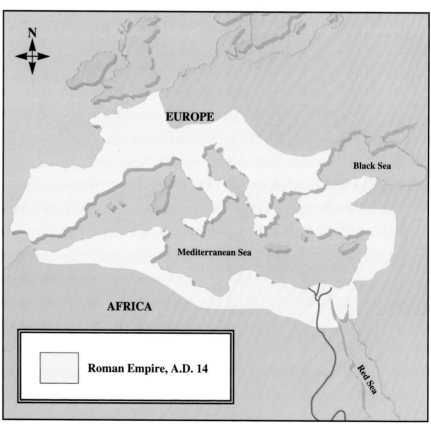

▲ *This map shows the Roman Empire in A.D. 14.*

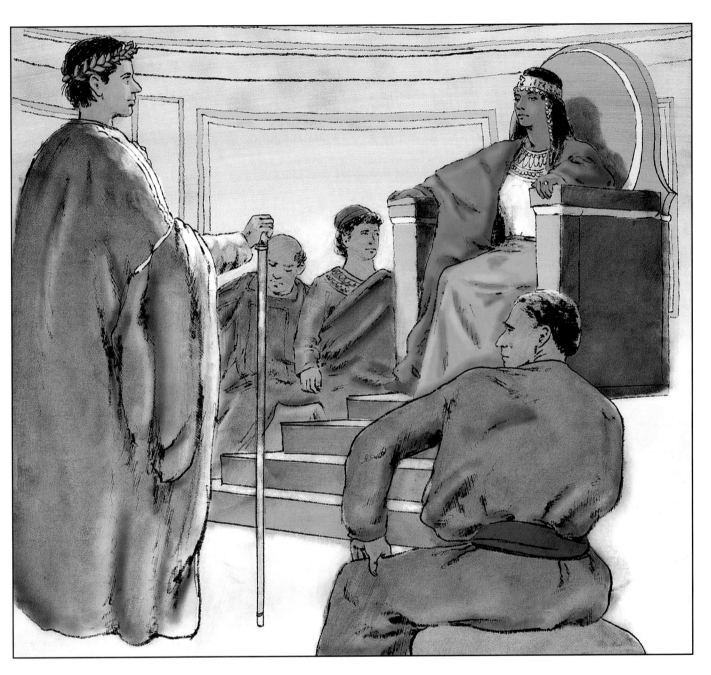

▲ *Marc Antony fell in love with Cleopatra, queen of Egypt. Octavian's army defeated Antony and Cleopatra in 31 B.C.*

A New Fight for Leadership

After Julius Caesar was assassinated, the Senate again wanted to **control** Rome. But so did Marc Antony, Caesar's second-in-command. And so did Octavian, Caesar's grandnephew and adopted son.

In 43 B.C., Marc Antony, Octavian, and a commander named Lepidus began to rule Rome as the Second Triumvirate. Finally, in 27 B.C., Octavian decided he had enough power to take control. He moved his army into the city and convinced the Senate to make him ruler of Rome. The Senate also gave him so many additional powers and titles that Octavian became an absolute ruler.

control: to run or be in charge of

Octavian Becomes Augustus

Even though Octavian had the power of an emperor, he did not call himself emperor. Instead, he chose the name Augustus, meaning "**revered** one." Rome seemed to need an absolute ruler at the time. Its many provinces needed better **management**. Many government officials did not do their jobs well and others were dishonest.

Augustus let the Senate **supervise** the treasury, foreign relations, and wars. Augustus set up another class of workers to run things from day-to-day. He chose these workers from the lower class of Roman society. This was the beginning of civil service in Rome.

management: the handling or running of something

revered: very highly thought of

supervise: to be in charge of

? THINK ABOUT IT:

What do we call government workers today?

What other ancient civilizations had civil service workers?

▲ *This is a statue of Augustus, the absolute ruler of Rome.*

▲ *This shows a view of the Roman Forum, where government offices were located, as it looks today.*

The New Government

The new government workers were very efficient. Some of these government workers were slaves. Others were former slaves called freedmen.

These workers and **administrators** ran police departments, fire departments, and libraries. They supervised systems of water delivery to public baths, fountains, and to the homes of the rich.

> **administrator:** one who oversees others in their work

> **? THINK ABOUT IT:**
>
> How do you think this new class of government workers changed Roman society?

▲ *This shows how a busy street might have looked in the ancient city of Rome.*

Life in the City

Although the government of Rome offered many services, the city still had problems. It was overcrowded and had no public **transportation**.

Life was hard for the poor of Rome. They lived in small, uncomfortable apartments over shops or in tenements. The mud-brick buildings were often cracked. Fire was a constant danger and destroyed many homes.

The streets of Rome had no street lights and were unsafe at night because of crime. Life in Rome was so dangerous, one Roman wrote of the times, "Anyone who goes out to dinner without making a will is a fool."

Life Outside Rome

In the country outside the city of Rome, wealthy people owned large houses called villas. While at their villas, men and women wore tunics, a simple **garment** slipped on and worn with a belt at the waist.

Poor people worked hard on farms all day. They even worked by lamplight at night, making bread, pottery, sandals, and tools.

In mid-December, all farm workers took a vacation for one month. In some parts of the countryside, the people celebrated a few holidays, just as people did who lived in the city. On these days, people sometimes watched a play on a grassy area set up as a theater.

donate: to give; to contribute

garment: an item of clothing worn on the body

? THINK ABOUT IT:

Why do you think farm workers took a vacation during December?

◀ *Some wealthy Romans **donated** money to build theaters for the people. This photograph shows the ruins of one theater.*

The Roman Rich

Society in the time of Augustus was divided into three classes: the rich, the middle class, and the poor.

Most of the rich of Rome were nobles. They wore white robes called togas. Some noblemen **presided** over the courts or were governors of provinces.

Some of the rich also owned farms. However, noblemen were never merchants or traders. The wives of noblemen supervised the slaves in their households and spent much of their day attending to fashion and beauty.

The rich lived in houses decorated with paintings and statues made of bronze and stone. However, the homes had only simple furniture—a few couches, chairs, benches, and small tables. Oil lamps provided light. Charcoal burners supplied heat in the winter.

preside: to run or rule over

? THINK ABOUT IT:

Could a Roman work hard and become a nobleman or noblewoman? Why or why not?

▶ *This painting shows a servant attending a wealthy Roman woman.*

▲ *Both rich and middle class people enjoyed the ritual of the daily bath in ancient Rome.*

The Middle Class

Rome's middle class included **native** Roman citizens, freedmen, and slaves. Augustus increased the number of people in the middle class by adding freedmen and slaves to those eligible to run the offices of government.

In addition to government workers, the middle class included farmers, laborers, shopkeepers, and soldiers. Noblemen only worked half a day at their jobs. The **middle class** worked all day, seven days a week, except for certain holidays.

Both the rich and the middle class alike went to the public baths. There they could enjoy exercise, conversation, and **soothing** waters and oils for their bodies.

middle class: the social class between the very rich and the lower working class; people in business, the professions, highly skilled workers, and well-to-do farmers

native: a person born in a certain city, region, or country

soothing: something that comforts and creates a nice feeling

? THINK ABOUT IT:

How did the life of a middle class Roman compare with the life of the average American citizen today?

▶ *This shows two Roman artisans working in a metal shop. Only people in lower classes did this kind of work.*

porridge: a cereal

? **THINK ABOUT IT:**

If you were emperor of Rome, would you help the poor people? Why or why not?

The Roman Poor

Many poor farmers lost their land while they were serving in the army. Poor people in the city often could not find jobs because slaves did most of the work.

Augustus did many things to try to improve the lives of the poor. He started public building programs to provide employment. He sent money to help people in provinces when natural disasters occurred. He gave land and money to soldiers when they left the army.

Augustus also gave the poor people free wheat. The poor ate very little meat. They made bread and **porridge** and ate some vegetables, olives, eggs, cheese, fruit, and honey.

Boys and Girls in Rome

Mothers taught children at home until the age of seven. Then for the next five years, boys and girls attended separate schools to learn reading, writing, and arithmetic. They studied from early morning until the middle of the afternoon.

When they reached 12 or 13, girls continued their learning at home. Many of them became highly educated women. Boys from noble families stayed in school for a few more years to prepare for a life of leadership.

▲ *This stone relief shows Roman children playing a game.*

? THINK ABOUT IT:

How does our system of education today differ from that of ancient Rome?

▲ *This picture shows the ruins of the Colosseum in Rome. Built after the time of Augustus, it could hold 50,000 people as they watched gladiators fight to the death.*

? **THINK ABOUT IT:**

Do you think giving the poor people entertainment was a good solution to their problems? Why or why not?

Chariots and Gladiators

Augustus wanted to keep the people happy. He was already providing them free wheat. He decided to give them free entertainment, too.

The Romans loved chariot races. The chariot drivers were heroes, and Romans bet money on the races. Battles between men, and between men and wild animals, were also very popular. These men, called gladiators, had to fight for their lives in these battles. Some gladiators became heroes to the people.

The Influence of Greece

Although Rome conquered Greece, the Romans copied many Greek ideas in education, art, science, architecture, and literature. Romans brought in Greek statues to decorate their homes and buildings. The Romans were better builders than the Greeks, but they copied Greek building styles.

Romans often chose Greeks as teachers for their schools. Augustus himself admired the Greek poets and often had them entertain his guests.

The Romans also adopted qualities of many of the Greek deities in their own gods and goddesses. Religion was important in the lives of Romans. They worshiped many gods and goddesses, including those of the earth, love, and war. They filled Roman cities with temples in which to praise the gods and goddesses. The Romans also built temples to Egyptian, Persian, and Greek deities. The Romans were tolerant of many different beliefs.

? THINK ABOUT IT:

What are some possible reasons the Romans copied Greek ideas?

▲ *A temple stands by the Tiber River where Rome began. This temple is shaped like the round huts of the first Romans. However, its columns show the influence of Greek architecture. You can see that it is being repaired.*

The "Pax Romana"

Augustus built 82 new temples to the gods and many bath houses for the people. He added libraries, theaters, and roads. Many streets in Roman cities were wide, well-paved, and clean. Augustus said he found Rome a city of sun-dried bricks and turned it into a city of marble.

Augustus developed an efficient postal system, built new highways to **remote** parts of the empire, and encouraged free trade among the Roman provinces.

Augustus ruled Rome for 41 years until his death in A.D. 14. Rome's past had been filled with war. Now, with a well-organized government, there was a time of peace called the Pax Romana. The Pax Romana lasted for 200 years.

Chapter Summary—Law and Government

Augustus was the first Roman emperor. He ruled over the many lands that had become part of the Roman Empire. Under his leadership, Rome entered a long period of peace called the Pax Romana.

After the death of Augustus, the Roman Empire continued to expand. Augustus had given the empire an efficient system of government. He encouraged people to build new highways, harbors, and waterways. These highways and waterways made travel easier and helped unify the Roman Empire. Rome was now a **vast** empire.

remote: distant; faraway

vast: of very great size; huge

? THINK ABOUT IT:

Why was Augustus able to rule Rome so much longer than anyone before him? What do you think Augustus meant when he said he turned Rome into a city of marble?

In what ways do roads help to unify a large area?

◀ *The ancient city of Timgad was built where six Roman roads came together. Its deserted ruins stand today in the mountains of Algeria in North Africa.*

CHAPTER 19
The Rise of Christianity and the Fall of Rome

3500 B.C.	3000 B.C.	2500 B.C.	2000 B.C.	1500 B.C.	1000 B.C.	500 B.C.	0	A.D. 500

Jesus is crucified (c. A.D. 37)
Fall of the Western Roman Empire (A.D. 476)

ERA: Early Civilizations
PLACE: The Roman Empire
PEOPLE: Jesus of Nazareth and the people of the Roman Empire
THEME: Law—a rule that tells people what they can or cannot do; and Government—a system for ruling a country

CHAPTER FOCUS: Rome slowly declined as a great power, but became the birthplace of Christianity.

◀ *"The Last Supper" is a painting of Jesus's final meal with his disciples.*

LINK

In the last chapter, you read about the beginning of the Roman Empire and the rise to power of Augustus. In this chapter, you will read about the birth of Jesus, the rise of Christianity, and the fall of the Western Roman Empire. As you read, think about how civilizations borrow ideas from earlier cultures.

The World

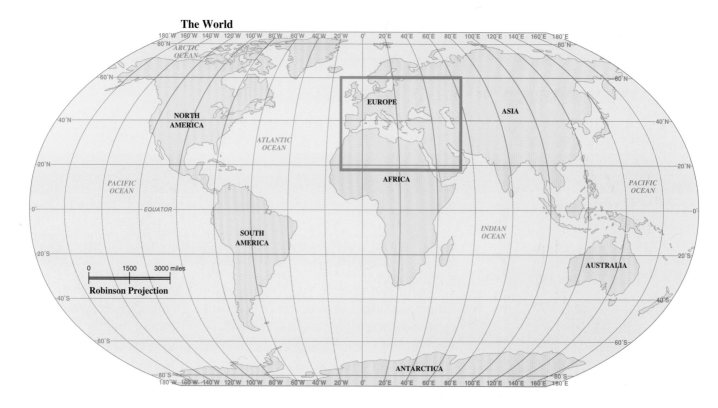

▼ GEOGRAPHY IN FOCUS

aqueduct: a bridge or other structure that helps move water in a certain direction

This aqueduct, built by the Romans, still stands today.

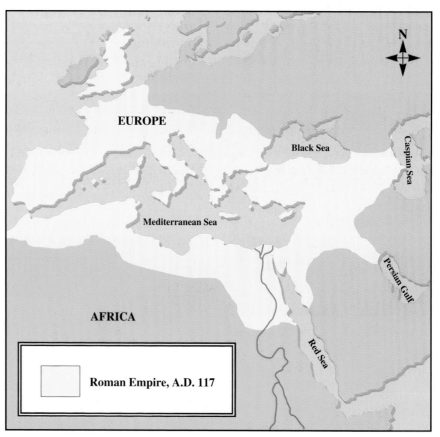

Roman Empire, A.D. 117

▲ *The map above shows the vastness of the Roman Empire at its peak in A.D. 117. Compare this with the Roman Empire in A.D. 14 on the map on page 262.*

The Birth of Jesus

The exact date of the birth of Jesus is not known. He was born sometime during the reign of the Emperor Augustus, probably around A.D. 4. The New Testament of the Christian Bible tells about the life of Jesus.

Augustus wanted to count all the people in the Roman Empire. He ordered people to return to their home towns to be counted. Mary and Joseph, the parents of Jesus, were Jews. They traveled to Bethlehem from their home in Nazareth to be counted in the Roman **census**. It was there that Jesus was born.

> **census:** a counting of citizens
>
> **stable:** a place where horses and other animals are kept

? THINK ABOUT IT:

What are some reasons a ruler might want to count the citizens in a country?

▲ Mary and Joseph could not find a place to stay in Bethlehem, so they made their bed in a *stable*.

▲ *This painting, "Christ Among the Doctors," shows a young Jesus teaching in the Jewish temple.*

? **THINK ABOUT IT:**

Is the "golden rule" still a good rule? Why or why not?

The Life of Jesus

Jesus was raised as a Jew. Early in his life he began to teach. Through his teaching and by his example, Jesus inspired people to love their neighbors. "And just as you want people to treat you, treat them in the same way," he advised. Today this is known as the "golden rule." It means acting toward others as you would want them to act toward you.

Jesus considered all of the teachings of the Torah to be important, but he said the most important of all was the commandment to love God and love your neighbor: "You shall love the Lord your God with all your heart and with all your soul, and with all your mind."

Jesus Teaches Forgiveness

Jesus taught about many things. To teach people about **forgiveness**, he told a **parable** about two sons. The younger son asked his father to give him his share of the family **estate**. He took the money and went to a far country. While he was there he wasted all the money on parties. When the money was gone, he had to take a job feeding pigs.

The son soon realized that his father's servants had a better life than he did, so he decided to go home and ask his father to let him work for him. Instead, when he got home, his father was so happy to see him he had a big feast to celebrate. The older brother was jealous and angry, but the father said it was right to celebrate because the son who was lost had returned.

This parable is one of many stories from the life of Jesus found in the Bible.

estate: everything one owns such as land, money, or property

forgiveness: the act of stopping feelings of anger toward a person

parable: a short, simple story that tells a lesson

? THINK ABOUT IT:

How does this story teach forgiveness?

▲ *This shows a father forgiving his "lost" son and welcoming him home with a feast.*

▲ *This shows Matthew, one of Jesus's followers, writing his gospel.*

The Romans Fear Jesus

Jesus **preached** mostly in desert areas around Palestine on the edge of the Roman Empire. He gathered around him 12 men called disciples. The disciples traveled to many places and helped spread Jesus's message.

In time, Jesus gathered many followers. They believed he was the "**Messiah**," or Christ. His followers became known as Christians. Some of these followers wrote about his teachings. These writings are collected today in the New Testament of the Christian Bible.

Jesus also had enemies. Although Romans were tolerant of many gods and religions, some Romans were afraid Jesus and his followers would **rebel** against the **authority** of Rome. Also, some Jews believed the teachings of Jesus were in **conflict** with their own religion.

authority: the rules giving one power

conflict: a difference that causes problems

Messiah: the expected leader or deliverer of the Jews

preach: to talk in public on a religious subject

rebel: to turn against

The Crucifixion of Jesus

Three years after he began teaching, Jesus led his followers into Jerusalem to celebrate the Jewish Passover holiday. He was arrested as a troublemaker and political rebel. He was questioned by the Roman governor, Pontius Pilate, then sentenced to death. Roman soldiers nailed Jesus to a cross and there he died. He was about 33 years old.

Before he was crucified, Jesus promised his followers that he would arise from the grave. According to the New Testament in the Christian Bible, Jesus did arise: "He has risen, just as He said." This became known as the **Resurrection**. Christians celebrate the Resurrection on Easter Sunday.

resurrection: a rising from the dead; a coming back to life; a renewal of life

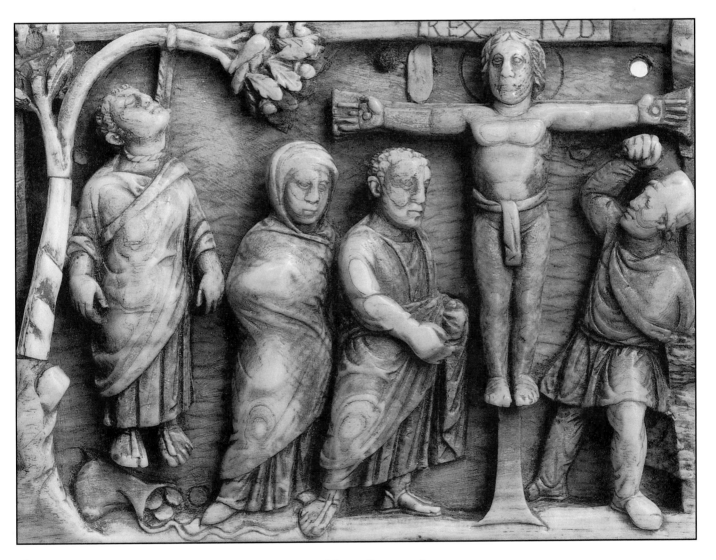

▲ *This ancient carving of the crucifixion of Jesus is one of the earliest ever done.*

condemn: to declare to be guilty of wrongdoing

libation: the ritual of pouring out wine or oil on the ground to honor a god

penalty: punishment for breaking a rule or law

persecute: to attack, injure, or bother constantly because of religion, politics, or race

treason: betrayal of one's country

? THINK ABOUT IT:

Why do you think Christians did not want to worship the Roman gods and goddesses and pour out a libation to the emperor? Why do you think the Romans wanted the Christians to worship the Roman deities as well as their own?

Why do you think the Christians did not change their actions when they were persecuted?

Christians Refuse to Worship Roman Deities

After the crucifixion of Jesus, the Christians continued to tell others about Jesus and his teachings. The beliefs of these Christians came into conflict with Roman beliefs.

Romans did not mind if the Christians worshiped in their own way. However, the Romans wanted them to worship the Roman gods and goddesses as well. They also wanted all the people to give allegiance to Rome by pouring out a **libation** to the emperor. Christians refused to do this.

Christians Condemned

When Christians refused to worship Roman gods and goddesses and pour out a libation to the emperor, they were charged with a crime and **condemned** for **treason** against the state. The **penalty** was death.

Some Romans also began to blame Christians for famines, sicknesses, and other disasters. Sometimes crowds of people attacked Christians. At other times, the Roman government **persecuted** them. Still, Christians grew in number.

▶ *Romans sometimes put condemned Christians into arenas to fight lions.*

▶ *Marcus Aurelius was one of Rome's great emperors.*

? THINK ABOUT IT:

How do the ways Marcus Aurelius helped the poor compare with the ways poor people are helped in the United States today?

The Reign of Marcus Aurelius

In A.D. 161, Marcus Aurelius (oh-RAY-lee-us) became emperor of Rome. Aurelius was one of the last of the great emperors of Rome. He made new laws to protect children, people in debt, and those who lived in the provinces.

Marcus Aurelius made other changes in the daily lives of Romans as well. He increased the number of people who could have free grain and made many cash gifts to the poor. To pay for these new programs and for all the people necessary to run them, Marcus Aurelius raised the people's taxes.

Soldiers Bring the Plague

By the reign of Marcus Aurelius, the Roman Empire had become so large that it was hard to defend its borders from invaders. Roman armies fought off the invaders; however, soldiers returning from battle brought with them a plague. They spread illness throughout each city as they came through. In Rome, 2,000 people died of this plague in a single day. Some small villages were entirely wiped out.

Even those who did not get sick felt the effects of the disease. Because so many people died, there were not enough workers to grow food for all the people. Transportation became disorganized. People went hungry. Nothing could be done to stop the plague.

? THINK ABOUT IT:

Do we have plagues today? What do we do to prevent them?

▲ *Ancient civilizations often were attacked by tribal peoples from outside their borders, as those shown here battling against Romans.*

The Eastern and Western Roman Empires

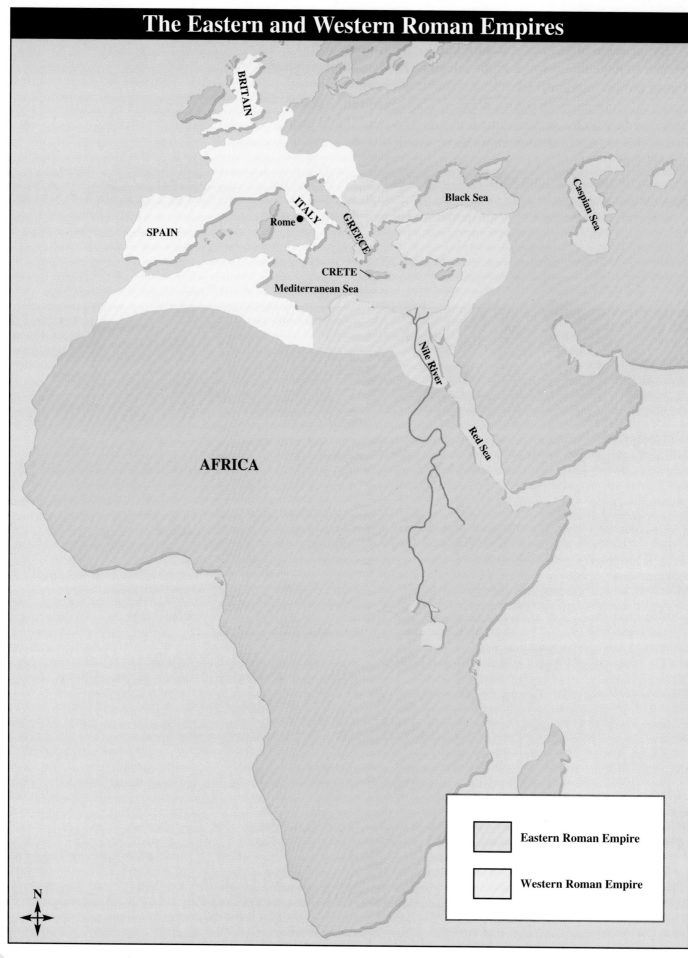

BRITAIN

ITALY

Rome

GREECE

SPAIN

Black Sea

Caspian Sea

CRETE

Mediterranean Sea

Nile River

Red Sea

AFRICA

N

Eastern Roman Empire

Western Roman Empire

More Wars, More Taxes

After the plague, invaders continued to attack the Roman borders. Marcus Aurelius had to spend much time and money on his armies. To pay his armies, Aurelius had to raise taxes again. Eventually, Marcus Aurelius went into battle himself. He became sick and died on the battlefield.

Rome Divided

After Marcus Aurelius died in A.D. 180, there were many problems in the Roman Empire. Tribal peoples continued to invade. The bureaucracy of government was expensive. People were forced to pay heavy taxes. The Roman government did not have enough money to pay for the large armies and all the government services. It was a time of chaos. The Pax Romana was over.

Finally, in A.D. 284, Diocletian (DY-uh-KLEE-shun) became emperor. He restored order in the empire. He also divided it into two separate states, the Eastern Roman Empire and the Western Roman Empire. He chose a co-emperor to rule the Western Roman Empire. He ruled the Eastern Roman Empire himself.

Diocletian also began greater persecution of Christians. Their treatment did not improve until Constantine came to power in the year A.D. 306. Constantine became a Christian in A.D. 313 and allowed Romans to follow any religion they wanted.

> **? THINK ABOUT IT:**
>
> What are the qualities that make a great leader?
>
> Why do you think Constantine decided to let the people follow any religion they wanted?

◀ *In A.D. 286, Emperor Diocletian divided the empire into two separate states, the Eastern Roman Empire and the Western Roman Empire.*

The Fall of Rome

separation: a dividing up

With the **separation** of the empire into two states, the Eastern Roman Empire prospered and managed to defend its borders. The Western Roman Empire, however, was attacked by invaders who swarmed into its land.

The Roman Empire was collapsing. By A.D. 476, the Western Roman Empire was destroyed, and the great city of Rome lay in ruins. The Eastern Roman Empire, however, survived for another 1,000 years. The Eastern Roman Empire later became known as the Byzantine Empire.

▲ *Ruins like these remind us of ancient Rome.*

? THINK ABOUT IT:

What are some reasons an empire could become weak? Could these reasons apply to nations today? Why or why not?

◀ *The Roman Pantheon was built in A.D. 130. Today, people from all over the world visit this classical building in the heart of Rome.*

Chapter Summary—Law and Government

The Roman Empire grew and prospered for many years. During the time of Augustus, Jesus was born. When Jesus grew to manhood, he began to preach. His followers became known as Christians. After only three years of teaching, Jesus was executed.

It seemed to be only a **brief** moment in Roman history at the time, but the belief in Jesus and his teachings lived long after him. Many people today still follow the teachings of Jesus.

In time, the Roman Empire grew so large it became difficult to run. Outside forces began to attack at its weakest points. In A.D. 476, the Western Roman Empire fell to invaders. The once great empire was no more. Its system of law and government, however, became a model for Western civilization.

brief: short; quick

? THINK ABOUT IT:

Was Rome destroyed forever?

In what ways are our lives influenced by the Romans? How can knowing about this ancient time help us today?

GLOSSARY

abandon   *capital*

A

abandon: (uh-BAN-dun) *v.* To leave.

absolute: (AB-soh-loot) *adj.* Unlimited.

abundance: (uh-BUN-dunz) *n.* A great supply; more than is needed.

accident: (AKS-i-dunt) *n.* Something that happens by chance.

accurate: (AK-yoor-it) *adj.* Free from mistakes.

acrobat: (AK-roh-bat) *n.* A performer who does tumbling or tricks on the trapeze or tightrope.

adapt: (uh-DAPT) *v.* To change to fit the environment.

administrator: (ad-MIN-us-tray-tor) *n.* One who oversees others in their work.

admire: (ad-MIYR) *v.* To like; look upon with pleasure.

adopt: (uh-DAHPT) *v.* To take or use as one's own.

adultery: (uh-DUL-tur-ee) *n.* The act of being unfaithful to a wife or husband.

adventure: (ad-VEN-chur) *n.* Exciting travel or event.

afterlife: (AF-tur-LIYF) *n.* Life after death.

afterworld: (AF-tur-WURLD) *n.* A world thought to exist after death.

aggressive: (uh-GRES-iv) *adj.* Starting fights or quarrels.

alliance: (uh-LIY-ins) *n.* Close association for a common purpose.

alloy: (AL-loi) *n.* A metal that is a mixture of two or more metals.

ally: (AL-liy) *n.* A friend, friendly nation, or group.

alternate: (AWL-tur-nit) *adj.* One that takes the place of another.

amateur: (AM-uh-chur) *n.* A person who does something for the fun of it, not for money.

ambition: (am-BISH-un) *n.* The desire to do or achieve something.

amulet: (AM-yoo-lit) *n.* A magic charm to keep away evil.

ancestor: (AN-ses-tur) *n.* A family member who lived long ago.

annals: (AN-uhlz) *n.* Yearly written account of events.

antler: (ANT-lur) *n.* A bone on the head of animals in the deer family.

aqueduct: (AK-wuh-DUKT) *n.* A bridge or other structure that helps move water in a certain direction.

Arabia: (uh-RAY-bee-uh) *n.* A peninsula in Southwestern Asia surrounded by the Red Sea, the Arabian Sea, and the Persian Gulf.

archer: (AHR-chur) *n.* A person who shoots with a bow and arrows.

arthritis: (ahr-THRIY-tis) *n.* A disease of the joints.

artifact: (AHR-ti-fakt) *n.* An object made by humans.

artisan: (AHR-tez-in) *n.* A person skilled at making things.

assassinate: (uh-SAS-i-nayt) *v.* To murder a politically important person by surprise attack.

assembly: (uh-SEM-blee) *n.* A group of people who meet together.

astrology: (uh-STRAHL-uh-jee) *n.* The study of the positions of the stars and planets to try to predict the future.

astronomer: (uh-STRAHN-uh-mur) *n.* A person who studies stars and other heavenly bodies.

Athenian: (uh-THEE-nee-un) *n.* One who lives in Athens.

Australopithecus boisei: (aw-stray-loh-PITH-uh-kus BOI-see-iy) *n.* Called "southern ape" because the first fossils were found in the southern part of Africa; Charles Boise helped pay for the Leakeys' exploration and they named the fossil after him.

authority: (uh-THOHR-i-tee) *n.* The rules giving one power.

B

Babylon: (BA-bi-lahn) *n.* An ancient city on the Euphrates River.

balance: (BAL-uns) *n.* Equal in value or weight; being in harmony.

balance of trade: (BAL-enz uhv trayd) *n.* The difference in value between all the imports and all the exports of a country.

bank: (bank) *n.* The side of a river.

barge: (bahrj) *n.* A large, flat-bottomed boat for carrying goods on rivers.

beacon: (BEE-kun) *n.* A fire or light to warn or call for help.

beg: (beg) *v.* To ask for something as a kindness or favor.

bilingual: (biy-LING-gwul) *adj.* In two languages.

boar: (bohr) *n.* A wild hog (with a hairy coat and a long snout).

boldly: (BOHLD-lee) *adv.* To do something strongly and without fear.

bondage: (BAHN-duhj) *n.* Slavery.

bookkeeping: (BUK-keep-ing) *n.* A record of trading or buying and selling.

booty: (BOOT-ee) *n.* Goods taken from the enemy.

boundary: (BOWN-duh-ree) *n.* A line or place that is the end or beginning of someone's land.

bribe: (briyb) *n.* Money or favors given in order to get something done unlawfully.

brief: (breef) *adj.* Short; quick.

brow ridge: (brow rij) *n.* The part of the forehead just above the eyes.

brutal: (BROO-tul) *adj.* Harsh; violent.

bundle: (BUN-dul) *n.* A number of things tied together.

bureaucracy: (byoo-RAH-kruh-see) *n.* Government through departments and officials.

butcher: (BUCH-ur) *v.* To cut up animals for meat.

C

camel caravan: (KAM-ul KAYR-uh-van) *n.* A group of people on camels traveling across the desert together.

canal: (kuh-NAL) *n.* A waterway built for irrigation.

capable: (KAYP-uh-bul) *adj.* Able.

capital: (KAP-i-tul) *n.* The main city of a country or state.

292

carve: (kahrv) *v.* To make a statue by cutting wood, bone, or stone.

cast: (kast) *v.* To form into a shape by pouring into a mold.

caste: (kast) *n.* A hereditary social class.

Çatal Hüyük: (chah-TUHL hoo-YUHK) *n.* In the Turkish language, *Çatal* means "fork" and *Hüyük* means "mound."

cataract: (KAT-uh-rakt) *n.* A large waterfall.

cavalry: (KAV-ul-ree) *n.* Troops on horseback.

cave: (cayv) *n.* An opening in a hillside.

ceiling: (SEEL-ing) *n.* The top of a room.

census: (SEN-sus) *n.* A counting of citizens.

Ceylon: (si-LAHN) *n.* An island to the south of India now called Sri Lanka.

channel: (CHAN-ul) *n.* A course through which water moves.

chant: (chant) *v.* To sing or say something without changing tone.

chaos: (KAY-ahs) *n.* Great confusion and disorder.

charioteer: (CHAYR-ee-uh-TEER) *n.* A chariot driver.

chivalrous: (SHIV-uhl-rus) *adj.* Showing the qualities of a gentleman, such as courage, fairness, courtesy, and protection of the poor.

citadel: (SIT-uh-dul) *n.* A walled place built on high ground to protect or defend a city.

citizen: (SIT-uh-sun) *n.* A member of a state or nation who has certain duties, rights, and privileges, such as the right to vote.

civil war: (SIV-ul wohr) *n.* War between two groups in the same country or group.

civil service: (SIV-ul SUR-vis) *n.* All the people who work for the government except people in the military, the people who make laws, and the judges.

cockfight: (KAHK-fiyt) *n.* A fight between birds trained to fight.

code: (cohd) *n.* A group of rules.

collapse: (kuh-LAPS) *v.* To fall in.

comet: (KAHM-it) *n.* An object that looks like a star and travels along a definite path around the sun.

command: (kuh-MAND) *v.* To order that something be done.

commandment: (kuh-MAND-munt) *n.* A law or order.

commerce: (KAHM-uhrs) *n.* The buying and selling of goods.

commit: (kuh-MIT) *v.* To do or be guilty of.

communicate: (kuh-MYOON-i-KAYT) *v.* To give information.

compile: (kuhm-PIYL) *v.* To gather and put together.

compose: (kuhm-POHZ) *v.* To make up; to create.

condemn: (kuhn-DEM) *v.* To declare to be guilty of wrongdoing.

confiscate: (KAHN-fus-kayt) *v.* To take private property for the government.

conflict: (KAHN-flikt) *n.* A difference that causes problems.

conquer: (KAHN-kur) *v.* To take over someone else's land.

conscience: (KAHN-shuns) *n.* A person's sense of right or wrong.

consul: (KAHN-sul) *n.* A government official with power to administer the law.

consult: (kuhn-SULT) *v.* To ask the advice of.

container: (kuhn-TAY-nur) *n.* A can, bottle, jug, box, or anything else for holding something.

content: (kuhn-TENT) *adj.* Happy with what one has; satisfied.

continually: (kuhn-TIN-yool-lee) *adv.* Over and over; without interruption.

control: (kuhn-TROHL) *v.* To run or be in charge of.

convenience: (kun-VEEN-yuhnz) *n.* Something useful; something that makes a person comfortable.

corrupt: (kuh-RUPT) *adj.* Willing to do wrong for money or other gain.

council: (KOWN-sul) *n.* A group of people who advise or govern.

court: (kohrt) *n.* The family, advisors, and attendants of a king or queen.

covenant: (KUV-i-nuhnt) *n.* A sacred agreement or promise.

covet: (KUHV-it) *v.* To want what another person has.

creative: (kree-AY-tiv) *adj.* Inventive; able to make something new or different.

crucify: (KROO-si-fiy) *v.* To kill a person by nailing their hands and feet to a cross made of wood.

cult: (kult) *n.* A system of religious worship or ritual.

cultivate: (KUL-ti-vayt) *v.* To prepare soil for planting.

cycle: (SIY-kul) *n.* A period of time in which certain regular events occur.

D

dagger: (DAG-gur) *n.* A short weapon with a sharp point.

damage: (DAM-ij) *v.* To harm or injure something; to break.

decay: (dee-KAY) *v.* To rot.

decipher: (dee-SIY-fur) *v.* To make out the meaning.

decline: (dee-KLIYN) *v.* To lose strength or power.

decorative: (DEK-uh-ruh-tiv) *adj.* Artistic; pleasing to the eye.

dedicate: (DED-i-kayt) *v.* To address a piece of art, music, or a book to a person (or deity) to honor or thank that person.

deed: (deed) *n.* Something done; an act.

defeat: (dee-FEET) *v.* To beat; win out over.

deity: (DEE-i-tee) *n.* A god or goddess.

deliver: (dee-LIV-ur) *v.* To set free or rescue.

delta: (DEL-tuh) *n.* A deposit of sand and soil at the mouth of some rivers; the delta is usually shaped like a triangle.

democracy: (duh-MAHK-ruh-see) *n.* Rule of the people.

desert: (DEZ-urt) *n.* A body of dry, sandy land with almost no water and few plants or trees.

dialect: (DIY-uh-lekt) *n.* The different sounds or words used by a group of people in a certain place that others using the same language do not understand.

dictator: (DIK-tay-tur) *n.* A ruler who has total power in government.

diplomat: (DIP-loh-mat) *n.* A representative of a government who conducts relations with another country.

293

disaster: (dee-ZAS-tur) *n.* A sudden event that causes great damage, loss, or destruction.

disband: (dis-BAND) *v.* To break up; dismiss from military service.

disciple: (di-SIY-pul) *n.* A student of a religious teacher.

discipline: (DIS-uh-plin) *n.* Strict control to make people obey rules.

discus: (DIS-kus) *n.* A heavy, round piece of metal thrown for distance as a test of strength and skill.

dispute: (dis-PYOOT) *n.* An argument or fight.

ditch: (dich) *n.* A long, narrow cut in the earth for carrying water.

divination: (div-uh-NAY-shun) *n.* The practice of trying to foretell the future.

divine right: (dih-VIYN riyt) *n.* The god-given right to be king.

diviner: (di-VIYN-ur) *n.* A person who tries to predict the future.

dolphin: (DAHL-fin) *n.* A mammal from the whale family that lives in the ocean.

donate: (DOH-nayt) *v.* To give; to contribute.

drain: (drayn) *n.* A pipe for carrying off water.

drama: (DRAH-muh) *n.* A story or play about people and their problems.

drive: (driyv) *v.* To force out.

drought: (drowt) *n.* A long period of dry weather; lack of rain.

drown: (drown) *v.* To sink into water, become unable to breathe, and die.

dynasty: (DIY-ni-stee) *n.* A line of rulers from the same family.

E

ebony: (EB-uh-nee) *n.* A hard, dark wood.

eclipse: (ee-KLIPS) *n.* Partial or complete darkening of the moon when the earth's shadow falls on it; or darkening of the sun when the moon comes between it and the earth.

economic: (ek-uh-NAHM-ik) *adj.* Having to do with the production, distribution, and use of wealth and resources.

efficient: (i-FISH-uhnt) *adj.* Able; capable.

elder: (EL-dur) *n.* An older person (with some authority).

embalmer: (em-BAHLM-ur) *n.* A person who preserves a dead body from decay by using special salts or chemicals.

embroider: (em-BROI-dur) *v.* To make a design on material using a needle and thread.

emergency: (ee-MUR-jen-see) *n.* A sudden situation that needs immediate action.

empire: (EM-piyr) *n.* A group of states or people ruled by one person or government.

enclosure: (en-CLOH-shur) *n.* An area surrounded by walls.

encounter: (en-COWN-tur) *v.* To meet or come upon.

encourage: (en-KUR-ij) *v.* To urge someone to do something.

endurance: (en-DUR-uns) *n.* The ability to keep trying to do something even though it is difficult.

engineering: (en-juh-NEER-ing) *n.* The planning, design, and construction of things such as roads, bridges, or large buildings.

envious: (EN-vee-uhs) *adj.* To want what another has.

erupt: (i-RUPT) *v.* To spill over or explode suddenly.

estate: (uh-STAYT) *n.* Everything one owns such as land, money, or property.

exaggeration: (eg-ZAJ-jur-RAY-shun) *n.* A statement that makes a thing seem bigger or better or smaller or worse than it really is.

excavation: (ek-skuh-VAY-shun) *n.* A hole made by digging.

exchange: (eks-CHAYNJ) *n.* A trade; giving back and forth.

execute: (EK-si-kyoot) *v.* To kill.

exhausted: (eg-ZAWST-ud) *adj.* Very tired.

exotic: (eg-ZAHT-ik) *adj.* From another place; not native.

expand: (ek-SPAND) *v.* To grow, spread out, or get larger in size.

expedition: (ek-spuh-DISH-un) *n.* A trip made to explore.

expel: (ek-SPEL) *v.* To force out.

expert: (EK-spurt) *n.* A person who knows a lot about a subject.

export: (ek-SPOHRT) *v.* To send goods to another place to sell or trade.

extinct: (ek-STINGKT) *adj.* None living.

extraordinary: (ek-STROHR-duh-NAYR-ee) *adj.* Very special.

F

fabric: (FAB-rik) *n.* Cloth.

false: (fawls) *adj.* Not real; not true.

famine: (FAM-in) *n.* Hunger caused by a widespread lack of food.

fast: (fast) *v.* To stop eating for a period of time.

feat: (feet) *n.* A great deed or act.

fertile soil: (FURT-ul soil) *n.* Soil good for growing food.

Fertile Crescent: (FURT-ul KRES-ent) *n.* A region of rich, fertile soil that stretched from the Mediterranean Sea, between the Tigris and Euphrates rivers, to the Persian Gulf.

figurine: (fig-yoo-REEN) *n.* A small figure that is carved or molded.

flake: (flayk) *n.* A thin piece cut from something.

flee: (flee) *v.* To run away or escape from danger.

fleet: (fleet) *n.* A group of ships sailing together.

flint: (flint) *n.* A very hard stone.

flock: (flahk) *n.* Small numbers of animals.

flourish: (FLUR-ish) *v.* To grow vigorously; to be at the peak of development.

flow: (floh) *v.* To move in a stream.

foothill (FOOT-hil) *n.* A low hill at the bottom of a mountain.

foreign: (FOHR-in) *adj.* From another country.

forgiveness: (fohr-GIV-nuhs) *n.* The act of stopping feelings of anger toward a person.

fortress: (FOHR-truhs) *n.* A structure or place that protects from an attack.

fossil: (FAH-sul) *n.* Hardened remains of a plant or animal.

fragment: (FRAG-munt) *n.* Broken piece.

frontier: (fruhn-TEER) *n.* The part of a country that borders another country or an undeveloped region.

fully upright: (FUL-lee UP-riyt) *adj.* Standing straight; not bent over.

functional: (FUNK-shun-ul) *adj.* Doing a certain job.

G

garment: (GAHR-munt) *n.* An item of clothing worn on the body.

genesis: (JEN-i-sus) *n.* The beginning; origin; creation.

genus and species: (JEE-nes and SPEE-sheez) *n.* A way of grouping plants and animals by their characteristics; the genus "Homo" means human; modern human beings are called Homo sapiens.

geologist: (jee-AHL-uh-jist) *n.* A person who studies the earth's crust (the outer layer).

geometric: (jee-uh-MET-rik) *adj.* Designs using lines and shapes.

glacier: (GLAY-shur) *n.* A large mass of ice and snow that forms faster than the snow can melt.

gladiator: (GLAD-ee-ay-tur) *n.* An armed fighter who battles another person or a wild animal as public entertainment.

glorify: (GLOHR-i-fiy) *v.* To surround with praise.

glorious: (GLOHR-ree-us) *adj.* Being at the height of prosperity or achievement.

gnat: (nat) *n.* A small insect that flies.

gorge: (gohrj) *n.* A deep, narrow pass with steep sides.

gourd: (gohrd) *n.* A fruit used for decoration.

granite: (GRAN-it) *n.* A hard stone used for building.

grid: (grid) *n.* A framework of parallel lines.

grip: (grip) *v.* To hold firmly with the hand.

H

hail: (hayl) *n.* Frozen raindrops; pieces of ice that sometimes fall during thunderstorms.

handicap: (HAN-dee-kap) *n.* Something that makes life difficult for a person.

handicraft: (HAN-dee-kraft) *n.* An art piece made by hand.

harpoon: (hahr-POON) *n.* A spear with a rope tied to it.

harrow: (HAYR-oh) *n.* A farm tool used to smooth the soil.

harsh: (hahrsh) *adj.* Extreme; severe; cruel.

hearth: (hahrth) *n.* The stones the fire sits on.

height: (hiyt) *n.* The highest point.

hemp: (hemp) *n.* A tall plant with tough fibers.

heritage: (HAYR-uh-tij) *n.* A person's culture and traditions passed down by one's parents.

hieroglyphic: (hiy-roh-GLIF-ik) *n.* A picture or symbol used in ancient Egyptian writing.

Hindu Kush: (HIN-doo kush) *n.* A mountain range in Central Asia.

hitch: (hich) *v.* To fasten or hook onto something.

hoe blade: (hoh blayd) *n.* A tool used for cultivating, weeding, or loosening the earth around plants.

honesty: (AHN-is-tee) *n.* Truthfulness.

honor: (AHN-ur) *v.* To show great respect for.

hut: (hut) *n.* A small house made of wood or branches.

hymn: (him) *n.* A song in praise of a deity.

I

ideograph: (ID-ee-oh-graf) *n.* A symbol representing an idea.

idol: (IY-dul) *n.* A picture or likeness of a false god.

imitate: (IM-uh-tayt) *v.* To copy.

impetuous: (im-PECH-yoo-us) *adj.* Acting suddenly with little thought.

import: (im-POHRT) *v.* To bring goods into one place from another.

imprison: (im-PRIZ-in) *v.* To put in prison or jail.

independent: (IN-dee-PEN-dent) *adj.* Not under the control of another.

influential: (IN-floo-EN-shul) *adj.* Powerful; having power over people because of one's position.

ingot: (ING-it) *n.* Metal cast into a bar.

inherit: (in-HAYR-it) *v.* To receive something as the result of another's death.

inscription: (in-SKRIP-shun) *n.* Something engraved (carved) on stones or coins.

insist: (in-SIST) *v.* To continue to ask or demand.

integrity: (in-TEG-ri-tee) *n.* Honesty; sincerity.

interact: (in-tur-AKT) *v.* To do things together.

intrigue: (in-TREEG) *n.* A plot in secret.

invade: (in-VAYD) *v.* To come in as an enemy.

invent: (in-VENT) *v.* To think up new ideas or ways to do things.

irrigate: (IR-uh-gayt) *v.* To supply with water.

island: (IY-land) *n.* A piece of land completely surrounded by water.

isolate: (IY-suh-layt) *v.* To stay apart; avoid others.

ivory: (IY-vuh-ree) *n.* The hard, white material of which the tusks of elephants and walruses are made.

J

Jawaharlal Nehru: (juh-wah-her-LAHL NAY-roo) *n.* Prime minister of India from 1947 to 1964.

jealous: (JEL-us) *adj.* Afraid of losing what one has or wishing for what another person has.

juggler: (JUG-lur) *n.* A person who performs tricks with balls.

K

Karnak: (KAHR-nak) *n.* A city in Egypt.

kidnap: (KID-nap) *v.* To take a person by force from one place to another.

kiln: (kiln) *n.* A very hot oven used to harden clay objects.

Korea: (kuh-REE-uh) *n.* A country east of China.

L

lancer: (LAN-sur) *n.* A soldier who carries a lance, a long wooden weapon with a sharp metal tip.

lava: (LAH-vah) *n.* Melted rock from a volcano.

legal: (LEE-gul) *adj.* Something that is right under the law.

legend: (LEJ-uhnd) *n.* A story handed down through generations; a myth.

legendary: (LEJ-uhn-DAYR-ee) *adj.* Famous.

levee: (LEV-ee) *n.* A special wall built along a river to keep water from flooding the land.

level: (LEV-ul) *n.* At the same height; not above or below.

libation: (liy-BAY-shun) *n.* The ritual of pouring out wine or oil on the ground to honor a god.

limestone: (LIYM-stohn) *n.* A kind of rock.

literature: (LIT-ur-uh-CHUR) *n.* Stories, poetry, and other writings.

living-floor: (LIV-ing-FLOHR) *n.* A place where people lived or camped.

local: (LOH-kul) *adj.* Of a certain place.

locust: (LOH-kust) *n.* A type of grasshopper.

loess highlands: (LOH-es HIY-lunds) *n.* A high area above the North China Plain covered by deep layers of windblown yellow soil called loess.

loom: (loom) *n.* A machine for weaving thread into cloth.

lotus: (LOH-tus) *n.* A water lily.

loyalty: (LOI-ul-tee) *n.* Being true to a friend, a country, or a cause.

luxury: (LUK-shur-ee) *n.* Something you would like to have, but don't need.

lyre: (liyr) *n.* A musical instrument.

M

Macedonia: (MAS-uh-DOH-nee-uh) *n.* An ancient kingdom north of Greece.

male: (mayl) *n.* Boy or man.

malnutrition: (mal-noo-TRI-shun) *n.* A condition caused by lack of healthy food.

management: (MAN-ij-munt) *n.* The handling or running of something.

mansion: (MAN-shun) *n.* A large, impressive house.

manufactured: (MAN-yoo-FAK-shurd) *adj.* Made in a factory or workshop.

martial: (MAHR-shul) *adj.* Having to do with war.

Mauryan: (MAHR-yuhn) *adj.* Name of a line of conquering kings.

maximum: (MAK-si-mum) *n.* The greatest amount possible.

maze: (mayz) *n.* A puzzling set of paths or passageways.

mechanical: (muh-KAN-i-kul) *adj.* Worked by machines.

medicinal: (muh-DIS-un-ul) *adj.* Healing.

meditation: (MED-i-TAY-shun) *n.* The act of thinking about spiritual things; in Buddhism, calming the mind.

memorize: (MEM-uh-riyz) *v.* To learn by heart.

Meroë: (MAYR-uh-wee) *n.* The capital of Kush.

Messiah: (muh-SIY-uh) *n.* The expected leader or deliverer of the Jews.

middle class: (MID-ul klas) *n.* The social class between the very rich and the lower working class; people in business, the professions, highly skilled workers, and well-to-do farmers.

migrate: (MIY-grayt) *v.* To move from one place to settle in another place.

military: (MIL-uh-TAYR-ee) *n.* People or places having to do with an army or navy.

mine: (miyn) *n.* A large hole dug into the earth from which copper, gold, or other minerals are taken.

minor: (MIY-nur) *adj.* Less important than others.

miracle: (MIR-uh-kul) *n.* Something almost beyond belief; an event or action that seems to go against scientific laws and is thought to have a supernatural cause.

misery: (MIZ-uh-ree) *n.* A condition of great pain; suffering.

missionary: (MISH-uh-NAYR-ee) *n.* A person sent to tell other people about a religion.

moderation: (MAHD-ur-AY-shun) *n.* Avoiding extremes.

mold: (mohld) *n.* A hollow form used to give shape to something poured into it.

monk: (muhnk) *n.* A man who joins a religious group and lives away from the rest of society.

monumental: (MAHN-yoo-MEN-tul) *adj.* Very large, solid, and long-lasting.

moral: (MOHR-uhl) *adj.* Having to do with principles of right and wrong.

mortar: (MOHR-tur) *n.* Dry powder that hardens when mixed with water.

mound: (mownd) *n.* A pile of dirt; a small hill.

mountain range: (MOWN-tuhn raynj) *n.* A group of mountains forming a line.

mummy: (MUHM-mee) *n.* A dead body that is handled in a special way to keep it from decaying.

murder: (MUR-dur) *v.* To kill.

musk: (muhsk) *n.* An oil from an animal used in making perfumes.

myrrh: (mur) *n.* A kind of gum or resin from a tree used in perfumes, medicines, or incense.

myth: (mith) *n.* A story told over and over that explains something about nature, the customs, or religious beliefs of a people.

N

native: (NAY-tiv) *n.* A person born in a certain city, region, or country.

Near East: (neer eest) *n.* The countries near or east of the eastern Mediterranean Sea.

niche: (nich) *n.* A small hole or hollow place in a wall.

noble: (NOH-bul) 1. *adj.* Having high moral qualities or ideals. 2. *n.* A person who is a member of the ruling family.

nomadic (noh-MAD-ik) *adj.* Having no permanent home; moving about in search of food.

O

oarsman: (OHRZ-mun) *n.* A person who rows a boat.

obedience: (oh-BEE-dee-unz) *n.* Doing what is ordered.

obelisk: (OHB-ul-isk) *n.* A tall pillar set up in honor of a special event, person, or deity.

obstacle: (AHB-stuh-kul) *n.* Something in the way that makes it hard to do what a person is trying to do.

occupation: (AHK-yoo-PAY-shun) *n.* Job.

offering: (AHF-ring) *n.* A gift made in worship.

oracle: (OHR-uh-kul) *n.* An announcement from a deity.

ore: (ohr) *n.* Rock or earth that has iron, silver, copper, or other metals in it.

organ: (OHR-gin) *n.* A part of the body which does certain work; the stomach, liver, heart, and lungs are organs.

ornate: (ohr-NAYT) *adj.* Heavily decorated.

ostrich: (AHS-trij) *n.* A very large bird that cannot fly, but can run very fast.

overseer: (OH-vur-SEE-ur) *n.* A person in charge of others; a supervisor.

P

palace: (PAL-us) *n.* A very large building in which kings, queens, and their families live.

papyrus: (puh-PIY-rus) *n.* A plant from which people of ancient civilizations made a paper-like material to write on.

parable: (PAYR-uh-bul) *n.* A short, simple story that tells a lesson.

paralyzed: (PAYR-ul-iyzd) *adj.* Not able to move.

parasite: (PAYR-uh-siyt) *n.* A person who lives at the expense of another without making a contribution.

pastime: (PAS-tiym) *n.* A way of spending spare time; hobby; anything done for amusement or recreation.

penalty: (PEN-ul-tee) *n.* Punishment for breaking a rule or law.

peninsula: (puh-NIN-suh-luh) *n.* A land area almost entirely surrounded by water.

permanent: (PUR-muh-nunt) *adj.* Made to last a long time.

persecute: (PUR-suh-KYOOT) *v.* To attack, injure, or bother constantly because of religion, politics, or race.

Persia: (PUR-zhuh) *n.* A country in western Asia now known as Iran.

pharaoh: (FAYR-roh) *n.* The leader or king of ancient Egypt.

pheasant: (FEZ-unt) *n.* A bird with a long, sweeping tail and brightly colored feathers.

philosopher: (fuh-LAHS-uh-fur) *n.* A person who thinks about and studies the basic questions of life.

plague: (playg) *n.* A disease that kills many people at one time.

plain: (playn) *n.* A stretch of flat, level country.

planet: (PLAN-it) *n.* A heavenly body that shines by reflected sunlight and revolves around the sun.

plaque: (plak) *n.* A thin, flat piece of wood, metal, glass, or clay used for ornamentation.

plaster: (PLAS-tur) *n.* A mixture of clay, sand, and water.

platform: (PLAT-fohrm) *n.* A part of the floor that is higher than the rest.

plot: (plaht) *n.* An area of ground.

plumbing: (PLUM-ing) *n.* A system of pipes through which water passes in and out of a building.

polish: (PAHL-ish) *v.* To smooth and brighten.

political: (puh-LIT-i-kul) *adj.* Having to do with government.

popular: (PAHP-yuh-lur) *adj.* Liked by people.

porridge: (POHR-ij) *n.* A cereal.

port: (pohrt) *n.* A city or town with a harbor where ships can load and unload goods.

possession: (poh-ZESH-uhn) *n.* Something a person owns.

potter's wheel: (PAHT-uhrz hweel) *n.* A turning wheel used to shape clay.

practical: (PRAK-ti-kul) *adj.* Useful.

preach: (preech) *v.* To talk in public on a religious subject.

prehistoric: (PREE-his-TOHR-ik) *adj.* The time before written history.

preserve: (pree-ZURV) *v.* To keep from spoiling or going bad.

preside: (pree-ZIYD) *v.* To run or rule over.

priest: (preest) *n.* A religious leader.

principle: (PRIN-suh-pul) *n.* A law upon which other laws are based.

produce: (PROH-doos) *n.* Farm products.

prohibit: (proh-HIB-it) *v.* To not allow.

Promised Land: (PRAHM-ist land) *n.* Canaan, in the Bible, the land promised by God to Abraham and his descendents.

properly: (PRAH-pur-lee) *adv.* Correctly; to do something as it should be done.

prosperous: (PRAHS-pur-us) *adj.* Successful; well-off.

province: (PRAHV-inz) *n.* Territory; region.

public: (PUB-lik) *adj.* For the use of all.

punish: (PUN-ish) *v.* To cause pain or suffering.

Punt: (punt) *n.* Probably present-day Somalia.

pursue: (pur-SOO) *v.* To chase or go after.

pyramid: (PIR-uh-mid) *n.* An ancient building where a dead body is placed; most are found in Egypt.

Q

quarry: (KWOHR-ee) *n.* A place from which stone is cut.

R

rage: (rayj) *v.* To show violent anger.

raid: (rayd) *v.* To make a sudden, hostile attack.

rank: (raynk) *n.* A social class.

raw: (rah) *adj.* In its natural, unchanged condition.

raw materials: (rah muh-TIR-ee-ulz) *n.* Things such as animal skins, wood, or gold that can be used to make other things.

realize: (REE-ul-iyz) *v.* To understand.

reap: (reep) *v.* To gather a crop by cutting.

rebel: 1. (REB-ul) *n.* A person who openly resists authority. 2. (ree-BEL) *v.* To turn against.

recite: (ree-SIYT) *v.* To speak aloud from memory.

refuse: (ree-FYOOZ) *v.* To not do as asked.

region: (REE-juhn) *n.* An area; a place.

reincarnation: (REE-in-kahr-NAY-shun) *n.* Rebirth of the soul in another body.

relief sculpture: (ree-LEEF SKULP-chur) *n.* A picture made by carving into wood, metal, or stone; the carved figures stand out from the background.

remain: (ree-MAYN) *v.* To stay.

remarkable: (ree-MAHR-kuh-bul) *adj.* Unusual; extraordinary.

remorse: (ree-MOHRS) *n.* A deep sense of guilt; regret.

remote: (ree-MOHT) *adj.* Distant; faraway.

repair: (ree-PAYR) *v.* To put back in good condition; to fix.

republic: (ree-PUB-lik) *n.* A government in which people elect their leaders.

resin: (REZ-in) *n.* A sticky material that comes from trees and plants.

result: (ri-ZULT) *v.* To cause to happen; to effect.

resurrection: (REZ-uh-REK-shun) *n.* A rising from the dead; a coming back to life; a renewal of life.

revered: (ree-VEERD) *adj.* Very highly thought of.

revolt: (ree-VOHLT) *v.* To turn or fight against.

rickets: (RIK-itz) *n.* A disease of the bones.

right: (riyt) *n.* Something a person has a just claim to, such as the right of free speech.

riot: (RIY-uht) *n.* Wild or violent disorder of a group of people.

rite: (riyt) *n.* A religious ceremony.

ritual: (RICH-yoo-uhl) *n.* A set form of religious rites.

river basin: (RIV-ur BAY-sun) *n.* The area drained by a river and its branches.

roam: (rohm) *v.* To move from place to place.

royal: (ROI-ul) *adj.* Belonging to the family of a king or queen.

rubbing: (RUB-ing) *n.* A picture made by placing a paper over the surface to be copied and moving a crayon or pencil back and forth.

rugged: (RUG-uhd) *adj.* Rough; severe; harsh.

ruins: (ROO-inz) *n.* The remains of a building or city.

ruthless: (ROOTH-lus) *adj.* Without pity.

S

Sabbath: (SAB-uth) *n.* A day set aside for worship; Saturday in the Jewish religion; Sunday in the Christian religion.

sacred: (SAY-krid) *adj.* Belonging to a god or goddess; holy.

sacrifice: (SAK-ri-fiys) *n.* An offering of the life of an animal or human.

sage: (sayj) *n.* A very wise person.

sanctuary: (SANGK-shoo-AYR-ree) *n.* A part of a church or temple.

scholar: (SKAH-lur) *n.* An advanced student; an educated person who may teach or do research.

scribe: (skriyb) *n.* A person who does the writing for others.

script: (skript) *n.* Written words.

scroll: (skrohl) *n.* A roll of parchment or paper, usually with writing on it.

scrounge: (skrownj) *v.* To try to find as best one can.

sea: (see) *n.* A large body of water, usually salt water.

second-class: (sek-UND klas) *adj.* Considered inferior; lower in value.

seek: (seek) *v.* To try to find; look for.

separation: (SEP-uh-ray-shun) *n.* A dividing up.

sermon: (SUR-mun) *n.* A speech giving instruction in religion.

servant: (SUR-vunt) *n.* A person who works in or around the home of someone else.

settlement: (SET-ul-munt) *n.* A village.

shadoof: (shah-DOOF) *n.* A device that consists of a long pole with a bucket on one end and a weight on the other to draw water to irrigate the fields.

shape: (shayp) *v.* To give a form or direction to.

shore: (shohr) *n.* The land bordering a large body of water.

shrine: (shriyn) *n.* An altar, chapel, or other place of worship.

siege: (seej) *n.* A type of warfare in which an army camps around a town and fights to destroy it.

sift: (sift) *v.* To pass through a screen; to separate.

silt: (silt) *n.* Soil or sand left behind by water.

site: (siyt) *n.* A place; location.

skeleton: (SKEL-uh-tun) *n.* The bones of an animal or person.

slag: (slag) *n.* Material left over when metal has been separated from ore.

slave: (slayv) *n.* A person who is owned by others and must work for and obey them.

smelting furnace: (SMEL-ting FUR-nis) *n.* A hot oven used to melt ore and separate it from slag.

society: (suh-SIY-i-tee) *n.* A community having shared traditions, activities, or interests.

solstice: (SOHL-stis) *n.* The point at which the sun is farthest north or south of the equator.

soothing: (SOOTH-ing) *adj.* Something that comforts and creates a nice feeling.

specialist: (SPESH-uh-list) *n.* A person who does a certain kind of work.

specimen: (SPES-uh-muhn) *n.* A sample or an example.

spiritual: (SPIR-i-choo-uhl) *adj.* Having to do with things of the spirit.

sportsmanlike: (SPOHRTZ-muhn-liyk) *adj.* Losing without complaining, winning without bragging, and treating others with fairness.

stable: (STAY-bul) *n.* A place where horses and other animals are kept.

stampede: (stam-PEED) *v.* To cause a sudden running away of a group of frightened animals.

standard: (STAN-durd) *n.* An object such as a flag or banner, used as a symbol of a group of people.

starvation: (stahr-VAY-shun) *n.* Becoming weak from hunger.

steatite: (STEE-uh-tiyt) *n.* A soft stone.

stele: (STEE-lee) *n.* An upright stone or pillar, engraved with writing.

stencil: (STEN-sul) *v.* To make a pattern by covering up places that will not be painted.

steppe: (step) *n.* A plain with few or no trees.

subcontinent: (SUHB-KAHN-tuh-nent) *n.* A large piece of land, somewhat separated but still a part of a continent.

subdue: (suhb-DOO) *v.* To conquer.

subject: (suhb-JEKT) *n.* A person under the authority or control of a group.

superior: (soo-PIR-ee-ur) *adj.* Higher in value, power, or authority.

supervise: (SOO-pur-viyz) *v.* To be in charge of.

surname: (SUR-naym) *n.* Last name; family name.

surplus: (SUR-plus) *n.* More than what is needed; extra.

surrender: (suh-REN-dur) *v.* To give in or accept defeat.

survive: (sur-VIYV) *v.* To live through.

suspect: (suh-SPEKT) *v.* To believe, but not be sure.

suspicious: (suh-SPISH-us) *adj.* To have no trust in.

swamp: (swahmp) *n.* Land that is very wet most of the time.

syllable: (SIL-uh-bul) *n.* A group of letters that make one sound.

symbol: (SIM-bul) *n.* A written mark that stands for an object or idea.

T

tanned: (tand) *adj.* Made into leather.

tanner: (TAN-ur) *n.* Someone who works with animal hides to make leather.

technology: (tek-NAHL-uh-jee) *n.* Progress in the use of tools.

temple: (TEM-pul) *n.* A building for the worship of a god or gods.

tend: (tend) *v.* To look after.

tenement: (TEN-uh-ment) *n.* Apartments that are rundown and overcrowded.

tension: (TEN-shun) *n.* A pull from two different directions; a strain.

terrace: (TAYR-us) *n.* An area of flat land, one above the other, on a hillside.

territory: (TAYR-uh-tohr-ee) *n.* Land or country.

terror: (TAYR-ur) *n.* Intense fear.

terrorize: (TAYR-ur-iyz) *v.* To cause fear by act or threat of violence.

terrors: (TAYR-urs) *n.* Things that make one afraid.

testimony: (TES-tuh-MOH-nee) *n.* Statement or evidence.

text: (tekst) *n.* A piece of writing.

throne: (throhn) *n.* The chair of a king, but also a symbol of the power of the king.

tidal wave: (TIY-dul wayv) *n.* A giant wall of water called a tsunami caused by a storm in the ocean, earthquake, or volcanic eruption.

timber: (TIM-bur) *n.* Wood suitable for building houses or ships.

token: (TOH-kun) *n.* A piece of clay that stands for something else (one token for each cow or sheep).

tolerance: (TAHL-uh-renz) *n.* Respect for the beliefs of others.

tomb: (toom) *n.* A building where a dead body is placed; grave.

Torah: (TOHR-uh) *n.* The sacred history and laws of the Israelites.

tournament: (TUR-nah-ment) *n.* Contest in a sport.

tradition: (truh-DISH-un) *n.* A story, belief, or custom handed down from parents or grandparents to children.

transform: (tranz-FOHRM) *v.* To change.

transportation: (TRANZ-pur-TAY-shun) *n.* A way to get from one place to another without walking.

treason: (TREE-zun) *n.* Betrayal of one's country.

treasure: (TREZH-ur) *n.* Valuables such as gold, silver, and jewels.

trench: (trench) *n.* A long narrow ditch.

tribune: (TRIB-yoonz) *n.* A Roman official appointed to protect the rights of the plebeians.

triumphantly: (triy-UM-funt-lee) *adv.* With pride in winning or being a winner.

triumvirate: (triy-UM-vur-it) *n.* Government by three people.

tung: (tuhng) *n.* An oil from a tree used in paint to give a shiny finish that is water-resistant.

turquoise: (TUR-koiz) *n.* A blue to blue-green substance found in rocks, used to make jewelry.

twin: (twin) *adj.* Describing one of two persons or things that are very much alike.

tyrant: (TIY-ruhnt) *n.* A cruel ruler.

U

uniformity: (YOO-nuh-FOHR-muh-tee) *n.* Always being the same; not changing.

unique: (yoo-NEEK) *adj.* Different from all others.

university: (YOO-nuh-VUR-suh-tee) *n.* A place of higher education; a group of colleges.

V

vain: (vayn) *adj.* To greatly admire one's own looks, possessions, or abilities.

vast: (vast) *adj.* Of very great size; huge.

vendor: (VEN-dur) *n.* A person who sells things.

vessel: (VES-ul) *n.* A container such as a vase, bowl, or pitcher, used for holding something.

Vietnam: (vee-uht-NAHM) *n.* A country south of China.

volcano: (vahl-KAY-noh) *n.* A hole in the earth's crust through which hot ashes or lava (melted rock) come out.

W

waterproof: (WAH-tur-proof) *v.* To make something so that it cannot soak up any water.

wealth: (welth) *n.* Much money or property; riches.

whim: (hwim) *n.* Sudden fancy or desire.

wreck: (rek) *v.* To tear apart, destroy, or ruin.

Y

yoga: (YOH-guh) *n.* A system of concentration and exercise used in the Hindu religion.

Z

ziggurat: (ZIG-uh-raht) *n.* A type of temple with a one-room shrine at the top.

Vowel Pronunciation Key

This pronunciation key shows how to pronounce the vowels, which are the most problematic sounds in English pronunciation.

SYMBOL	KEY WORDS
a	ant, man
ay	cake, May
ah	clock, arm
aw	salt, ball
e	neck, hair
ee	ear, key
i	chick, skin
iy	five, tiger
oh	coat, soda
oi	boy, coin
ohr	board, door
oo	blue, boot
ow	cow, owl
u	foot, wolf, bird, and the schwa sound used in final syllables followed by 'l,' 'r,' 's,' 'm,' 't,' or 'n,' for example, children (CHIL-<u>drun</u>)
uh	bug, uncle, and other schwa sounds, such as, kangaroo (kang-<u>guh</u>-ROO)

Source: The vowel pronunciation key is derived from the *American Heritage Dictionary of the English Language*, 1981; *Oxford American Dictionary: Heald Colleges Edition*, 1982; and *Webster's New World College Dictionary, Third Edition*, 1990. Please note that the surrounding letters may affect the vowel sound slightly.

INDEX

Photography and Illustration Credits

(t=top, b=bottom, l=left, r=right)

Page: 4-5, Des & Jen Bartlett/Bruce Coleman, Inc.; 6-7, Keith Neely; 7 (1t) Lower Paleolithic pointed hand axe, courtesy John Keeping, photograph by Sally Mittuch; 8-9, Des & Jen Bartlett/Bruce Coleman, Inc.; 10, ©Des Bartlett, Science Source/Photo Researchers; 11, Des & Jen Bartlett/Bruce Coleman, Inc.; 12, Keith Neely; 13, (l) Keith Neely (r) Des & Jen Bartlett/Bruce Coleman, Inc.; 14, ©Des Bartlett, Science Source/Photo Researchers; 16-17, Keith Neely; 18, Alaska Division of Tourism; 19, (l) neg. #260298 courtesy The Library, American Museum of Natural History (r) Keith Neely; 20, ©David L. Brill, 1985; 21, 23, 24, 25, 27, Keith Neely; 28-29, 31-32, Flo Buchanan; 33, (l) Keith Neely (r) Jerry Pase, courtesy Dr. Philip E. Smith and Time-Life Books, Inc.; 34, Keith Neely; 35, ©David L. Brill, 1985; 37, (l) ©David L. Brill, 1985 (r) Réunion des Musées Nationaux/Art Resource, NY; 38-39, Keith Neely; 40-41, Leilani Trollinger; 42, Keith Neely; 43, ©The World Bank, photograph by Yosef Hadar; 44, Keith Neely; 47, (l) Leilani Trollinger (r) Keith Neely; 48, Leilani Trollinger; 49, (l) Leilani Trollinger (r) Keith Neely; 50, Leilani Trollinger; 51, Keith Neely; 52-53, Keith Neely; 56, The University of Pennsylvania Museum (neg. #T4-283c2 & T4-420c2); 57, ©Copyright The British Museum; 58, Fujiko Miller; 59, All rights reserved, The Metropolitan Museum of Art, Fletcher Fund, 1940 (40.156); 60, 62, Keith Neely; 63, Scala/Art Resource, NY; 64, (l) Réunion des Musées Nationaux/Art Resource, NY (r) Ashmolean Museum, Oxford; 65, Keith Neely; 66, Fujiko Miller; 68-69, Elaine Elwell; 71, Patricia P. Miller; 72, Egyptian Tourist Authority; 73, Fujiko Miller; 74, All rights reserved, The Metropolitan Museum of Art, Rogers Fund and Edward S. Harkness Gift, 1929 (29.3.1 & 29.3.2); 75, All rights reserved, The Metropolitan Museum of Art, Museum Excavations, 1919-1920, Rogers Fund, supplemented by contributions of Edward S. Harkness (20.3.11); 76, All rights reserved, The Metropolitan Museum of Art; 77, Fujiko Miller; 78, Elaine Elwell; 79, ©The Field Museum, neg. #A90388, Chicago; 80-81, The Metropolitan Museum of Art, Rogers Fund and Edward S. Harkness Gift, 1920 (20.3.1) Photograph ©1983 The Metropolitan Museum of Art; 81, (t) The Metropolitan Museum of Art, 1919-20, Rogers Fund and Edward S. Harkness Gift, 1920 (20.3.1detail), Photograph ©1983 The Metropolitan Museum of Art; 82-83, Patricia P. Miller; 84-85, Egyptian Expedition of The Metropolitan Museum of Art, Rogers Fund, 1930 (30.4.21) Photograph ©1978 The Metropolitan Museum of Art; 86, 88, Keith Neely; 89, ©Copyright The British Museum; 90, (l) Dr. Charles Bonnet, photographer (r) The Griffith Institute, Oxford; 91, Fujiko Miller; 92, (t) photograph ©2004 Museum of Fine Arts, Boston (b) Keith Neely; detail used, Museum Expedition, courtesy Museum of Fine Arts, Boston; 94, photograph ©2004 Museum of Fine Arts, Boston; 95, (b) photograph ©2004 Museum of Fine Arts, Boston (t) Keith Neely; 96, The Walters Art Museum, Baltimore; 97, Timothy Kendall, photographer; 98, photograph ©2004 Museum of Fine Arts, Boston; 99, courtesy The Oriental Institute of The University of Chicago; 100-101, courtesy Ebrahim Nakhuda and Salim Chohan; 103, Don Weiss; 104, courtesy Ebrahim Nakhuda and Salim Chohan; 105, (t) *Seal with Two-horned Bull and Inscription.* India, Indus Valley civilization, c. 3000-1500 B.C. Steatite, 3.2 x 3.2 cm. ©The Cleveland Museum of Art. Purchased from the J.H. Wade Fund 73.160 (b) *Seal with Unicorn and Inscription.* India, Indus Valley civilization, c. 3000-1500 B.C. Steatite, 3.5 x 3.6 cm. ©The Cleveland Museum of Art. Purchased from the J.H. Wade Fund 73.161; 106, (l) courtesy Ebrahim Nakhuda and Salim Chohan (r) Keith Neely; 107, 109, Keith Neely; 110, National Museum of Pakistan, Karachi, Department of Archaeology and Museum Government of Pakistan; 111, (l) National Museum of Pakistan, Karachi, Department of Archaeology and Museum Government of Pakistan (rt) neg. #207069 courtesy The Library, American Museum of Natural History (rb) National Museum of Pakistan, Karachi, Department of Archaeology and Museum Government of Pakistan; 112, (l) (r) National Museum of Pakistan, Karachi, Department of Archaeology and Museum Government of Pakistan; 113, courtesy Ebrahim Nakhuda and Salim Chohan; 116-118, Keith Neely; 119, Art Resource, NY; 120, Keith Neely; 121, Fujiko Miller; 122, Keith Neely; 123, Professor Glen Yocum; 124, Fujiko Miller; 125, All rights reserved, The Metropolitan Museum of Art, Gift of the Kronos Collections, 1985 (1985.392.1), Photograph by Bruce White, Photograph © 1994 The Metropolitan Museum of Art; 126-130, All rights reserved, The Metropolitan Museum of Art, Gift of the Kronos Collections and Mr. and Mrs. Peter Findlay, 1979 (1979.511); 131, Keith Neely; 132-133, Fujiko Miller; 135, Don Weiss; 136, 138, Keith Neely; 140, (l) The J. Paul Getty Museum, Villa Collection, Malibu CA (r) Réunion des Musées Nationaux/Art Resource, NY; 141, Keith Neely; 142, Gladys Smith; 143, Fujiko Miller; 144, (l) Elaine Elwell (r) photograph courtesy Frank Ratnam; 145, courtesy The Griffith Observatory, E. C. Krupp; 146, Fujiko Miller; 147, Gladys Smith; 148-149, Keith Neely; 150-151, Elaine Elwell; 152, Keith Neely; 153, Bridgeman-Giraudon/Art Resource, NY; 154, Keith Neely; 155, Erich Lessing/Art Resource, NY; 156, Werner Forman/Art Resource, NY; 157, Keith Neely; 159, (l) Keith Neely (r) The Avery Brundage Collection, #B60B764, © Asian Art Museum of San Francisco, used by permission; 161-162, Fujiko Miller; 164-165, Keith Neely; 166, Jim De Forge; 168, Fenollosa-Weld Collection, courtesy Museum of Fine Arts, Boston; 169, Werner Forman/Art Resource, NY; 170, Fujiko Miller; 171, Gina Capaldi; 173, Keith Neely; 174, Mary Altier; 175, © The British Museum; 176, Cultural Relics Publishing House; 177, Dr. Stanley Jones; 178, Cultural Relics Publishing House; 180-181, New China Pictures Company; 182, Marvin J. Malecha, FAIA; 183, Elaine Elwell; 184, Cultural Relics Publishing House; 185, Bibliothéque nationale de France; 186-187, Cultural Relics Publishing House; 188, William Amory Gardner Fund and Annie Anderson Hough Fund, courtesy Museum of Fine Arts, Boston; 189, Cultural Relics Publishing House; 191, Gina Capaldi; 192, Don Weiss; 193, Werner

Text Credits

Forman/Art Resource, NY; 194, With permission of The Royal Ontario Museum ©ROM; 196-197, Scala/Art Resource, NY; 198, Gina Capaldi; 200, Israel Government Tourist Office; 201, Erich Lessing/Art Resource, NY; 202, Alinari/Art Resource, NY; 203, Keith Neely; 204, The J. Paul Getty Museum, Los Angeles; 205, Original artwork and photograph ©Vatican Museums; 206, Keith Neely; 207, Alinari/Art Resource, NY; 208, Keith Neely; 209, Original artwork and photograph ©Vatican Museums; 210, Keystone-Mast Collection (X122374) UCR/California Museum of Photography, University of California, Riverside; 212-213, Keith Neely; 215, Hellenic Republic Ministry of Culture; 216, Patricia P. Miller; 217-218, Keith Neely; 219, Audrey Gottlieb; 221, Louis S. Glanzman/National Geographic Image Collection; 222, Kunsthistorisches Museum, Vienna; 223, Allison Mangrum; 224, Keith Neely; 225, The J. Paul Getty Museum, Villa Collection, Malibu, CA; 226, American School of Classical Studies at Athens: Agora Excavations; 227, Hellenic Republic Ministry of Culture; 228-229, Scala/Art Resource, NY; 230, Gina Capaldi; 231, Fujiko Miller; 232, Professor Spyros Amourgis; 233, Fujiko Miller; 234, Keith Neely; 235, Hellenic Republic Ministry of Culture; 236, from *Great Ages of Man: Classical Greece* Photograph by David Lees 1965 ©The Kerameikos Museum, Athens, Greece; 237, Keith Neely; 238, Gladys Smith; 240, Keith Neely; 241, Scala/Art Resource, NY; 244-245, Keith Neely; 247, Burt Glinn/Magnum Photos, Inc.; 248, Istituto Archeologico Germanico; 249, Scala/Art Resource, NY; 250, Keith Neely; 252, Fujiko Miller; 253, Réunion des Musées Nationaux/Art Resources, NY; 254, ©Bildarchiv Preußischer Kulturbesitz/Art Resources, NY, 1990, Jurgen Liepe; 255, Keith Neely; 256, The Royal Collection ©2004, Her Majesty Queen Elizabeth II; 257, Anne Laskey; 258, Keith Neely; 260-261, Scala/Art Resource, NY; 263, Keith Neely; 264, Original artwork and photograph ©Vatican Museums; 265, Scala/Art Resource, NY; 266, Keith Neely; 267, Professor Paul Helmle; 268, The Metropolitan Museum of Art, Rogers Fund, 1903 (03.14.5) photograph ©1986 The Metropolitan Museum of Art; 269, Keith Neely; 270, Alinari/Art Resource, NY; 271, Original artwork and photograph ©Vatican Museums; 272, Gladys Smith; 273, Anne Laskey; 274, Mme. Ray Delvert; 276-277, Scala/Art Resource, NY; 278, Professor Paul Helmle; 279, Lotto, Lorenzo, *The Nativity,* Samuel H. Kress Collection, Image ©1994 Board of Trustees, National Gallery of Art, Washington; 280, Kunsthistorisches Museum, Vienna; 281, Scala/Art Resource, NY; 282, The J. Paul Getty Museum, Los Angeles; 283, © The British Museum; 285, Keith Neely; 286, Allison Mangrum; 287, Keith Neely; 290, Anne Laskey; 291, Panini, Giovanni Paolo, *The Interior of the Pantheon, Rome,* Samuel H. Kress Collection, Image ©1994 Board of Trustees, National Gallery of Art, Washington.

Colored by Ronaldo Benaraw:
6, 19, 23, 27, 30, 34, 38, 39, 42, 47, 49, 50, 51, 58, 62, 86, 87, 91, 95(t), 107, 118, 122, 131, 138, 143, 162, 171, 203, 218, 234, 250, 258, 263

Photo Research: Connie Stanyer and Sara Whitacre

9, From *Disclosing the Past*, by Mary D. Leakey, New York: McGraw-Hill, 1986; **31**, From *The Emergence of Man*, by John E. Pfeiffer, New York: Harper & Row, 1969; **65**, From *TimeFrame 3000-1500 BC: The Age of God-Kings,* Alexandria, VA: Time-Life Books, 1987; **73**, From *Egypt of the Pharoahs: An Introduction*, by Sir Alan Henderson Gardiner, Oxford: Clarendon Press, 1961; **139**, From *Historic India*, by Lucille Schulberg, New York: Time-Life Books, 1968; **145**, From *Historic India*, by Lucille Schulberg, New York: Time-Life Books, 1968; **156**, From *The Columbia History of the World*, edited by John A. Garraty and Peter Gay, New York: Harper & Row, 1972; **160**, From *Ancient China from the Beginnings to the Empire*, by Jacques Gernet, translated by Raymond Rudorff, Berkeley, CA: University of California Press, 1968; **179**, From *Confucian Analects*, translated by Ezra Pound, Bournemouth, England: Boscome Printing Co., 1933; **183**, From *TimeFrame 400 BC-AD 200: Empires Ascendant,* Alexandria, VA: Time-Life Books, 1987; **187**, From *The Horizon History of China*, by C. P. Fitzgerald, edited by Norman Kotker, New York: American Heritage Publishing Company, 1969; **190**, Adapted from *The Emperors of China*, by Christopher Hibbert, Chicago: Stonehenge Press, Inc., 1981; **203**, From Exodus 2:14, *Holy Bible*, New International Version; **204**, From Exodus 3:6, *Holy Bible*, New International Version; Exodus 3:10, *Holy Bible*, New International Version; **205**, From Exodus 3:11, *Holy Bible*, New International Version; **206**, From Exodus 5:1, *Holy Bible*, New International Version; Exodus 11:4, *Holy Bible*, New International Version; **207**, From Exodus 14:21, *Holy Bible*, New International Version; **208**, From Exodus 16:3, *Holy Bible*, New International Version; **209**, From Exodus 6:7, *Holy Bible*, New International Version; **266**, From *Greece and Rome: Builders of Our World*, National Geographic Book Service, Washington: National Geographic Society, 1977; **280**, From Luke 6:31, *Holy Bible*, New American Standard Bible; Matthew 22:37, *Holy Bible*, New International Version; **283**, From Matthew 28:6, *Holy Bible*, New International Version

Every effort has been made to trace the copyright holders. We apologize in advance for any unintentional errors or omissions. We would be pleased to insert the appropriate acknowledgment in subsequent editions of this book.